D1355954

OUR KING

CHARLES III: THE MAN AND THE MONARCH REVEALED

Robert Jobson is a No.1 international bestselling author and award-winning journalist. He co-authored the 2002 *New York Times* and *Sunday Times* bestselling book *Diana: Closely Guarded Secret* with the princess's personal protection officer, Inspector Ken Wharfe.

Jobson has written several other acclaimed books about the British royal family, including *Charles at Seventy*, *The Royal Family Operations Manual* and *Prince Philip's Century 1921–2021*.

He has reported on the British royal family since 1991 as royal correspondent for British newspapers including the *Sun*, *Daily Express* and currently the *Evening Standard*. He was the recipient of the London Press Club *Scoop of the Year* award in 2005 for his world exclusive revealing the engagement of Charles and Camilla Parker Bowles and was dubbed 'The Godfather of Royal Reporting' by the *Wall Street Journal* in 2011.

Jobson is Royal Editor for the Australian breakfast show *Sunrise* on Channel 7, as well as a contracted royal contributor for *Good Morning America* on the US network ABC. He regularly appears on British television and royal documentaries as a royal expert.

OUR KING

CHARLES III: THE MAN AND THE MONARCH REVEALED

ROBERT JOBSON

First published in the UK by John Blake Publishing
an imprint of Bonnier Books UK
4th Floor, Victoria House
Bloomsbury Square
London WC1B 4DA
England

Owned by Bonnier Books
Sveavägen 56, Stockholm, Sweden

www.facebook.com/johnblakebooks
twitter.com/jblakebooks

First published in 2023 by John Blake Publishing

Hardback ISBN: 978-1-78946-704-8
Trade paperback ISBN: 978-1-78946-705-5
Ebook ISBN: 978-1-78946-706-2
Audiobook ISBN: 978-1-78946-707-9

British Library Cataloguing-in-Publication Data:
A CIP catalogue record for this book is available from the British Library.

Design by www.envydesign.co.uk

Printed and bound in Great Britain by Clays Ltd, Elcograf S.p.A

1 3 5 7 9 10 8 6 4 2

All names and locations have been changed to protect the identity of the victims
and all those involved.

Every reasonable effort has been made to trace copyright-holders of material reproduced in
this book, but if any have been inadvertently overlooked the publishers would be glad to hear
from them.

John Blake Publishing is an imprint of Bonnier Books UK
www.bonnierbooks.co.uk

Queen Elizabeth's was a life well-lived; a promise with destiny kept and she is mourned most deeply in her passing. That promise of lifelong service I renew to you all today.

KING CHARLES III'S FIRST SPEECH ON 9 SEPTEMBER 2022, IN WHICH HE REFERENCED HIS LATE MOTHER'S PLEDGE TO THE PEOPLE OF ALL COMMONWEALTH COUNTRIES IN 1947 THAT: 'MY WHOLE LIFE WHETHER IT BE LONG OR SHORT SHALL BE DEVOTED TO YOUR SERVICE.'

Contents

Introduction

I set out to write an authentic and honest portrayal of our King, Charles III. A deep-thinking, spiritual man, he is not only a worthy recipient of the Crown, but an anchored monarch we are blessed to have in these times of uncertainty. He is not cynical but intuitive, instinctive, and perhaps a little sentimental and overemotional at times. Mostly, he is somebody who cares very deeply about those he serves: in the UK, the realms and the wider Commonwealth, and the planet on which we all live, today and for the future. He may have been born into a family with huge wealth and privilege, but he has always tried his best to justify that good fortune by working tirelessly to improve the lot of others less fortunate than himself.

He would be the first to admit he is not perfect, far from it. He can be obsessive, a little eccentric, and he does have a short fuse, but his temper is invariably short-lived. Prince Harry writes in his controversial memoir *Spare* that when his father watched the BBC news on television, he would often end up throwing the remote control at the screen out of frustration.

A passionate, driven man, he has a great love of the arts, too – of books, Shakespeare (his favourite is *Henry V*), and J.K. Rowling's *Harry Potter*, of the Goons, the poetry of Dylan Thomas, the music of Bach, Hubert Parry and Leonard Cohen; of art, particularly the work of Johan Joseph Zoffany, and the classical architecture of Rome, Christopher Wren and, more recently, Quinlan Terry. He loves to wake up and literally smell the roses, due to his heightened sense of smell.

It seems to me a little absurd for an author to write a fair and contemporaneous biography about a living person without having met them, or at least watched them at close quarters. It is different for historians, for, short of inventing a time machine, what other options are open to them apart from digging deep and relying on the source material they unearth? But it is implausible for a biographer to claim to have some idea of a person's real character from only second- or third-hand accounts.

In the writing of this book, I have been privileged to have had access to the King and several of those in his circle. I have been able to observe closely what he does now, as King, and what he did as heir to his late mother, Queen Elizabeth II. In my thirty-three years as a journalist covering the British Royal Family, I have also been fortunate to be honoured by my peers for my work: I was the recipient of the London Press Club's prestigious 'Scoop of the Year' award for breaking the story that Charles would marry Camilla in the *London Evening Standard* in 2005, and the following year at the British Press Awards I was highly commended in the Hugh Cudlipp Award for excellence in popular journalism.

During my work as a royal correspondent, I have met and chatted with the King on numerous occasions when I have chronicled the Royal Family and as I have followed him at home and abroad. In February 2015, Charles and Camilla visited the *Evening Standard* offices, which were then in Kensington, west London, and a year later he also collected a special Londoner of the Decade award at the *Evening Standard* Progress 1000 party honouring the capital's innovators, which was held at the Science Museum. It was an idea that I had put to the deputy editor, Ian Walker, and I was on hand as the newspaper's owner Evgeny Lebedev presented the prince with the special front page. Charles jokingly described it to me as 'one of your better front pages'.

More importantly, I have been granted interviews with the King twice, when he was the Prince of Wales, to discuss issues that he is clearly passionate about. On both occasions he was gracious and generous with his time, and candid in what turned out to be two meaningful and enlightening conversations.

The first was in April 2018, on a jet flying back to Australia from Port Vila, the capital of Vanuatu, the South Pacific nation made up of eighty islands. Everyone was in high spirits on the return flight from Vanuatu, where Charles had been photographed in a grass skirt and a garland after the local Council of Chiefs made him 'Chief Mal Menaringmanu'. He had then drunk kava with them and met some of the tribal leaders of Tanna, where his father, Prince Philip, was revered as a god.

The especially configured Boeing 737 Business Jet was designed to fly the Australian prime minister and VVIPs. This time I was one of only twenty-five people on board, including the Australian foreign minister, Julia Bishop, and, of course, Charles and his team of advisers. The prince, referred to as 'The Boss' by his staff, sat at the front of the luxury jet working though his correspondence in a sealed-off private section. Outside was an adjoining corridor leading to the pilots and crew at the front and the open area equipped with large, luxury, cream leather seats for the officials.

I was beckoned forward by his then communications secretary, Julian Payne, into the middle section of the plane where Charles's staff were all seated. 'The Boss', he said, would be very happy to have a conversation with me for a few minutes.

Charles is complex. As he himself said in an interview with his biographer Jonathan Dimbleby in 1994, 'I am one of those people who searches. I'm interested in pursuing the path, if I can find it, through the thickets.' It is Charles's character – that of a man who admits to getting carried away by enthusiasm in his bid to try to improve things, not just his position in society and royal status – that makes him interesting to write about.

The prince was sitting at his desk in a comfortable, dark-grey leather chair surrounded by papers and his handwritten letters. We shook hands and I told him that I felt his visit to Vanuatu had been a 'triumph'. Charles was immaculate, sitting in his seat with his lightweight-wool Anderson & Sheppard tailored suit and silk tie still on, and a silk pocket handkerchief.

He does not seem to take praise that well, but he smiled warmly and said, 'Yes, I was very touched by the warmth of the welcome.' It had, he added, felt like something from 'history, from another time'. He was right. The power of the energy created by the hundreds of dancers performing a traditional *kastom* dance (a pidgin word derived from the English pronunciation of 'custom') had seemed almost hypnotic and overwhelming to one watching it for the first time.

Our conversation was wide-ranging. One minute we were discussing the future of the Commonwealth and climate change, the next the built environment and Poundbury, his visionary traditionalist village in Dorset. This is so often unfairly mocked as a 'feudal Disneyland', but a growing and diverse community has settled there and developed over time, suggesting it has achieved its objective.

Had I been, Charles asked me. I nodded in the affirmative and expressed my genuine approval. I have, in fact, visited Poundbury three times on media days arranged by his Clarence House office and, essentially, I agree with the concept.

Introduction

My conversation with the prince was not exclusively serious. There was humour, too – with Charles that is almost inevitable. He is a very funny man, with a quirky sense of humour formed from his love of Spike Milligan and the Goons. When I commended his amusing speech at a governor general's reception in Brisbane, where he had his audience in stitches, he was typically humble. He had joked that he would never again fit into a pair of skin-tight 'budgie smugglers' and said, somewhat alarmingly, that his advancing years coincided with 'bits falling off'.

'You're very kind,' he said with a smile, before adding, 'But I've never even owned a pair of budgie smugglers in my life,' with perfect comic timing. The way he put emphasis on the words 'budgie smugglers' made me chuckle.

My five-minute 'brush-by' had turned into twenty-five minutes of intriguing, enlightening and meaningful conversation with the future king. I returned to my comfortable seat for the remainder of the two-and-a-half-hour flight, sipped a perfectly chilled glass of Australian Sauvignon Blanc and made contemporaneous notes of our conversation. Charles continued with his work, prepping for his next engagement. He had short biographies to read on all the people he would meet. Nothing was left to chance.

My second one-to-one interview with the future king was on 25 October 2019 at the British ambassador's residence in Tokyo. Charles had been in Japan, his fifth visit, for the enthronement of Emperor Naruhito, who had succeeded his father Akihito the previous May. The following day Charles attended a garden party, hosted by the British ambassador to Japan, Paul Madden. He was keen to talk about a subject close to his heart, a sustainable economy. We exchanged pleasantries, and I told him I had just been on a visit to Pakistan with his son Prince William and before that with Prince Harry in South Africa. Then we got down to business.

He immediately stressed the importance of financial institutions reducing their investments in sectors such as oil and gas and redirecting it towards schemes that deliver sustainable returns. Our conversation took place shortly after Typhoon Hagibis hit Japan, causing at least eighty deaths, and he stressed that action was needed quickly before the planet passed a point of no return.

'But you see, there is no good waiting until it is a complete crisis, because then it is terribly difficult to rectify the situation. So often in the history of humanity we've waited until something becomes a total catastrophe before doing something about it. This time it is more critical than ever.'

Charles then talked to me with great passion about the importance of sustainable investment into the regeneration of forests, the oceans, and agriculture for several more minutes, and then he was gone and off to his next engagement.

The first time I saw him after he had become King was on 16 November 2022, at a reception to promote small businesses that he hosted at Buckingham Palace, as he stepped out from the White Room, where he had been chatting to business leaders including billionaire Peter Jones, star of the television series *Dragons' Den*. He spotted me as I was covering the royal rota. I bowed my head and addressed him, 'Your Majesty', and he asked how I was. It was a nice touch.

Fundamentally, I believe the picture that emerges from my research, and I hope is reflected in this book, is of a thoroughly decent man, a person of integrity and honour who has always striven to do his best as a public servant and tried to put duty before himself. This is my attempt to tell the true story of his remarkable journey from a shy prince to our first king of the twenty-first century.

Robert Jobson,
February 2023

CHAPTER I

My Beloved Mother

May flights of angels sing thee to thy rest.

**KING CHARLES III'S TRIBUTE TO HIS LATE MOTHER,
HER MAJESTY ELIZABETH II.**

King Charles III delivered his first televised address as sovereign on Friday, 9 September 2022, the day after the death of his mother, Queen Elizabeth II, the oldest and longest-reigning monarch in British history. It was a poignant and deeply moving tribute to a remarkable woman, public servant and much-loved monarch. His words were heartfelt, poetic and personal.

His pay-off line, 'May flights of angels sing thee to thy rest,' was a quote taken from Act V, Scene II of William Shakespeare's *Hamlet*, when Horatio pays tribute to the Prince of Denmark as he dies in his friend's arms. It was a mark of respect by Charles for the woman who had been his guiding light, which had now been extinguished.

The Queen had passed away peacefully in her bed aged ninety-six at 3.10 p.m. on 8 September at Balmoral Castle. It was the first time a British monarch had died in Scotland since James V in 1542. Charles and his sister Princess Anne, the Princess Royal, had fortunately both been in Scotland when they were first alerted that the Queen's health had suddenly deteriorated. Charles, who had been at a function at Dumfries House in Ayrshire on the evening of 7 September, helicoptered the next morning to Balmoral Castle, on the Queen's 52,000-acre estate in the Scottish Highlands, and soon joined his sister at the Queen's bedside.

Anne never left her side. Charles, however, after a few hours with the Queen, returned to Birkhall, his nearby estate on Royal Deeside that he had inherited from the late Queen Mother. With its sloping lawn, the secluded, L-shaped property is embraced by the surrounding woodland. As the defining moment in his life approached, Charles went out foraging for mushrooms in the wild woods, carrying a basket and with his walking stick in hand, while the sound of the River Muick, a tributary of the River Dee, filled the air.

He was understandably lost in thought and at one with nature, as he liked most, acutely aware that he was on the cusp of the start of his reign and perhaps preparing himself for the grief that he would soon feel on the death of his mother. It was while he was out on this solo walk that one of his Scotland Yard personal protection officers, who had given Charles some space but knew what part of the woods he was in, alerted him that his mother's condition had taken another dramatic turn for the worse. The prince was advised to return to Balmoral in haste, which he did. At the end of the Queen's life, Charles, his wife Camilla and the Princess Royal were the only family present.

More than three hours were to pass before Buckingham Palace officially announced the death of the monarch at 6.30 p.m. that day. The Princess Royal later registered her mother's death. Douglas James Allan Glass is noted as the certifying registered medical practitioner and the only cause of death listed was 'old age', with no other contributing factors.

No other members of her immediate family members made it

to Scotland in time to see Her Majesty before her death. Her two other children, Prince Andrew, Duke of York, and Prince Edward, Earl of Wessex, together with his wife, Sophie, Countess of Wessex and her grandson and direct heir, Prince William, then Duke of Cambridge, took an RAF Dassault Falcon flight from RAF Northolt at 2.39 p.m., arriving at Aberdeen airport at 3.50 p.m., by which time it was too late.

With Prince William at the wheel of a royal Range Rover, his Uncle Andrew in the front passenger seat, Edward and Sophie in the rear seats and the security in a vehicle behind, the family group did not arrive at the Scottish Highlands estate until shortly after 5 p.m., almost two hours after the Queen had died. Prince Harry had decided to travel separately and took a private jet to Scotland, not getting there until just before 8 p.m. Close sources said he had elected not to fly with his brother and uncles after a disagreement over the attendance of his wife, Meghan. When he insisted that Meghan must accompany him to Balmoral, it was his father who told him she could not come.

'It did not go down well with the family, they were all shocked by his behaviour,' an insider said.

Secret contingency plans about what should happen in the event of the death of the Queen in Scotland had long been established. The arrangements, signed off by the Queen personally, even had a codename: 'Operation Unicorn' – for the mythological creature that has been Scotland's national animal since the fifteenth century. The plans included a ceremonial procession along the Royal Mile in Edinburgh to St Giles' Cathedral, and a 24-hour period of lying-in-state, which would be open to the public.

After that, her body would be flown to England where Operation London Bridge would kick in, with elaborate state ceremonies, filled with pomp and pageantry, culminating with the state funeral at Westminster Abbey as the nation bid her a final farewell on 19 September 2022. In a personal touch, the wreath adorning the Queen's coffin had a handwritten note written by the King, which read, 'In loving and devoted memory. Charles R.' Finally, the late Queen was laid to rest at St George's Chapel, Windsor, alongside her cherished Prince Philip, her late husband of seventy-three years, who had died seventeen months earlier, aged ninety-nine.

In the days before her passing, the Queen, despite her frailty, had insisted on personally welcoming her new prime minister, Liz Truss, for the 'kissing hands' ceremony, the traditional ritual that formally installs the prime minister of the United Kingdom.[1] There had been talk of the Queen returning to Buckingham Palace, but her doctors ruled that out. Ultimately, the Queen compromised and invited the outgoing prime minister Boris Johnson and Liz Truss to Balmoral, rather than her flying back to London.

She stood her ground, telling medical staff and family, 'It's my job,' when they counselled against it. 'Nothing was going to stop her,' close sources confirmed, although the official meetings with Johnson and Truss 'took an awful lot out of her'.

One of the last house guests she hosted at Balmoral was the Right Rev Dr Iain Greenshields, the moderator of the general assembly of the Church of Scotland, who described how the Queen's evident frailty was eclipsed by her vital conversation and 'amazing' memory. The Queen spoke to him about being 'at peace' and her love of Balmoral – where so many of her happiest memories were forged, from her secret engagement to Philip in 1946 to family barbecues – and of her sustaining faith.

'When I first saw her, I was struck by how frail she looked,' said Dr Greenshields, who had dinner and lunch with her the weekend before she died. He said, 'She just was absolutely engaged with good conversation, asking about my family, and the one thing that stood out was [her] memory. For somebody of her age to have the clarity of looking back to the past and remembering the things that she did was amazing. She didn't need prompting by anybody around her.'

The Queen's love of her Highland surroundings came across 'very, very strongly', too, he remarked. 'She said it gave her a great deal of peace and pleasure to be at Balmoral. She wandered over to the window and she was looking out, explaining to me the garden and how it had developed.' She was on fine form. At the end of the evening, she even cracked a joke. After dinner she asked him where he was staying in the castle, knowing full well his room was in the tower of the castle. She told him, 'Now your Queen is sending you to the Tower!'

Dr Greenshields went on, 'She mentioned how important her faith had been to her right through her life, and that there were particular people who'd had a significant influence on that.' The churchman brought a gift of a wooden cross, crafted by prisoners at HMP Glenochil from recycled church pews. 'Her leaving the room holding that cross will be my enduring memory,' he said.[2]

Her son Charles had prepared all his life for, as well as dreaded, this moment. Of course he would wholeheartedly embrace the role of monarch, but he always knew that when he did so it would be because of the sad passing of his beloved mother and the sovereign whom he had served as liegeman all his adult life. He rose to the occasion. Now King, he drafted a consummate speech, which he would pre-record the following day when he returned to Buckingham Palace. It would set the tone for the start of his reign and the period of official mourning.

That evening, after his siblings and wider family had pledged their allegiance to him, Charles and Camilla returned to the sanctuary of Birkhall, where they were joined by his son and heir

Prince William for a private dinner. Harry, who was greeted at Balmoral by his aunt, the Princess Royal, remained with the other members of his family at the castle, as the family-run funeral directors William Purves looked after the Queen's body.

The King flew back to Buckingham Palace the next morning and his powerful words in the televised address following the Queen's passing are worth revisiting in full here. For his speech to the nation is not only a loving tribute to Her late Majesty Queen Elizabeth II, whose reign of 70 years and 214 days was the longest in British history, it also sets out his position as our new monarch and gives an indication of how he intends to reign.

There is no procrastination. He appoints William as Prince of Wales immediately and he also clarifies his wife's position as Queen Consort. There is a sense that this is a man on a mission; a man in a race against time. He spoke from the same room that the Queen had often used for her televised Christmas broadcasts, the Blue Drawing Room at Buckingham Palace. Dressed in a black suit, white shirt and black tie, with a top pocket handkerchief of black and white squares, his tone was mostly sombre.

Here is the King's address in full:

I speak to you today with feelings of profound sorrow. Throughout her life, Her Majesty the Queen – my beloved mother – was an inspiration and example to me and to all my family, and we owe her the most heartfelt debt any family can owe to their mother; for her love, affection, guidance, understanding and example. Queen Elizabeth's was a long life, well lived; a promise with destiny kept and she is mourned most deeply in her passing. That promise of lifelong service I renew to you all today.

Alongside the personal grief that all my family are feeling, we also share with so many of you in the United Kingdom, in all the countries where the Queen was head of state, in the Commonwealth and across the world, a deep sense of gratitude for the more than seventy years in which my mother, as Queen, served the people of so many nations. In 1947, on her twenty-first birthday, she pledged in a broadcast from Cape Town to the Commonwealth to devote her life, whether it be short or long, to the service of her peoples. That was more than a promise: it was a profound personal commitment which defined her whole life.

She made sacrifices for duty. Her dedication and devotion as sovereign never wavered, through times of change and progress, through times of joy and celebration, and through times of sadness and loss. In her life of service, we saw that abiding love of tradition, together with that fearless embrace of progress, which make us great as nations. The affection, admiration and respect she inspired became the hallmark of her reign. And, as every member of my family can testify, she combined these qualities with warmth, humour, and an unerring ability always to see the best in people.

I pay tribute to my mother's memory, and I honour her life of service. I know that her death brings great sadness to so many of you, and I share that sense of loss, beyond measure, with you all. When the Queen came to the throne, Britain and the world were still coping with the privations and aftermath of the Second World War, and still living by the conventions of earlier times. In the course of the last seventy years, we have seen our society become one of many cultures and many faiths. The institutions of the state have changed in turn. But, through all changes and challenges, our nation, and the wider family of realms – of whose talents, traditions and achievements I am so inexpressibly proud – have prospered and flourished. Our values have remained, and must remain, constant.

The role and the duties of monarchy also remain, as does the sovereign's particular relationship and responsibility toward the Church of England – the church in which my own faith is so deeply rooted. In that faith, and the values it inspires, I have been brought up to cherish a sense of duty to others, and to hold in the greatest respect the precious traditions, freedoms and responsibilities of our unique history and our system of parliamentary government.

As the Queen herself did with such unswerving devotion, I too now solemnly pledge myself, throughout the remaining time God grants me, to uphold the constitutional principles at the heart of our nation. And wherever you may live in the United Kingdom, or in the realms and territories across the world, and whatever may be your background or beliefs, I shall endeavour to serve you with loyalty, respect and love, as I have throughout my life.

My life will, of course, change as I take up my new responsibilities. This is also a time of change for my family. I count on the loving help of my darling wife, Camilla. In recognition of her own loyal public service since our marriage seventeen years ago, she becomes my Queen Consort. I know she will bring to the demands of her new role the steadfast devotion to duty on which I have come to rely so much. It will no longer be possible for me to give so much of my time and energies to the charities and issues for which I care so deeply. But I know this important work will go on in the trusted hands of others. As my heir, William now assumes the Scottish titles which have meant so much to me. He succeeds me as Duke of Cornwall and takes on the responsibilities for the Duchy of Cornwall, which I have undertaken for more than five decades.

Today, I am proud to create him Prince of Wales, Tywysog Cymru, the country whose title I have been so greatly privileged to bear during so much of my life and duty. With Catherine beside him, our new Prince and Princess of Wales will, I know, continue to inspire, and lead our national conversations, helping to bring the marginal to the centre ground where vital help can be given. I want also to express my love for Harry and Meghan as they continue to build their lives overseas. In a little over a week's time we will come together as a nation, as a Commonwealth and indeed a global community, to lay my beloved mother to rest. In our sorrow, let us remember and draw strength from the light of her example.

On behalf of all my family, I can only offer the most sincere and heartfelt thanks for your condolences and support. They mean more to me than I can ever possibly express. And to my darling Mama, as you begin your last great journey to join my dear late Papa, I want simply to say this: thank you. Thank you for your love and devotion to our family and to the family of nations you have served so diligently all these years. May 'flights of angels sing thee to thy rest'.

His sorrow was immense, real and raw. His moment of destiny was now upon him.

CHAPTER 2

Born to Be King

It has just been announced from Buckingham Palace that
Her Royal Highness Princess Elizabeth, Duchess of Edinburgh
was safely delivered of a prince at 9.14 p.m. and that
Her Royal Highness and her son are both doing well.

BBC NEWSREADER JOHN SNAGGE, BBC HOME SERVICE,
14 NOVEMBER 1948

Within weeks of exchanging her marriage vows with Prince Philip at Westminster Abbey on Thursday, 20 November 1947, the heir presumptive, Princess Elizabeth, Duchess of Edinburgh was pregnant. Buckingham Palace, however, chose not to announce the news publicly. Instead, the princess effectively hid her baby bump under loose-fitting blouses and boxy coats, and eventually retreated from public life when it became so pronounced that she could no longer hide it, reflecting the general attitude toward pregnancy at the time.

There was never any official confirmation that the royal couple were expecting their first child. Buckingham Palace simply released a statement announcing that Elizabeth would not be seen in public for the foreseeable future. It read: 'Her Royal Highness the Princess Elizabeth will undertake no public engagements after the end of June.' It was as close to official confirmation as the press, which had been busy speculating about a baby, was going to get.

Princess Elizabeth, at just twenty-two, delivered a baby boy weighing a healthy 7lb 6oz at 9.14 p.m. on 14 November 1948, via Caesarean section carried out by Royal Surgeon-Gynaecologist Sir William Gilliatt and assisted by John Peel, in the Buhl Room at Buckingham Palace. Ordinarily it was used as a guest room, but it had been especially converted into what was described as a 'miniature hospital' specifically for the important royal birth. Her husband Philip, however, was not at his wife's bedside during the birth. It was not common practice in the 1940s for fathers to be present during the delivery of a baby.

Instead, he got so restless pacing up and down an equerry's room waiting for news that his private secretary, Commander Michael Parker,[1] took him off for a game of squash on the palace court. It was the King's private secretary, Sir Alan 'Tommy' Lascelles, who gave Philip the good news. He was ecstatic and ran to the Buhl Room, where, still wearing the sporting flannels and open-neck shirt he had been wearing on the squash court, he held his firstborn son in his arms.

Philip declared to his wife and those in the room that his newborn son looked just like a 'plum pudding'. As she was hazy and feeling nauseous, Princess Elizabeth's medical team decided to administer her extra oxygen when the anaesthetic wore off. It was then that her overjoyed husband presented her with a beautiful bouquet of flowers, red roses and carnations, which Parker had sent out for, and popped open a bottle of champagne. At Philip's insistence, for which he got the King's backing, the new parents were not joined by any senior government officials, such as the home secretary, as had been the custom for royal births, including that of Princess Elizabeth herself, over the centuries.[2]

A proclamation was posted on the palace railings just before midnight announcing: 'Her Royal Highness Princess Elizabeth has been safely delivered of a son who has been named Charles Philip Arthur George.' Outside, loyal fans had gathered and started chanting, 'We want Philip,' such was the popularity among the public for this handsome Royal Naval officer. A forty-one-gun salute was fired to mark the new arrival by the King's Troop, Royal Artillery, and in Trafalgar Square the fountains were floodlit blue, as almost four thousand people gathered outside Buckingham Palace to watch the comings and goings of the medical team.

According to Philip's cousin, Princess Marina, Duchess of Kent, he was equally entranced by the new arrival. 'I am so happy for Philip, for he adores children and also small babies,' she wrote in a letter to her mother, Grand Duchess Elena Vladimirovna of Russia. 'He carries it [the baby] about himself quite professionally, to the nurse's amusement.' Nevertheless, Philip showed no inclination for being a nappy-changing, hands-on kind of father of the modern era. At the time, he not only had his career in the Royal Navy to consider, but he was also scheduled to carry out royal duties, while still trying to maintain a remnant of his former bachelor lifestyle through late-night outings with his close friend Mike Parker.

Indeed, Philip saw nothing wrong in handing his baby son over to the care of nursery staff. He had himself been effectively raised by a nanny, Miss Emily Roose, the daughter of a bookmaker from Plymouth and a trained nurse.[3] So, each morning at 9.00 a.m., baby Charles would be taken to see his mother. In the evening, if her engagement schedule allowed it, Princess Elizabeth would join her baby in the nursery. Essentially, the infant and his parents lived separate lives. 'To my knowledge, she never bathed the children,' recalled Mike Parker's first wife, Eileen. 'Nanny did all that.'[4]

It was therefore down to his nanny to nurture and comfort the shy, sensitive Charles, and to whom he naturally turned for the affection he needed. Helen Lightbody, the daughter of an Edinburgh textile worker, whom he called 'Nana' and the press dubbed 'No nonsense Lightbody', was the one who got him up in the morning, dressed him, slept in the same room as he did and comforted him if he awoke frightened during the night.

Of course he adored his mother, but it was from afar. She was, according to Charles's biographer Jonathan Dimbleby, a 'remote and glamorous figure who came to kiss you goodnight, smelling of lavender and dressed for dinner'. Aside from this nightly ritual, Elizabeth was physically undemonstrative by nature and she found overt signs of affection towards her son difficult. She was not keen on hugging or kissing him, preferring to leave such tactile displays of emotion to the nannies.[5]

It was to be one of the happiest periods of Philip and Elizabeth's married life. They were very much in love and there was a mutually strong physical attraction between them. Philip romanced his young wife, buying her flowers and love tokens as well as taking her dancing, which she loved.

In October 1949, Philip was posted to Malta as the second-in-command of the destroyer HMS *Chequers* and Elizabeth first flew to join him there on 20 November, their second wedding anniversary. Elizabeth then divided her time between Malta, where Philip's maternal uncle, Lord Louis Mountbatten and his wife, Edwina, played host to the couple, and Britain, where she carried out her public duties as heiress presumptive. Their son Charles did not join his parents when they were in Malta; instead, he was cared for at their London residence, Clarence House.

Prince Philip's Royal Navy career was flourishing. He had been promoted to lieutenant commander and then appointed to his first and, as it transpired, only command, the frigate HMS *Magpie*, a modified Black Swan-class sloop, on 2 September 1950.

He had every reason to believe he was on the rise. He felt he was at last fulfilling his potential and was clearly destined for a highly successful career in the Royal Navy.

For Elizabeth, the time she spent in Malta with her husband was filled with fun. It was a carefree existence where she could forget about her royal destiny and the responsibility she faced on becoming Queen, and try to lead as normal a life as possible. Between 1949 and 1951, the couple lived in the townhouse Villa Guardamangia, in Pietà, which was leased by the owners to Lord Mountbatten.

Lady Pamela Hicks, Mountbatten's daughter and Philip's cousin, said, 'It was a period that he [Philip] described as among the happiest days of his sailor life, as well as being the closest he and his young bride came to living an ordinary married life. It was the only place where she felt she could live without the pressure of being next in line to the throne. The princess really loved Malta, because she was able to wander through the town and do some shopping. She was able to live the life of a naval officer's wife, just like all the other wives. It was wonderful for her and it's why they have such a nostalgia for Malta.'

When she was six months' pregnant with her second child, Princess Elizabeth returned home for good, and Princess Anne was born in August 1950. By now Philip was well on the way to an accomplished career as commander of HMS *Magpie*. An ambitious officer, he always had his eye on the main chance and hoped, even then, to go right to the top of the Admiralty. It is no overstatement to say that he felt that it was his destiny.

Then in the summer of 1949, George VI had his first brush with death. His condition was so worrying, the idea of a regency while he recovered was flirted with as he lay in bed in Buckingham Palace following an operation to block a nerve at the base of his spine. Speculation circulated that he was dying, or, at best, would not recover sufficiently to take up the reins of state again. Prime minister Winston Churchill observed that 'Bertie now walked with death.'

The lumbar sympathectomy was designed to counteract the arteriosclerosis, a stiffening of arteries, that the King suffered from because of too much stress and smoking far too many cigarettes every day. Miraculously, the King made an excellent recovery, although it took its toll on him. The traumatic times through which he led Britain had left him physically and mentally exhausted and those close to him, including his wife the Queen, believed it contributed to his faltering health.

On Sunday, 23 September 1951, sombre crowds gathered outside the palace awaiting news of their King following the announcement that he needed to have an operation to remove part of his lung. In the days before social media or 24-hour news, a bulletin on his health posted on the palace gates in the afternoon read: 'Anxiety must remain for some days... but his immediate post-operative condition is satisfactory.' It was signed by the five doctors who attended the monarch and who spent the night prior to the operation at the palace.

Many feared the worst. The situation was so worrying that the Labour prime minister, Clement Attlee, flew back to London from Scotland. He was kept informed of the King's progress at 10 Downing Street. Special prayers were being said in churches throughout the country for George VI's recovery. Remarkably, he did get better. But by February 1952 his doctors confirmed what they had feared: he had lung cancer.

As preparations were made for Princess Elizabeth to take on more of his royal duties, Prince Philip had no choice but to support her and to leave the Royal Navy on 'indefinite leave', flying home from Malta in July. A successful tour to Canada and America followed and, at the end of January the next year, Philip and Elizabeth prepared to travel to Kenya on a stopover en route to Australia and New Zealand.

Frail and wan, and ironically with a pack of his favoured strong Chesterfield cigarettes in his pocket, the King went to London airport to see off his beloved daughter and son-in-law. He was greeted with a cheer from his loyal supporters and responded with a customary gesture of acknowledgement. It was a bitterly cold evening and he waved them goodbye. As his daughter climbed aboard a royal flight bound for Africa, he looked heartbroken. He then turned and told Margaret 'Bobo' MacDonald, Elizabeth's loyal assistant, 'Look after the princess for me.' Miss MacDonald later disclosed that she had never seen him so upset. He was a very ill man, determined to do his duty to the last.

Charles admits that he did not really know either of his grandfathers. Philip's father, Prince Andrew, died on 3 December 1944 in the Metropole Hotel, Monte Carlo, aged sixty-two, before Charles was born, and he can recall only one hazy childhood memory of the King that he cherishes.

It was of the photoshoot he did with his grandparents on 14 November 1951. It was Charles's third birthday and the prince and his sister were taken to Buckingham Palace to pose for photographs with both the King and Queen, the first images taken of the monarch after his lung operation two months previously. At the other end of the sofa the Queen sat holding Anne as the strong studio lights shone on the group. Immaculately dressed in a dark Benson & Clegg bespoke tailored suit, the King is pictured with his arm round his grandson, wearing a short-sleeved shirt and shorts, and smiling warmly. It is a memory that stayed with Charles for the rest of his life.

King George VI, who had been in fine form the evening before, died peacefully in his sleep at Sandringham House in the early hours of the morning on 6 February 1952, having never fully recovered from the lung surgery the previous September. He was found unresponsive in his bed at 7.30 a.m. by his loyal valet, James MacDonald. Dr James Ansell, the Surgeon Apothecary to the Royal Household, was called soon afterwards and declared that the King was dead.

At 8.45 a.m. the late King's principal private secretary, Sir Alan Lascelles, telephoned his assistant Sir Edward Ford in London with the codeword for the monarch's demise: 'Hyde Park Corner'. He instructed Sir Edward to go personally and tell prime minister Winston Churchill and Queen Mary, the King's mother, of the monarch's passing. At 9.00 a.m., Sir Edward finally arrived at 10 Downing Street, the bearer of what he described as 'bad news' for the prime minister.

'Bad news?' a shocked Churchill replied, saying it was 'The worst!' news.

Oblivious to events in Norfolk and London, Princess Elizabeth and Philip had spent the night in Aberdare Forest in Kenya at the remote Treetops Hotel, accessible via a ladder, where they watched the baboons in the jungle. She then went up to a lookout point at the top of the tree to see the dawn breaking. The duke's closest friend and confidant, Mike Parker, who was accompanying the royal couple on the visit, was at her side when they spotted an eagle hovering overhead. 'I never thought about it until later, but that was roughly the time when the King died,' he recalled later.

Elizabeth was already Queen, but she knew nothing about it. Lady Pamela Hicks later remarked: 'She goes up as a princess. The King dies that night. She comes down the ladder as a Queen.'[6]

Secret ciphers announcing the King's death were sent by the

British embassy to the governor's residence in Nairobi, Kenya, but the coded messages could not be read because the codebook was locked in a safe and the governor, Sir Philip Mitchell, the only person with a key, had already left for the coast. When the news finally reached royal aides, Elizabeth was at Sagana Lodge, near Nyeri.[7]

Martin Charteris, Elizabeth's private secretary, was in a restaurant in the Outspan Hotel when he was contacted by the editor of the *East African Standard* by telephone and asked if reports of the King's death were true. As soon as he had confirmed the sad news, Charteris contacted the lodge, and asked to speak to Commander Parker. Once Martin Charteris had imparted the news, it fell to Parker to tell Philip of the King's death. Parker later admitted that when he told the duke the news, it was 'as if you'd dropped half the world on him'.

Philip steeled himself as he prepared to tell his wife, now the sovereign, and invited her for a walk in the garden. At 2.45 p.m., local time, Princess Elizabeth finally learned that she was now the Queen. Her stoicism and deep sense of duty to the Crown, her late father and the people of her country somehow gave her strength in her hour of need.

Martin Charteris had then to open the sealed accession documents, which had been taken on the trip due to the seriousness of the King's medical condition. The new Queen, Elizabeth II, formally requested that no photographs be taken at this point exposing her private emotions to the public. It was a more deferential age and the gentlemen of the press obliged, every one of them lowering their cameras out of respect. With her permission, she was photographed later walking through Sagana Lodge alongside Sir Philip Mitchell, Governor of Kenya, a few hours after learning of the King's death.

Once the plane from Nairobi had touched down at London

airport and taxied, the Queen's mourning outfit was taken aboard so that she could change. When the aircraft door finally opened, her uncle, the Duke of Gloucester, walked up the steps, followed by the late King's private secretary, Sir Alan Lascelles, and went inside to offer his condolences to his new queen.

Conscious that the world's cameras were waiting, Elizabeth took a few extra moments to compose herself. She then descended the steps alone; her husband, in what would become a familiar routine, was told by the notoriously forthright Lascelles to wait at the top of the steps for a second or two. She was then greeted officially by the welcoming party including prime minister Winston Churchill, the leader of the opposition, Clement Attlee, and Anthony Eden, the foreign secretary.

The new Queen did not go straight to Sandringham to comfort her grieving mother, Queen Elizabeth, and sister, Princess Margaret, as she had to carry out several formal functions connected with the Accession in London. So, on the morning of 8 February, Elizabeth went directly to attend the Accession Council at St James's Palace. It was there, with her assembled ministers and privy councillors standing, as they always do, that she read out her Declaration of Sovereignty. She said, 'I pray that God will help me to discharge worthily this heavy task that has been laid upon me so early in my life.' Tired and emotional, she managed to get through it without faltering, despite having to mention her father several times.

Her father had tried to prepare his precious daughter and heiress for her future role, but he just ran out of time. Elizabeth would now have to learn the complexities of the role of monarch while on the job. Her lifetime of duty and sacrifice had started. At only twenty-six, the new Queen had to figure it out for herself. Wisely, she chose not to make major changes to the running of the Royal Household or the institution. Cautious by nature, the new Queen felt it best to follow the template for kingship established by her father, George VI, and by her grandfather, George V.

'So often she would say, "My father did it this way, my father told me that,"' said the long-serving courtier Lieutenant Colonel Sir Malcolm Ross, who served the Queen for nearly twenty years.

On 2 June 1953, London was once again the media centre of the world. News that the New Zealander Edmund Hillary and Nepalese Sherpa, Tenzing Norgay, of the British expedition led by Colonel John Hunt, had become the first people to reach the summit of Mount Everest was released on the morning of the coronation. Many interpreted it as a portent for a reinvigorated British Commonwealth after the painful and slow death of the British Empire. Hotels and boarding houses were full, and it was said that wealthy Americans were in exclusive occupation of the rooms overlooking the coronation parade.

The Queen admitted years later that she had been deeply moved by the entire experience of the religious service. In 1937, as an eleven-year-old, she had watched her father's crowning. Now her son, Charles, aged only four, was among the 8,251 guests in the Abbey and, like his mother, he witnessed the coronation. (Princess Anne did not attend the ceremony, as at the age of two she was considered too young.) Charles received a special, hand-painted children's invitation to his mother's coronation and watched history unfold alongside his beloved grandmother, now the Queen Mother. Charles was only four at the time, and he became the first child to witness his mother's coronation as sovereign.

He was understandably fascinated by his mother's crown, the Imperial State Crown, which weighs more than 1kg and is adorned with 2,901 precious stones, including the infamous Cullinan II diamond.[8] Lady Anne Glenconner, a close friend and lady-in-waiting of Princess Margaret who had been a maid of honour at the coronation, revealed in a podcast by the jeweller Annoushka Ducas, *My Life in Seven Charms*, how Charles tried to get his hands on it.

'Prince Charles got his paws on it when we got back to Buckingham Palace,' she said, recalling how he made a beeline for it when the Queen put it on the table. 'We thought he was going to drop it. We thought, *oh my goodness, that would be a bad omen*. But luckily, I think my mother, as a lady-in-waiting, seized it from him and took it away.' Lady Anne also revealed that the Queen would wear the crown while she was writing letters, saying, 'I think Prince Charles says he remembers going in and seeing her [wearing it]. He asked her why she was wearing it and she said she was practising.'

Charles would say later, 'I have vivid memories of the coronation. I remember my mother coming to say goodnight to my sister and me while wearing the crown, so that she could get used to its weight on her head before the coronation ceremony. I recall thousands of people gathered in The Mall outside Buckingham Palace chanting, "We want the Queen" and keeping me awake at night.'

CHAPTER 3

Colditz in Kilts

*Children may be indulged at home, but school is expected to be
a spartan and disciplined experience in the process of developing
into self-controlled, considerate and independent adults.*

**PRINCE PHILIP IN A PREFACE TO A HISTORY OF HIS AND
CHARLES'S OLD PREPARATORY SCHOOL, CHEAM**

In May 1954, after six months away on their groundbreaking tour
of the Commonwealth, Elizabeth and Philip, the world's new star
couple, were reunited with their children in the port city of Tobruk,
on Libya's eastern Mediterranean coast. Their 500 engagements
in Commonwealth countries that spanned the globe, on what
is still the longest-ever royal tour, had helped to unify the new
Commonwealth under Her Majesty's banner and to cement her
position as symbolic leader of much of the so-called free world, the
old British Empire. It had been a great success, with huge crowds
greeting the royal couple wherever they went, especially in New
Zealand and Australia.

It had, however, come at a cost to their family life. Despite the
long separation from their parents, Prince Charles and Princess
Anne, who had sailed to Tobruk aboard the new royal yacht HMY
Britannia, were not met with loving hugs or kisses by their mother
and father. Instead, in public at least, the Queen and Philip, who
had entrusted their children to the care of the Queen Mother and

their nannies, simply shook hands with their five-year-old son and three-year-old daughter. The Queen later joked, 'They were terribly polite. I don't think they knew who we were at all!'

The truth is, for whatever reason, Elizabeth and Philip were simply not demonstrative parents. The duke, like many contemporary fathers, was inclined to be strict with his children. Such was his sense of humour that he tended to poke fun at them, with little appreciation of his son Charles's sensitive nature.

Anne, however, was close to her father. After she was born, he allegedly told everyone, 'It's the sweetest girl.' Philip encouraged her boisterous behaviour as a youngster, which might explain her strong and opinionated personality. She was much more a 'chip off his old block' than Charles. Anne coped better with her father's unique 'banter' and shared his sense of humour. She also appeared to have inherited some of her father's characteristics. Anne would cheerfully brave his taunts, not taking them too seriously, unlike her older brother, who would visibly recoil. He would freeze in apparent awe of his loud father, and gravitated towards his quieter, more sympathetic mother.

Charles's innate sensitivity as a child did not sit well with alpha male Philip's parenting style. He practised the 'authoritarian parenting' style, perhaps in a bid to toughen up his son. It meant to outsiders, who did not see the whole picture, that some of Philip's actions appeared too harsh. Even family members, such as the Queen Mother, frowned upon his brashness and the way he treated Charles. It is also true that many of its practices would be frowned upon today. Philip would set very strict rules and expect Charles to meet incredibly high standards. It was a way to exert control over his behaviour or activities. There was little warmth towards his son, and, growing up, Charles often felt lonely and isolated.

In Philip's defence, he believed those around Charles, perhaps overly conscious of his unique status, were adding to his son becoming overindulged. In particular, he clashed with his mother-in-law Queen Elizabeth, the Queen Mother, whom he felt pandered to the prince. He believed that introducing a 'tough love' approach would counteract Charles being spoiled. In fairness, Philip's own challenging upbringing had taught him to be resourceful and to cope with whatever life threw at him.

His father, Prince Andrew of Greece and Denmark, who faced execution after a military coup in Greece before eventually being exiled, had effectively abandoned him as a teenager to live a playboy existence in the South of France, and he had been separated from his mother, Princess Alice of Battenberg,[1] ever since she was sectioned by her own family after she was diagnosed with schizophrenia and committed to a sanatorium. His go-to phrase throughout his life was, 'Just get on with it.' He expected his children to follow the same philosophy.

Perhaps unaware of the reasons for Philip's stance, many who witnessed the father/son dynamic felt his behaviour towards Charles was tantamount to bullying. Philip was often publicly dismissive of his son's achievements and could be sarcastic in his tone when talking to him. It made the already reserved boy even more nervous when he was in his father's presence. When Charles was sitting with his parents during teatime, the atmosphere was often tense.

'Somehow even those contacts were lacking in warmth,' recalled Sir Martin (later Lord) Charteris, the Queen's former senior aide. 'The Queen is not good at showing affection either.'

Of course, as with any family, there were lighter moments away from prying eyes, but they were sporadic. When Charles was four, the Queen tried to teach her son to ride a horse but, unfortunately, said Charteris, he found the idea of the horse bolting to be frightening. Again, Anne outshone him, as she was a natural in the saddle.[2]

Philip's matter-of-fact approach to life extended to his choice of school for his son. After her accession in 1952, Queen Elizabeth had made it clear that she would defer to her husband on family matters, and in particular their children's education. The Duke of Edinburgh's attitude seemed to be, 'What is good enough for me, is good enough for him.' It did not seem to matter to him that he and his son were like chalk and cheese. The boisterous Philip excelled at sports and outdoors endeavours as a child, while Charles, although still an accomplished sportsman, was more reserved and sensitive, a boy who preferred the comfort of his nanny's company.

Philip's determination that Charles went to his own alma mater, the remote Scottish boarding school Gordonstoun, has since been deemed an error of judgement by some, including the Queen and the late Queen Mother, and it damaged Charles's relationship with his father for many years.

Previously unpublished letters written to her daughter reveal that the Queen Mother, who viewed Charles as her favourite grandchild, tried to sway his parents' choice of schooling, because she rightly predicted that attending Gordonstoun would bring him misery. She felt that Eton College should be the preferred option, given that it was situated in the shadow of Windsor Castle, and she believed the style of teaching and the attitude of his peers would be to Charles's advantage.

'I have been thinking such a lot about Charles,' the Queen Mother wrote to the Queen, in a missive addressed to 'My Darling Lilibet' and dated 23 May 1961. 'I suppose that he will be taking his entrance exam for Eton soon. I do hope he passes, because it might be the ideal school for one of his character and temperament.

However good Gordonstoun is, it is miles and miles away and he might as well be at school abroad.'

She added, 'All your friends' sons are at Eton, and it is so important to growing up that you and Philip can see him during school days and keep in touch with what is happening. He would be terribly cut off and lonely in the far north. I do hope you don't mind my writing my thoughts on this subject, but I have been thinking and worrying about it all (possibly without cause).'[3]

The Queen Mother knew she had good cause, but Philip proved intractable. He was adamant that if his son was to become the first Prince of Wales to be educated at school, it would be at his old school, Gordonstoun, in Elgin, Moray, Scotland. The duke ruled out Eton College, saying it was far too close to Windsor and the prince would be harassed by the media if it was decided that he study there. Philip believed his diffident eldest son, given his role in life, needed to experience the unrestrained atmosphere of Gordonstoun to strengthen his character. He got his way and Charles started his first term there in April 1962.

Elizabeth and Philip saw their children only after breakfast and after teatime. It may not seem to be appropriate by twenty-first-century standards, but it does not mean that they were dreadful people. 'She had been brought up in that style herself,' Robert Lacey, the historical adviser for Netflix's *The Crown*, and author of *The Crown: The Inside History*, explained to *Town & Country* magazine, referring to the formality of the parent/child relationship and the relative lack of daily contact that she and Philip had with their two older children. He further added that the Queen thought it best to have nannies raise her children while she was travelling, rather than bring them along with her.

In contrast, the Queen Mother knew how to nurture him. I think the key to their relationship is that she saw in him the same sort of insecurity she saw in her husband George VI. In other words, she knew that Charles needed to be given a lot of support and to be bolstered emotionally, which is what she did very well, rather better than his parents.

Charles took every opportunity to escape Gordonstoun and visit the Queen Mother at her Scottish home, Birkhall. Once there, in his book *Charles: A Biography*, Anthony Holden recounts, 'The Queen Mother listened to Charles's plaintive outpourings about his loneliness, his homesickness, the impossibility of blending into school like other boys.'

'She provided a much-needed shoulder to cry on,' the Queen Mother's biographer Hugo Vickers wrote in *Elizabeth: The Queen Mother*. 'You must remember that, when the Queen was away on her tour of the Commonwealth, from November 1953 until May 1954, the Queen Mother was really Prince Charles and Princess Anne's guardian. They were very young then and they would share weekends [with her] at Royal Lodge in Windsor Great Park, and they spent a long Christmas holiday together at Sandringham. I think it was then that Charles bonded with his grandmother.'

They had a mutual adoration. Their sense of humour was the same, they enjoyed the same activities, and the Queen Mother instilled a love of culture in him. He recalled the 'sheer joy' he experienced when she took him to the Royal Opera House to see the Bolshoi Ballet and, when he was very young, she would walk him through the corridors of Windsor Castle explaining all the paintings. Until her death, she kept a boyhood photo of Charles on her desk, and her letters about him radiate affection. 'Charles is a great love of mine. He is such a darling,' she says in one, later telling the Queen, 'He is intensely affectionate. I'm sure that he will always be a very loving and enjoyable child.'

Her personal letters to the prince are perhaps the most doting.

She was thrilled when he sent her flowers after an appendix operation in 1964, saying, 'My darling Charles, I can't tell you how touched and delighted I was.' He in return tried to make light of his misery. Even when he was feeling down, he would joke to her about the teachers and about his own inadequacies.

However, returning to Gordonstoun after a break filled Charles with dread. 'I hate coming back here and leaving everyone at home... I hardly get any sleep at the House because I snore and get hit on the head the whole time. It is absolute hell,' he noted about boarding at the school, in a letter of 9 February 1963.

Charles would later let slip to his sons that he was 'persecuted' as a boy and was sent to the school by his parents to 'toughen him up', according to Harry's memoir, *Spare*. He confided that he was bullied horrendously because he was one of the sensitive, bookish types. Harry remembers his father 'murmuring ominously to himself, "I nearly didn't survive."' How did he manage it? By clinging on to his teddy bear, which for years afterwards went everywhere with Charles, according to his younger son.

One event irritates Charles to this day, especially the punishments that were meted out to those involved: the so-called 'Cherry Brandy incident'.[4] On a sailing trip to the Isle of Lewis, a cinema visit had been arranged to see a Jayne Mansfield film at the Stornoway Playhouse after dinner at the local pub, the Crown Inn. The barmaid Christine Matheson had no idea who Charles was and asked him what he wanted to drink. The fourteen-year-old prince innocently said the first drink that entered his head and ordered a cherry brandy for two shillings and sixpence. It became a huge scandal, because also in the bar was a freelance journalist, who transmitted the story of the heir to the throne's underage drinking to the world's press.

When Charles first arrived at the school, his housemaster warned the other boys that to be caught bullying the heir to the throne would risk expulsion. This had, unsurprisingly, the opposite effect. Charles was picked on at once, 'maliciously, cruelly and without respite'. A prince, let alone an insecure prince, would have found it hard enough to befriend his peers. 'Even to open a conversation with the heir to the throne was to court humiliation, to face the charge of "sucking up" and to hear the collective "slurping" noises that denoted a toady and a sycophant,' Jonathan Dimbleby observed in his book *The Prince of Wales: A Biography*.

The prince took this abuse on the chin. He never complained to his teachers or his parents. He was far too proud to let his frustrations show. But privately he was miserable and hated returning. To be sent to one of the toughest schools in Britain was a ghastly mistake.

Charles later described the school as being like 'Colditz in kilts'. 'It was like penal servitude,' agreed William Boyd, the bestselling novelist and screenwriter and a Gordonstoun contemporary of Charles. 'I happen to know, from his own lips, that Prince Charles utterly detested it.'

'He was bullied,' recalled Ross Benson, the late *Daily Mail* correspondent, who was also a contemporary of the prince at the school. 'He was crushingly lonely for most of his time there. The wonder is that he survived with his sanity intact.' For the school was filled with toughs, according to Benson. 'Had their parents not been rich enough to pay the fees – a third higher than those at Eton – these pupils would probably have ended their educational careers in prison rather than at a public school.'

His father did not see it. Charles struggled dutifully on, head held high, and said nothing. To be fair, the Duke of Edinburgh had enjoyed a happy time at the school in the 1930s. He admonished his son in letters, urging him to be more resourceful. 'This did not help,' Jonathan Dimbleby wrote in his 1994 authorised biography of Charles. As the prince and his peers matured, however, his school environment improved markedly, as did his attitude towards it. His school life was still not to his liking, but nor was it all hell.

At seventeen, Charles was given a break from the numbing Scottish regimen with two terms at the Australian outback school, Timbertop. It helped him to grow as a person. 'I took him out there a boy,' said his acting equerry, David Checketts, 'and brought back a man.' Charles's return to Gordonstoun was triumphant, first being appointed head of house, then Guardian (head boy) of the school.

'In many ways,' summed up Ross Benson, 'Charles was worthy of that responsibility placed upon him. He was honest, honourable, and hardworking. If his judgement was sometimes flawed, he erred only on the side of compassion. Along the way, however, he had to acquire a hard veneer of self-absorption to protect the vulnerability that had been such a mark of his young character – but was now, forever, lost from sight.'

In 2002, in a controversial examination of Her Majesty by the respected writer Graham Turner in the *Daily Telegraph*, the Queen was portrayed as a distant mother who failed to provide her children with firm guidance. In the article, an unnamed 'private secretary' was quoted as saying that the Royal Family would have been in a far better state had the Queen 'taken half as much trouble about the rearing of her children as she has about the breeding of her horses'. Turner also quoted the former Dean of Windsor, Michael Mann, who recalled how Anne herself came to see him before her second wedding and complained that she had been unable to talk to her mother about it.

Instead of aligning herself with Charles – whose biographer Jonathan Dimbleby had been told that the Queen spent just an hour and a half a day with him when he was a child and suggested that she lacked warmth – Princess Anne was furious with what she regarded as her brother's self-indulgence and the book's suggestion that the Queen had been an 'uncaring mother'. She publicly defended their mother as a loving parent and said she disagreed with Charles's recollections that he felt 'emotionally estranged' from his parents and all his life had yearned for a different kind of affection that they'd been 'unable or unwilling to offer'.

In an interview for a four-part BBC TV documentary, *Queen & Country*, to mark the Queen's Golden Jubilee in 2002, Anne said it was 'extraordinary' for anybody to claim her mother had ever not cared about her children, although protocol demanded that her children and grandchildren had to bow or curtsey to her, and she spent a lot of time apart from them. Anne said, 'I simply don't believe there is any evidence whatsoever to suggest that she wasn't caring. It just beggars belief.'

Charles, however, was quoted as saying that the people who raised him were not his parents, but 'inevitably the nursery staff'. In her 2005 book, *The Firm*, Penny Junor went further, saying that Philip did not show much affection towards his son. Ms Junor wrote, 'The Duke of Edinburgh was and is a bully and was sparing in his affection.' She claimed Philip was 'rough' with his son and 'frequently reduced the boy to tears', causing 'irretrievable damage' to the father/son relationship.[5]

In the mid-1960s, being Queen may not have been exactly easy, but Elizabeth had become more comfortable in her role and what was expected of her. By now, a decade after having given birth to Princess Anne, she had two more children – Prince Andrew, born on 19 February 1960, and Prince Edward, born on 10 March 1964. She had learned to manage her time better and to ensure that she left space in the schedule for her family, too.

Unlike the awkward meals she had once shared with Charles

when he was a young boy, Elizabeth spent time cycling and chasing her two younger children through the palace and even running behind them as they pedalled along the long corridors. Once a week, Edward and Andrew's nanny Mabel Anderson was given the night off and Elizabeth would take over; something that would never have happened when Charles and Anne were small.

The Queen began to refer to nanny Mabel's night off as her favourite night of the week. She enjoyed putting the boys to bed and even 'happily got up in the night' when they would wake and need soothing before falling back to sleep. She was certainly a more hands-on parent than she was the first time round. Sadly, though, there is no rewind and do it over again when it comes to raising children.

When pressed, Philip clearly did not want to get drawn on his parenting. All that he would say on the record was that he and Elizabeth did the best they could as parents. Lady Kennard, a distant cousin of the Queen and one of her closest friends, went further and told Jonathan Dimbleby that their best was not so bad. Philip, she insisted, was a 'wonderful parent. He played with his children, he read them stories, he took them fishing, he was very involved.' Of course, everything is a matter of perspective, and as a self-effacing young boy Charles saw it differently.

Philip's praise for his younger sons when they were children had irked the teenage Charles. Of course he loved his brothers but, privately, close sources said, he felt a degree of injustice. Andrew's 'macho action-man' image had previously been seen as a positive, but the duke did not hold back later from criticising his son's apparent transgressions, and, later still, he was furious at the way Andrew allowed the Royal Family to be tainted by the sordid Epstein affair.[6]

Philip always shared a unique bond with his youngest child,

Prince Edward. Before she gave birth to him, the Queen spent some time perusing women's magazines and read of the advantages of fathers being present for the birth of their children. Philip agreed and held her hand as their son Edward was born. Typically, he lightened the mood in the delivery room (a bathroom at Buckingham Palace), saying, 'Only a week ago, General de Gaulle was having a bath in this room.'

The Queen was thrilled to be a mother for the fourth time. 'What fun it is to have a baby in the house again,' she is reported as saying. Philip and Elizabeth were able to spend a lot more time with their younger children, Andrew and Edward, than they had been able to with either Charles or Anne at the outset of her long reign. With the large age gap of nearly ten years between Anne and Andrew, it was almost as if they had a new young family.

Charles had been made Prince of Wales at the age of nine, when his mother issued the Letters Patent, published on 26 July 1958. But at the time, she said an investiture would be held when she felt her eldest son would fully appreciate its significance. When Charles reached the age of twenty, the palace announced that the date for the investiture ceremony was to be on 1 July 1969 at Caernarfon Castle, the medieval fortress in Gwynedd, north-west Wales, at the mouth of the River Seiont.

After taking his A levels and leaving Gordonstoun in 1967, Charles had departed from royal tradition by not joining the armed forces, instead choosing to read Archaeology and Physical and Social Anthropology at Trinity College, Cambridge. He had gained an upper second class in his Part One examination in 1968, and was enjoying his academic life, having selected to study history in his second year. He joked, 'The tables will now be turned, and I will be envisaged as a princely swot!'

However, Charles's future was again in the hands of his father. Philip believed it was important that Charles be sent to study for a term at the University College of Wales in Aberystwyth to master the Welsh language ahead of his investiture. The switch of colleges was a political decision rather than simply a cultural one. Philip felt that if his son completed a period of academic study in Welsh, it might help to quell the surge in the revival of nationalism in Scotland and Wales.

Just before his departure to the Welsh college, Charles recorded his first ever radio interview for the BBC Radio 4 *Today* programme on 1 March 1969. The interviewer, Jack de Manio, talked about the prince's student theatrics as part of the 'Revolution' revue at Cambridge, and Charles did his impressive *Goon Show* impersonations, but he was also asked about his attitude towards the apparent hostility against him in Wales.

He answered frankly, saying, 'It would be unnatural, I think, if one didn't feel any apprehension about it. One always wonders what's going to happen. As long as I don't get covered in too much egg and tomato, I'll be all right. But I don't blame people demonstrating like that. They've never seen me before. They don't know what I'm like. I've hardly been to Wales, and you can't really expect people to be overzealous about the fact of having a so-called English prince to come amongst them.'

Prince Philip insisted that Charles's stint in Wales must go ahead regardless, as to cancel the university term in Wales would have been a public relations disaster for both the government and for the prince himself. The Queen and the Labour prime minister, Harold Wilson, agreed with Philip, and felt to pull Charles out would be perceived as weakness – and worse, be seen as bowing to extremist terrorist threats, of which there had been several by Welsh nationalists.[7]

Upon his arrival at Pantycelyn Hall, where he would share accommodation with 250 other students, Charles was met by a 500-strong cheering crowd, which left him 'deeply touched'. In fact, the students were not at all antagonistic towards him and embraced him as one of their own. In the end, Charles thoroughly enjoyed his time at the university and acknowledged later that he was treated very kindly in Aberystwyth.

Charles wrote to a friend, 'If I have learned anything during the last eight weeks, it's been about Wales. They feel so strongly about Wales as a nation, and it means something to them, and they are depressed by what might happen to it if they don't try and preserve the language and the culture, which is unique and special to Wales, and if something is unique and special, I see it as well worth preserving.'[8]

Years later, he said the time he spent studying there had left him with his fondest memories of the time he spent in the principality. He recalled with pleasure the 'memorable times spent exploring mid-Wales during my term at Aberystwyth University', where he learned 'something about the principality and its ancient language, folklore, myths and history.'

On the eve of the investiture ceremony, Charles and his parents boarded the Royal Train, used to convey senior members of the British Royal Family, bound for North Wales. All three of them knew that this pageant had to win over the public and were hoping for a positive response from the people. They had no choice but to trust in the stringent security already put in place by the police and the army. Welsh nationalist fanatics had formed what they called the Free Wales Army and their actions had put them on the radar of the British security service, MI5.

A wake-up call came when an RAF warrant officer was seriously injured in an incident the Free Wales Army had planned. A few days later, the same gang planted a bomb that destroyed the Temple of Peace in Cardiff. Another bomb was found in the lost luggage department of the city's railway station. Clearly an attempt by the Welsh nationalists to maximise publicity, police also received an anonymous warning that Prince Charles had been placed on their target list. It left the twenty-year-old heir to the throne understandably uneasy about the investiture ceremony.

But the event, again with Philip pulling the strings behind the scenes, was a carefully choreographed spectacle brilliantly arranged by Lord Snowdon, Princess Margaret's husband. With a colourful mix of old and new, the investiture was modelled on the previous one arranged for Prince Charles's great-uncle, David (later King Edward VIII and Duke of Windsor), at Caernarfon Castle, on 13 July 1911, when he too was sworn in as the Prince of Wales. Lord Snowdon, however, ensured that this time there would be more than a nod to the epoch and towards the future.

A UK television audience of 19 million, nearly a third of the country, tuned in to watch on 1 July 1969 as the Queen installed her son as the Prince of Wales. Before the ceremony, the prince was driven through Cardiff in an open carriage on his way to the castle past cheering crowds. Then as the guests and choir sang 'God Bless the Prince of Wales', he was conducted to the dais and knelt before the Queen, wearing a robe by royal warrant holders Ede & Ravenscroft, whose skilled tailors had crafted it from handwoven purple velvet lined with ermine, and finished it with an ermine cape and collar fully lined with white silk, similar to the robe made for the previous Prince of Wales, including original solid gold clasps.

Charles was invested with the Insignia of his Principality and the Earldom of Chester: a sword, coronet, mantle, gold ring and gold rod. Television footage shows that the prince was a little awkward, perhaps overawed by the spectacle, with him centre stage. He acquitted himself well as he gave his formal response. 'I, Charles, Prince of Wales, do become your liegeman of life and limb and of earthly worship and faith and truth I will bear unto you to live and die against all manner of folks.'

Philip, the proud father, watched from his vantage point among the 4,000 VIP guests at the ceremony as his eldest son swore his allegiance to the Queen, just as the duke had done at his wife's coronation sixteen years earlier.

Charles would later write that he found it profoundly moving when he placed his hands between his mother's and spoke the oath of allegiance. The Queen then presented the prince to the crowd at Eagle Gate and at the lower ward to the sound of magnificent fanfares. After that he was again paraded through the streets before retiring aboard the royal yacht at Holyhead for a well-deserved dinner, an emotionally exhausted but very happy prince.

Buoyed by the experience, Charles noted, 'As long as I do not take myself too seriously, I should not be too badly off.'

The next day the newly installed Prince of Wales set off alone to undertake a week of solo engagements around the principality. He recalled being 'utterly amazed' by the positive reaction he received. As the tour progressed into England, the crowds grew even bigger. At the end of it, Charles arrived exhausted but elated at Windsor Castle. He retired to write up his diary, noting the silence after the day's cheers and applause, reflecting that he had much to live up to and expressing the hope that he could provide constructive help for Wales.

But if the young man was looking for praise from his mother and father, he would be disappointed. That was not their style.

CHAPTER 4

The Feeling of Emptiness

*In a case like yours, the man should sow his wild oats and have
as many affairs as he can before settling down, but for a wife, he
should choose a suitable, attractive, and sweet-charactered girl
before she has met anyone else she might fall for.*

**LETTER WRITTEN BY LORD LOUIS MOUNTBATTEN
TO PRINCE CHARLES, 1974**

'I don't make friends easily, I find the position one is in builds up a
little bit of a barrier,' said a young, awkward Prince Charles, who was
put on the spot by the BBC television presenter Cliff Michelmore.
The television special had been arranged for transmission on 26
June 1969, five days ahead of his investiture at Caernarfon Castle,
encouraged by Prince Philip.

In a joint production between HTV and BBC, Charles,
who looked younger than his twenty years, was questioned by
Michelmore and ITV's Brian Connell on a wide range of subjects,
from his ability to make friends and to forge relationships, his
apparent shyness and his love of acting, to his concerns over
Welsh nationalists.

Charles, speaking in a stereotypical cut-glass, upper-class
accent, admitted to still being 'fairly shy', but said he was trying
to overcome his natural reticence. Michelmore, best known for
the BBC television programme *Tonight*, which he presented

from 1957 to 1965, prodded further, trying to give the viewer a better understanding of the future king. Was he like others from his 'protest' generation, dissatisfied with what he saw going on in the country? 'A little bit,' Charles responded, but, showing his patriotism, he chose to steer away from making controversial comments that Fleet Street editors might pounce on. Instead, he stressed that people in Britain did not realise 'how lucky they were' to live here, compared to what faced people in some other countries.

Out of the blue, Connell, a trim-bearded individual who was renowned for keeping a signed photo of Prince Philip on his desk, asked Charles a more personal question. 'Do you have any thoughts about the lady the Prince of Wales should marry, should she still be a royal or titled lady?'

Charles laughed nervously and licked his lower lip before he answered.

'You see, it's awfully difficult, because you've got to remember when you marry in my position you are going to marry somebody who perhaps one day is going to become Queen, and you've got to choose somebody very carefully, I think, who could fulfil this particular role, because people like you would expect quite a lot from somebody like that, and it's got to be somebody pretty special. And the one advantage of marrying a princess for instance, or somebody from a royal family, is that they do know what happens. The only trouble is I feel I would like to marry somebody English, or perhaps Welsh... British.'

As ridiculous as the boyish-looking heir to the throne sounded, he was right. For in those days it was expected of him that he would choose a future wife who would be an aristocrat and a virgin, and not a Roman Catholic. Moreover, she would be a person able to cope with the rigours of royal life. Marriage, however, was not his paramount concern at this stage of his life. Indeed, in his early twenties, he intended to follow his mentor Lord Mountbatten's rather lewd advice to 'sow his wild oats and have as many affairs' as possible, before settling down.[1]

For Charles, as his interview showed, it was never going to be as simple as falling in love with a girl and marrying her. His marriage was always going to be a national event.

Charles met his first real love, Lucia Santa Cruz, when he was an undergraduate at Trinity College, Cambridge. The Latin linguist, the daughter of the Chilean ambassador to the Court of St James Victor Santa Cruz, was twenty-eight when she and Charles met in Cambridge in 1970 – six years older than the prince, who was then twenty-two. She spoke four languages and had just published a book titled *Three Essays on Chilean Women*.

He was impressed by her intellect, as she already had degrees from King's College, London and St Antony's College, Oxford, as well as by her beauty. At the time, Lucia was employed as a research assistant by the Master of Trinity College, Lord 'Rab' Butler. The two hit it off immediately and enjoyed a carefree romance. Charles even introduced the Roman Catholic academic to the Queen, and, even though this first love affair petered out, the two remained friends.

However, his focus at Cambridge was not on finding a bride. Charles had personal ambitions, such as learning to fly, and in his second year as an undergraduate at Trinity College he had asked for flying lessons to be arranged with the Royal Air Force. It had been a passion of his father's and perhaps he was trying to make Philip proud, too. With Philip's backing, the Queen eventually agreed and in 1968 Charles was filmed taking to the skies with his instructor in a red de Havilland Chipmunk, a single-engine, two-seater trainer, at RAF Tangmere.

After studying Archaeology, Anthropology and History at Cambridge, Charles graduated in 1970 with a 2:2 degree. He then trained as a jet pilot at Royal Air Force Cranwell, Lincolnshire, before enrolling in the Britannia Royal Naval College for a six-week course of study, arriving in his Aston Martin in the uniform of an acting sub lieutenant to a parade in his honour, put on by the naval cadets. He began his Royal Navy service on the guided missile destroyer HMS *Norfolk* on 5 November 1971.

Earlier that year, Lucia Santa Cruz had moved into a flat in Stack House in Belgravia, London, one of a quartet of seven-storey towers built in the 1950s. A social young woman, she became close to one of her neighbours, the spirited debutante Camilla Shand, who shared the flat she rented with her friend Virginia Carrington, daughter of the future foreign secretary Lord Peter Carrington.

While Charles was paying a visit to Lucia at her apartment in 1971, his hostess invited Camilla to join them for a drink, believing her friend and the prince would hit it off and were well suited. It was there that Lucia referred to the fact that Camilla's great-grandmother, Alice Keppel,[2] had been a mistress of his great-great-grandfather, King Edward VII, which both her guests found amusing. She reportedly added, 'Now you two watch your genes,' because of their ancestors' adultery.[3] It was the start of a brief, but nonetheless passionate, love affair.

By the time Charles first met Camilla, at twenty-three, he had already had several girlfriends, but his relationships with them were somewhat chaste. Instead, his sexual education was to be gained with more experienced women, preferably married.

Lady Tryon, an Australian married to an English peer and nicknamed 'Kanga' by the prince, is said to have been one such lover. Her maiden name was Dale Harper, and she was the vivacious blonde daughter of a wealthy Melbourne printing magnate. Charles first met her in Australia in 1966 when he was a teenager, while he spent two terms at Geelong Grammar School in Victoria. They renewed their friendship when she moved to Britain to work as a public relations officer for the Australian airline Qantas. Charles found her lack of deference refreshing.[4]

Charles had been concerned for some time about how he would find the right woman with whom to share his life and responsibilities. He knew that whoever he wed would be as much married to the institution of monarchy as to him and it weighed heavily on his mind. In the witty and confident Camilla Shand, with whom he was besotted, he saw a woman he believed was compatible with him, but also somebody who had the qualities needed to handle the job of being a princess. She was not fazed by him or monarchy and she had the right social credentials, she was a member of the Church of England, and he had fallen head over heels in love with her. By late autumn of 1972, they had become inseparable. Her sexual energy excited the rather naive prince like no one else previously.

There was a catch, however, because at that time in her life Camilla did not feel the same as he did. While she was extremely fond of Charles, her passion burned for the man she had previously dated since she was eighteen, cavalry officer Andrew Parker Bowles, nine years her senior. Sadly for Charles, she was still captivated by the dashing British Army captain. It was only when Parker Bowles was posted to Germany in 1972 that Camilla felt the relationship was over for good, and she was free to start her liaison with Charles.

His great mentor Lord Mountbatten encouraged the relationship, as he saw Camilla as 'good mistress material', although he also rightly believed that Charles was more devoted to her, and that she was still in love with her eventual first husband, Andrew Parker Bowles.

Charles's next Royal Navy posting would prove to be the end of their first romance. In early December 1972 he was commanded to join his new ship, the frigate HMS *Minerva*, and was set to sail on her for an eight-month visit to the Caribbean in January.

The narrator on a British Movietone News film made at the time announced: 'Whatever his royal duties on shore, at sea he gives and obeys orders like any other member of the ship's company,' signing off with, 'So hold that course, Lieutenant, and no falling asleep on watch.'

Camilla joined Charles on a tour of the ship before it sailed, and they had lunch on board. She returned the following weekend and he bemoaned the fact that it would be 'the last time I shall see her for eight months'.

It was to prove, for him, much worse than that. For Camilla gave no promise to wait for him and when Andrew Parker Bowles returned to the UK, she and the handsome officer rekindled their romance and became engaged in March 1973. Andrew was a good catch – the fact that he was a philanderer and everyone wanted him made him even more tempting. Camilla regarded her relationship with Charles as a fling and jumped at the opportunity to wed the man she had been in love with for years just weeks later, in July the same year.

After arriving in the Caribbean on HMS *Minerva*, Charles had joined HMS *Fox* for a month and moved on to Antigua, where he was delighted by English Harbour, which had originally been Admiral Lord Nelson's dockyard during the eighteenth-century wars with the French. It was here that news reached him of Camilla's engagement to Andrew Parker Bowles. In May, he received a letter from his father informing him that his sister, Princess Anne, who had herself previously dated Parker Bowles, had agreed to marry army captain Mark Phillips of

1st The Queen's Dragoon Guards, an Olympic gold medal-winning horseman for Team GB.

It appeared to Charles that everything he held dear to him at home was being taken away. He had been completely blindsided by Camilla. Devastated at the news, he wrote to Lord Mountbatten that it seemed so cruel that fate should be this way. 'Such a blissful, peaceful, and mutually happy relationship… I suppose the feelings of emptiness will pass eventually.' In fact, Charles and Camilla remained friends over the next seven years, and she became one of his most trusted confidantes. On his return from sea, in 1974 when the Parker Bowles' first child, Tom, was born, Camilla asked Charles to be a godfather and he accepted.

Charles, now free to date whoever he wanted, was once again one of the most eligible bachelors in the world and continued to play the field. The actress Susan George caught his eye and enjoyed several intimate dinner dates with him before she met her long-time husband, the actor Simon MacCorkindale. Now an Arabian horse dealer, Susan George was hotly sought after on the social scene at the time and her fame soared after her performance in the 1971 film *Straw Dogs*. Their relationship was never confirmed but an informed source, who was very close to her, said even at their most intimate moments she still called him 'Sir'. She always referred to the prince as her 'special individual', but publicly denied any romantic involvement.

Charles knew that in time he must marry a woman who was suitable to be his Queen Consort. He was later to comment, 'I've fallen in love with all sorts of girls, and I fully intend to go on doing so, but I've made sure that I haven't married the first person I've fallen in love with. I think one's got to be aware of the fact that falling madly in love with someone is not necessarily the starting point to getting married. Marriage is basically a strong friendship, so I'd want to marry someone whose interests I could share.'

In January 1974, Charles flew on an RAF VC10 to Tengah Airbase in Singapore, before joining HMS *Jupiter*, a 2,200-ton frigate docked at ANZUK Naval Base. Now a full lieutenant, he would serve as communications officer under the ship's captain, Commander John Gunning. On the ship he was treated as one of the officers, but whenever the *Jupiter* arrived in port it always caused a commotion, as the prince was on board. When the frigate sailed into San Diego, there was a frenzy of excitement, with several television cameras waiting to greet it out of the fog. The prince served on the frigate until her return to the UK later that year.

It was while on shore leave that Charles pursued his friendship with the Hollywood star Barbra Streisand, with whom he formed a close bond in the 1970s. He later recalled during a radio programme called *Music and Memories with* HRH The *Prince of Wales* in 2022 – part of the UK's national Thank You Day honouring Britain's National Health Service for their dedication during the COVID-19 pandemic – how he met the singer for the first time.

'In 1974, when I was serving in the Royal Navy... as a young lieutenant in the frigate HMS *Jupiter*, we called in to the United States navy's base in San Diego, California... when I heard that she was currently making the film [*Funny Lady* – sequel to *Funny Girl*]. I was lucky enough to visit the set and to meet her there. I shall never forget her dazzling, effervescent talent and the unique vitality and attraction of her voice and her acting ability. This next song, "Don't Rain on my Parade", is therefore full of special memories of – I hardly dare think of it now – forty-seven years ago.'

Streisand was equally effusive about Charles in an interview with the British television presenter Ross King. Responding to the prince's compliments about her, she said that 'it was so sweet' of him to share some of those 'special memories'. 'We became friends,' said Streisand, 'and I loved spending some time at Highgrove for a weekend fundraiser and going through his gardens.' She explained that their friendship all took place 'before he met Diana,' adding, 'I had a very funny line on stage when he came to see [my] show. I said, "You know, if I played my cards right, I could have wound up being the first Jewish princess!"'

Once back in the UK, Charles threw himself into improving his flying skills and qualified as a helicopter pilot at Royal Naval Air Station Yeovilton. From there he joined the 845 Naval Air Squadron aboard the aircraft carrier HMS *Hermes*. Then, in February 1976, Charles commanded the coastal minehunter HMS *Bronington* for nine months. It was while serving on the mahogany-hulled boat in his final year of service that the prince was involved in an incident off the coast of North Wales, which ultimately cost the Royal Navy several thousand pounds. One of the *Bronington*'s former company, Paul Henke, revealed what happened in the 2015 documentary *Charles, Prince of Wales: A Life Full of Madness*.

He said, 'When we came to anchor up in the morning to move as a squadron, Prince Charles pulled his anchor up to find the truss channel telephone cable was hooked on the flukes of his anchor. They spent a long time trying to get rid of that cable. Finally, they had to ditch one and a half shackles of phosphor-bronze chain, which is probably the most valuable thing that naval minehunters carry.'

It later transpired that Charles was criticised by his Royal Navy superiors for his role in this incident. He was upset by the whole event, but he had served his time and by then he was more than ready to move on with the next stage of his life. Three months later, Charles stood down from active service in a planned departure.

When the time came, he was given the unusual send-off – which involves the wearing of a toilet seat round the neck.

Despite his considerable wealth and resources, Charles has devoted his entire life to public duty, supporting the Queen in her role as head of state as well as being a global philanthropist. Later that year, using his £7,400 severance pay from the Royal Navy, he started up the Prince's Trust, his charity dedicated to funding community initiatives that support disadvantaged youth.

Charles entered the world of green activism early on. His first speech on the environment was in 1968 – years before the phrase 'global warming' was widely in use.[5] Now, Charles's 'inner dissident' began to surface. After he left the Royal Navy he started to develop a reputation for being outspoken as heir to the throne, and faced an avalanche of media criticism for raising concerns close to his heart. Throughout the late 1970s and early 1980s, he found himself a lost voice as he called for harmony and balance in society and the way we all live together. As a teenager, it is true, as he put it, that he 'minded' about the 'white heat' of so-called progress and technology, and the determination of big business to suppress nature, the uprooting of trees and hedgerows, the draining of wet places and destruction of interesting habitats.

'Most critics imagined that I somehow wanted to turn the clock back to some mythical golden age, when all was a perfect rural idyll. But nothing could be further from the truth,' he would write later in his book, *Harmony: A New Way of Looking at Our World*, co-written with Tony Juniper and Ian Skelly.[6]

On 19 February 1970, at just twenty-one, Charles made his first landmark speech about the environment and warned of the threats from plastic waste and chemicals dumped into rivers and seas, and air pollution from industry, vehicles and planes. Back then the ideas, now mainstream, were dismissed. 'We are faced at this moment with the horrifying effects of pollution in all its cancerous forms,' he said at the 'Countryside in 1970' conference, Steering Committee for Wales, Cardiff.

His robust language raised eyebrows among the political class and in the corridors of Whitehall. He did not hold back, happy to confirm himself as an environmental radical. He went on, 'There is the growing menace of oil pollution at sea, which almost destroys beaches and certainly destroys tens of thousands of seabirds. There is chemical pollution discharged into rivers from factories and chemical plants, which clogs up the rivers with toxic substances and adds to the filth in the seas. There is air pollution from smoke and fumes discharged by factories and from gases pumped out by endless cars and aeroplanes.'

Speaking about the reaction to the speech when it was made in 1970, Charles said, 'I was considered rather dotty, to say the least, for even suggesting these things, rather like when I set up a reed-bed sewage treatment system at Highgrove all those years ago – that was considered completely mad!'[7]

Ultimately, of course, many of his 'dotty' ideas would prove to be spot on and are mainstream today. The specially built reed-bed sewage system, which attracts clusters of dragonflies at its treatment end, is now used for all the waste water at Highgrove.

CHAPTER 5

End of an Era

It made me want to die too.

THE PRINCE OF WALES ON HEARING OF THE MURDER OF
LORD MOUNTBATTEN BY AN IRA BOMB

While serving in the Royal Navy, Charles had made several official overseas visits on behalf of the Queen. In 1970, he and Anne made a two-day informal visit to Washington as guests of President Richard Nixon at the White House. The president told twenty-one-year-old Charles and his nineteen-year-old sister, 'I want you to feel very much at home,' and he would do his part by trying to stay out of sight. The weekend was hosted by the president's daughters, Tricia and Julie, and Julie's husband, David Eisenhower, who planned a round of sightseeing and parties.

Even before leaving the military, Charles stepped up and toured Australia and New Zealand with the Queen, the Duke of Edinburgh and Princess Anne. He made solo visits to Fiji's centenary celebrations in 1974, and the coronation of Nepal's King Birendra the following year, along with the independence celebrations of Papua New Guinea in September.

His foreign forays were increased after his active military service ended, and he visited the 1976 Olympics in Montreal, Canada, along with other members of the Royal Family, to see his sister

Anne compete in the three-day equestrian event on the Queen's horse Goodwill. In 1977, the year of the Queen's Silver Jubilee, Charles made solo visits to Kenya, Ghana, Ivory Coast, Monaco, France, Canada, the USA, Australia and West Germany.

Meanwhile, although sympathetic to his great-nephew's heartbreak, Lord Mountbatten was not overly concerned when he heard that Camilla had returned to Andrew Parker Bowles. He felt Charles was far too young to settle down. She was from a well-off family – her mother was the Hon Rosalind Maud Shand (née Cubitt), the daughter of 3rd Baron Ashcombe – but she was not of high birth. Mountbatten had also counselled Charles, 'I think it is disturbing for women to have experiences if they have to remain on a pedestal after marriage.' However backward it appears now, Charles's princess-to-be would have to be of 'pure' reputation, and Camilla was not a virgin.

Charles did not languish and enjoyed his role as the world's most eligible bachelor. Not all the women he dated were seen as potential brides, but Lady Jane Wellesley, the daughter of the Duke of Wellington, certainly was one of them. They stepped out together from 1973 to 1974, although amid intense media interest, Lady Jane once said, 'Do you honestly believe I want to be Queen?' No romance took off between the couple, but they remained friends.

Still in his early twenties, Charles was in no rush to wed and in 1975, he said, 'I personally feel that a good age for a man to get married is around thirty.' He was free to enjoy the company of a variety of women and did. In 1977, Charles was linked to Lady Sarah Spencer (the older sister of Diana). But all chances of a match evaporated when she spoke to the tabloids about the prince. In an interview, she was reported as saying that she'd had 'thousands of boyfriends', and shared, 'I wouldn't marry anyone I didn't love – whether it was the dustman or the King of England. If he asked me,

I would turn him down. He doesn't want to marry anyway. He's not ready for marriage yet.' Shortly afterwards the prince saw the article and told her, 'You've just done something incredibly stupid.'

Another girlfriend, Davina Sheffield, was embraced by Charles's family. The granddaughter of industrialist Lord McGowan and a cousin of Samantha Sheffield, wife of the future prime minister David Cameron, she was considered a marriage contender, before apparently being ruled out after a boyfriend announced that they had lived together.

After Charles hit the age milestone that he had set himself in 1978, the media took him literally and started adding to the pressure for him to choose a bride. Charles's mentor Mountbatten thought that Amanda Knatchbull, who was Mountbatten's granddaughter and Charles's second cousin, was a perfect match. The prince even proposed to her in 1979, but Amanda did not feel any passion between them and turned him down – becoming a full-time royal did not appeal to her.

Charles also dated Anna Wallace, a Scottish heiress. But she decided to end the relationship because she felt he paid too much attention to Camilla Parker Bowles. Despite being married with two young children, her romantic relationship with the prince had resumed at around that time.

The intimacy between Charles and Camilla, who had always remained friends after she married, returned after the birth of Camilla's daughter Laura, who was born in April 1978, when her husband Andrew returned to his philandering ways. Camilla was drawn to the prince again and an adulterous affair ensued. She was not the first married woman to move in royal circles and have an affair, nor was she to be the last. Charles was fully aware of the danger in conducting an affair with a married woman, but he was prepared to take the risk.

Even if she were to end her marriage, Camilla would still not make a potential bride for the prince; as a divorcee, she would be unacceptable. Besides, Charles enjoyed his bachelor existence, and having his soulmate Camilla as his mistress suited him.

Yet this did not change the fact that he needed to marry.

Dawn on 27 August 1979, a bank holiday, was bright and sunny at Classiebawn Castle near the fishing village of Mullaghmore, County Sligo, in the Republic of Ireland. After days of rain, despite security advice and warnings from the Garda, Earl Mountbatten of Burma, former Chief of the Defence Staff of the United Kingdom and great-grandson of Queen Victoria, decided to take a small party of seven with him lobster-potting and tuna fishing in a wooden boat, the *Shadow V*. On board with Mountbatten were his daughter Lady Patricia, her husband Lord John Brabourne, their fourteen-year-old twins Timothy and Nicholas, and Lord Brabourne's mother, the dowager Lady Doreen Brabourne. Paul Maxwell, aged fifteen, a friend of the family who worked on the boat, was also on board.

Unbeknown to Lord Mountbatten, IRA member Thomas McMahon had slipped onto the unguarded boat that night and attached a radio-controlled 50-pound (23kg) bomb. The bomb was detonated by remote control at 11.39 a.m., when the boat was about two hundred yards from the harbour. Mountbatten, Nicholas Brabourne and Maxwell were killed immediately. Lady Brabourne died the next day, and the others survived serious injuries.

The IRA were quick to admit responsibility for carrying out the bombing, saying it was designed to 'bring to the attention of the English people the continuing occupation of our country'. At the time of the explosion, McMahon, then thirty-one, was seventy miles away, in police custody; by chance he and a second man, gravedigger Francis McGirl, aged twenty-four, had been stopped at a checkpoint after he had laid the explosive. But McMahon had flakes of green paint from Lord Mountbatten's boat and traces of nitroglycerin on his clothes. He and McGirl were charged with murder.

Gerry Adams of Sinn Féin said of Mountbatten's death, 'The IRA gave clear reasons for the execution. I think it is unfortunate that anyone has to be killed, but the furore created by Mountbatten's death showed up the hypocritical attitude of the media establishment.' Adams went on, 'As a member of the House of Lords, Mountbatten was an emotional figure in both British and Irish politics. What the IRA did to him is what Mountbatten had been doing all his life to other people; and with his war record, I don't think he could have objected to dying in what was clearly a war situation. He knew the danger involved in coming to this country. In my opinion, the IRA achieved its objective: people started paying attention to what was happening in Ireland.'

In the end, there was insufficient evidence to place McGirl at Mullaghmore; he was found not guilty of murder and died in 1995. McMahon was sentenced to life imprisonment but was released from jail in August 1998 as part of the Good Friday peace agreement.

On 20 May 2015, local people gathered to greet Charles and his wife, the Duchess of Cornwall, when they visited the Pier Head Hotel in Mullaghmore, where the dead and injured had been brought on makeshift stretchers on that dreadful day. Among those there was Peter McHugh, who helped to pull the bodies from the sea and who described to Charles the events of that day. 'I didn't want to be too sombre. I just gave him the briefest outline of what happened,' he said.

Timothy Knatchbull, Mountbatten's grandson, who was badly injured in the blast, guided Charles's gaze out to where the boat had set off on its fateful trip that morning. Knatchbull has since been vocal in applauding the reconciliation process, having found his own path to 'forgiveness and peace'.

The other child victim, schoolboy Paul Maxwell, had been on holiday from Enniskillen and was earning pocket money as a boat hand. His father John, a teacher, had to steel himself to attend the royal visit, but did so, saying it was the right thing to do. For Paul's mother, Mary Hornsey, it was her first time in Mullaghmore since the day of her son's death, but she had accepted the invitation to meet Charles on a visit she said was 'extending the hand of forgiveness'.

Richard Wood-Martin, who with his wife Elizabeth was in a boat behind Mountbatten's, recalled how they pulled Timothy Knatchbull from the sea: 'There was a puff of smoke, a loud bang, a shower of bits of timber and the boat was gone. One person was blown to the left and it was Timothy. I managed to pull him into the boat. He was face down in the water.'

Understandably, Charles was profoundly affected by the murder of his beloved mentor and great-uncle, Lord Mountbatten. At the time he said that it 'made me want to die too'. To this day, he has said, during quieter, solitary moments he talks to his departed loved ones and in that way keeps Mountbatten and many other dearly missed spirits alive in his heart. In many ways, I believe his great-uncle's death has contributed to Charles's fatalistic attitude towards his own mortality.

On Australia Day of 1994, in Tumbalong Park, Sydney, when a twenty-three-year-old protester called David Kang stormed a stage and fired two blank shots at Prince Charles, he was about to deliver a keynote speech in which he referred to the republican issue.[1] I was among the reporters who were there that day and watched the drama unfold.

Charles's personal protection officer, Superintendent Colin Trimming, barged him out of the line of fire as the rest of the Scotland Yard security detail restrained Kang, along with the 1994 Australian of the Year, Ian Kiernan, who had just received his honour, and was one of the first to subdue the attacker. The Cambodian university student, who claimed later he intended no harm to Charles, was protesting about the treatment of hundreds of Cambodian asylum seekers being held in detention camps in Australia.[2]

After Superintendent Trimming had checked that the attacker was on the ground, he secured the prince, who remained cool, if a little bemused, throughout.

'Suddenly a man leapt out of the crowd to the right and started running flat out towards the dais, firing a pistol as he ran,' he recalled. As it turned out, the gun proved to be a starting pistol. Later, Charles even joked about the incident. Turning to an aide, he recounted an anecdote about how he was charged by a bull elephant while in Kenya. He said the African encounter was far more frightening.

A few years later, during an official visit to Latvia on 8 November 2001, I was inches away from another serious incident when the prince was attacked by a young person, later identified as sixteen-year-old schoolgirl Alina Lebedeva, who slapped him round the face with three red carnations during a walkabout in a protest over NATO's involvement in bombing raids in Afghanistan. He later joked privately about returning home with facial scars from a 'crazed assault by a carnation-wielding, adolescent Latvian Bolshevik' (she was a Latvian communist of Russian ethnicity), which he admitted 'frightened me rigid'.[3]

The Latvians, Charles said, were mortified by this incident. The prince pleaded for her to be treated leniently and she was spared prison, but sentenced to a year of educational measures by a court. He applauds the great strides that former communist countries have made towards freedom, although he remains sceptical about how so many former communists in all these countries suddenly succeed in becoming the wealthiest businesspeople, and yet do not seem to be prepared to take any corporate responsibility for providing social assistance within the community. He has said that it shows how 'crooked' the whole system was in the past.

Charles's view on his own personal security is that he must leave it to the professionals who surround him and just get on with his job. If advised not to do something, he will always take that advice, but he is not going to hide away. He once famously said to reporters during a reception trip in Spain, 'There is nothing you can do if your name is on the bullet.'

Indisputably, Lord Mountbatten was crucial to Charles's development from boy to man in almost every area. He was effectively the grandfather Charles never had, having lost George VI so early in his life and never knowing his paternal grandfather. The anger and devastation Charles felt at the manner of his loss cannot be overstated.

The two men wrote long and meaningful letters to one another, and the urbane Lord Louis became his most trusted mentor early on in his journey, filling the void left by Charles's more complicated relationship with his father, Prince Philip, Mountbatten's nephew. There was nothing he could not share with Mountbatten, nothing that the old man did not seem to have a handle on, from affairs of the heart to advice on matters of state or his military career. Mountbatten had always been there for him, just like his beloved grandmother, the Queen Mother. When the IRA detonated that deadly bomb, it robbed the prince of his wisest male adviser. He was lost without him.

End of an Era

'At the time I could not imagine how we would come to terms with the anguish of such a deep loss,' Charles told an audience in the nearby town of Sligo years later in 2015. 'Through this dreadful experience, I now understand in a profound way the agonies borne by others on these islands of whatever faith or political persuasion.'

CHAPTER 6

Lady Di

I like to be a free spirit. Some don't like that,
but that's the way I am.

PRINCESS DIANA

It was not until Lady Diana Spencer spent a weekend at the Queen's Balmoral estate as the guest of the Prince of Wales in September 1980 that news of their fledgling romance was to reach the public consciousness. On 8 September, the *Sun* newspaper proclaimed on its front page, 'He's in Love Again, Lady Di is the new girlfriend for Charles.' It was the first time Diana had been called 'Lady Di' in the press.

Arthur Edwards, the notorious Fleet Street and royal photographer, had taken a picture of Lady Diana in July at a polo match in which the Prince of Wales had been playing. Arthur had vaguely recognised her and the gold 'D' hanging round her neck, and had taken some pictures for his files, in case he needed to verify who she was. At Balmoral, while he was on assignment photographing Prince Charles fishing by the River Dee, Edwards had spotted Diana again, this time at Charles's side. He quickly figured out this was the same girl from the polo match in July and pulled the picture out of his file to check. He knew instantly he had his major scoop.

Lady Diana had first met Charles in November 1977, when she was only sixteen and he was attending a grouse shooting party at Althorp, the Spencer family estate in west Northamptonshire. Charles's relationship with her older sister Sarah had later fizzled out when she shared the story of her royal romance with two reporters.

Charles and Diana met again three years later, in July 1980, when they were both invited to a weekend barbecue at Philip de Pass's house, Petworth, in West Sussex. 'I was asked to stay with some friends in Sussex and they said, "Oh, the Prince of Wales is staying," and I thought, I hadn't seen him in ages,' Diana told her speech coach, the British actor Peter Settelen, on a tape that was later used for the Channel 4 documentary *Diana: In Her Own Words*.

She added, 'He'd just broken up with his girlfriend and his friend Mountbatten had just been killed. I said it would be nice to see him. I was so unimpressed. I sat there and this man walked in, and I thought, well, I am quite impressed this time round. It was different.' According to Diana, the prince appeared to be taken by her, too.

She said in the tapes: 'He was all over me,' adding, 'We were talking about Mountbatten and his girlfriend, and I said, "You must be so lonely." I said, "It's pathetic watching you walking up the aisle with Mountbatten's coffin in front, ghastly, you need someone beside you." Whereupon he leapt upon me and started kissing me and I thought, urgh, this is not what people do. And he was all over me for the rest of the evening, following me around like a puppy.'

Diana also spoke of how difficult she found those early days of dating the prince. 'He wasn't consistent with his courting abilities. He'd ring me every day for a week, then wouldn't speak to me for three weeks. Very odd. I thought, fine. Well, he knows where I am if he wants me. The thrill when he used to ring up was so immense and intense. It would drive the other three girls in my flat crazy.'

Once Charles's relationship with Lady Diana Spencer was public, Prince Philip became increasingly concerned by what he saw as the unruly behaviour of the photographers and reporters camped outside her west London apartment, Flat 60 in Coleherne Court, an Edwardian mansion block on the Old Brompton Road. She had bought it using £50,000 of inheritance, and shared it with three close girlfriends, Carolyn Bartholomew (née Pride), Anne Hill (née Bolton) and Virginia Clarke (née Pitman). According to Andrew Morton's best-selling book *Diana: Her True Story – In Her Own Words*, Diana described her years at the property as 'the happiest time' of her life.[1]

She was pursued by the press relentlessly, with scores of reporters and photographers turning up every day ready to pounce as she left the flat, to fire in questions and take photographs and splash them across the papers the next day. The nineteen-year-old was caught up in the excitement.

'They chased me everywhere,' recalled Diana, on the tapes recorded years later by Peter Settelen. 'We are talking thirty of them.' She received no practical support from Charles, the police or from media advisers at Buckingham Palace. Charles, of course, felt duty-bound to protect his new girlfriend but, effectively, he was powerless to do so.

On one occasion the editor of this book, Barry Johnston, who lived opposite Diana's apartment at the time and saw first-hand the media attention she was forced to endure, witnessed another side to the story. Late one afternoon he was buying an *Evening Standard* from the newspaper stall at the bottom of Earl's Court Road when Diana came up and stood next to him. When she saw the headline on the newspaper claiming that she had said she was ready to marry soon, she said furiously, 'I didn't say that!', then paid for the paper and walked quickly back to her flat. The next day she issued a denial, perhaps worried that she might scare off Charles by speaking to the press, as her elder sister Sarah had done, or by seeming too keen on getting married to him.

Something decisive needed to be done to protect Diana, and fast. Prince Philip, along with the Queen, was keen for the prince to marry a suitable bride and, in time, to start a family and hopefully produce an heir to the throne. Given that Charles was approaching thirty-two, Philip felt it appropriate to write to his eldest son about it, stressing that he felt the prince should either propose marriage to Lady Diana or let her go.

It was a warm and encouraging letter from father to son, not an abrupt order or ultimatum, as some critics of the duke have interpreted it to be. Contrary to a popular narrative on this subject, Charles did not in any way blame his father or his mother for what some viewed as effectively forcing him into an ill-conceived marriage to Lady Diana.

'It was measured and sensitive,' said Lady Pamela Hicks, who claimed to have read the letter her cousin Philip sent to Charles. Some unfairly use this as evidence that Charles felt he was 'bullied into marriage' by his parents and claim that Philip said he could go back to his mistress, Camilla, if things did not work out. But that is neither fair nor true, and Charles did not feel that.[2]

What is undeniably true is that once the powerful press machine gathered momentum, Charles could see no way out but to marry Lady Diana Spencer. He explained to a close friend years later, 'To have withdrawn [from the marriage], as you can no doubt imagine, would have been cataclysmic. Hence I was permanently between the devil and the deep blue sea.'[3] He went on,

'Things were very different in those days. The power and influence of the media driving matters towards an engagement and wedding were unstoppable.'

Charles was right, of course. The so-called Fourth Estate was all powerful and the tabloid editors drove the royal romance story because it sold newspapers, lots of newspapers. If Charles blamed anyone for what turned out to be a disastrous marriage being played out in public, it was a ferocious media, 'aided and abetted by somebody rather close to me [Diana]', whom he believed, towards the end of their marriage, 'lived hand to mouth with the press'.

As the pressure on him increased, Charles did not need a letter from his father to remind him of his responsibilities as a gentleman, but he confessed to a friend, 'I'm terrified sometimes of making a promise and then perhaps living to regret it. It is just a matter of taking an unusual plunge into some rather unknown circumstances that inevitably disturbs me, but I expect it will be the right thing in the end.'

On 6 February 1981, he took the leap and proposed to Lady Diana Spencer. To his surprise, she quickly agreed to marry him. Charles, at last, had found his bride.

The couple had dated mostly through phone calls in those early days, with sources saying they met only thirteen times before Charles went on to propose. It was all a bit cringeworthy, Diana would disclose years later to the author Andrew Morton. She had secretly recorded her memories on tapes that she supplied to Morton via a go-between, Dr James Colthurst.

'It was like a call to duty, really,' recalled Diana. 'He said, "Will you marry me?" and I laughed. I remember thinking, this is a joke, and I said, "Yeah, OK," and laughed. He [Charles] was deadly serious. He said, "You do realise that one day you will be queen." And a voice said to me inside, "You won't be queen, but you'll have a tough role." So, I thought, OK, so I said, yes. I said, "I love you so much, I love you so much.'"

In truth, neither Charles nor Diana was in love with the other, although both may well have been enamoured with the idea of it. This was effectively the last of the great arranged royal marriages, in an age when divorce had become acceptable, even commonplace.

The bottom line was that Charles and Diana were not a compatible couple. The Wales's so-called 'fairytale' marriage was doomed from the start, and Charles knew it. The couple shared that infamous and deeply awkward engagement interview when they were asked about love. 'I had a long time to think about it, because I knew the pressure was on both of us. And, um… it wasn't a difficult decision in the end. It was what was wanted,' Diana said, adding quickly, 'It's what I wanted.'

Asked if they were in love, Charles followed up Diana's quick 'of course' with that infamous and damning line, 'Whatever "in love" means.' They were words that would be repeated on air, in books and in newspapers time and again and established the *parti pris* narrative of an uncaring older husband who wilfully wrecked the life of the pure young woman who was devoted to him.

Even before their relationship disintegrated, Charles was deeply unsure of Diana's suitability as his wife and, after a few meetings, he believed they were totally incompatible. He told his close circle of friends, 'I desperately wanted to get out of the wedding in 1981, when during the engagement I discovered just how awful the prospects were, having had no chance whatsoever to get to know Diana beforehand.' When referring to the 'awful' prospects, Charles was arguably speaking of Diana's bulimia and her mood swings and temper, which he found impossible to deal with.

In the middle of one conversation in the weeks leading up to the wedding, Charles was talking to Diana about his day and his work commitments, when she stared back at him blankly. She seemed incapable of grasping the thread of what he was saying. Then for no apparent reason, he recalled to friends, she welled up and burst into tears. A sympathetic man, Charles was at a total loss as to what to do (although he did later seek professional help for her.)

Charles was not the only one to have second thoughts. Only days before the wedding, Diana told her sisters, Lady Jane and Lady Sarah, that she did not think she could marry Charles, because he was still besotted with Camilla Parker Bowles.

The wedding, described by the Archbishop of Canterbury, Robert Runcie, as the 'stuff of which fairy tales are made', went ahead on 29 July 1981. But there would be no 'happy ever after' for this marital union. Unfortunately, Charles almost immediately regretted his predicament. Issues that had been swept aside, such as Diana's youth and the short time they had spent together before marrying, grew into insurmountable problems.

There are many who persist in lambasting Charles over his treatment of Diana and choose to ignore the obvious good in the man and his lifetime of service, his vision and his passion for the world and humanity. Not that it excuses his behaviour, but they were both in a very pressured and nuanced situation. Even so, Charles's detractors repeat his apparent neglect of his young bride and his subsequent adultery (whilst seemingly ignoring her own affairs), which in their view marks him out as deeply flawed, a pariah and unsuitable for kingship.

The King has long accepted there is no point in fighting against this distorted portrayal of his character, particularly in the aftermath of Diana's death. For some, as far as he is concerned, the mud has stuck and no amount of hard work on his part will remove the stains. Charles also knows that the failings of his first marriage and the tragic circumstances of Diana's death continue to dent his popularity severely. The truth is that he has agonised over his mistake for years. He believes he let down not only the monarchy, but himself and Diana, too, through his inability to call off the wedding.

What frustrates the King to this day is that one version, Diana's version, is so ingrained in the popular psyche that it has gone down as the truth when, in his view, it is a tissue of lies fed to a sympathetic press. Now, after years of soul searching, those close to him say that Charles would like the untrue stories promulgated about him by Diana and the media to be corrected, because he feels they are in danger of wrongly becoming 'historical fact' and distorting what really happened.

One of the falsehoods disseminated widely at the time was the 'news' that he and Diana had spent two nights together, one on board the Royal Train, which Diana and her family denied. The Duke of Edinburgh was reportedly furious about this and is said to have sent his eldest son a strongly worded letter – although nobody other than the sender or recipient has ever seen it – warning Charles that his reputation as a gentleman and Lady Diana's honour would both be under threat if he did not propose to her.

That tryst-on-the train story was a well-publicised and often-recited one that heaped pressure on Charles unfairly, because the incident never actually happened. The timing of the *Sunday Mirror* story was certainly sensitive, as was the subject matter. The editor, Bob Edwards, insisted he had an impeccable source (as it turned out, one of the local policemen assigned to watch the train overnight in the sidings). The Queen's press secretary, Michael Shea, was robust in his response and made it clear the palace took 'grave exception' to the report. After making further checks, Edwards refused to print an apology and said he would print their correspondence, thus giving himself another splash story – under the banner headline 'Prince Charles and Lady Diana' – agreed by the palace.

Diana herself was deeply shocked and upset by the story. After all, she knew that it was not her who had secretly visited the Royal Train. She was devastated, too, by the implication that her boyfriend had been two-timing her while she was tucked up in bed miles away. By December 1980, Diana's infuriated mother, Frances Shand Kydd, was growing tired of the slights against her daughter's good character and wrote an uninhibited letter to the editor of *The Times* for publication, protesting in the strongest terms about the 'lies and harassment' that Diana had been forced to endure since the romance with Charles had been made public. 'She [her daughter] had denied with justifiable indignation, her reported presence on the Royal Train.'

It is a fabrication that has haunted Charles ever since it was first circulated. It still irritates him to this day, quite possibly because it is the one story that, more than any other, set him on a course to the altar out of protecting his own and Lady Diana's honour, even though there was not a shred of truth in it.

He explained to a close friend, 'The most extraordinary and pernicious of these is that first of all I secreted Diana on board the Royal Train on the eve of our wedding. This was endlessly denied at the time. The truth is the *Daily Mirror* [*sic*] had mistaken a private secretary's blonde secretary for Diana. The press obstinately stuck to this story. Then, years later, they pushed the invention even further, claiming it was Camilla [on board the Royal Train] after all.'[4]

In 2007, the *Daily Telegraph* wrote, 'Her [Camilla's] unpopularity was such that an irate shopper was reported to have thrown a bread roll at her in a supermarket in Wiltshire.' Charles went on, to friends, 'Another persistent lie is that the duchess had bread rolls thrown at her by angry shoppers in a store in Chippenham. This was in fact a totally fabricated media exercise stunt, which involved actresses throwing bread rolls at one another. A lookalike actress was employed and placed in the store in Chippenham.'

The bad omens were everywhere. Charles was apparently furious when he took a group of his closest friends, including Winston Churchill's grandson, Tory MP Nicholas Soames, to White's Club in St James's for his stag night dinner. They tucked into a dinner of canapés, cold meats, potatoes, cheese soufflés and beans, washed down with a lot of very, very expensive booze. Everyone had been sworn to secrecy, but when they arrived there were several photographers waiting. Charles left shortly after midnight, by which time more photographers had arrived.

The following day, the prince and his fiancée Diana attended a garden party at Buckingham Palace, and she indiscreetly revealed that on his return they had argued. 'There was a terrible row last night between Charles and me. It had been his stag party,' she said.

Charles 'wept' the night before his 1981 wedding to Lady Diana Spencer as he felt torn between her and his feelings for his former girlfriend Camilla. It is also claimed, once again totally falsely, that he smuggled his then-married mistress into his suite of rooms at Buckingham Palace for a secret tryst on the same night, just hours before marrying Diana. Charles regards this as 'monstrous'.

He told a close friend, 'One of the worst lies of all is that Camilla was smuggled into Buckingham Palace the night before our wedding in 1981. The idea that this could even have happened and that I could have done any such thing is beyond belief, and yet this monstrous nonsense has persisted.' He added, 'There are doubtless endless other lies and inventions that I have no idea about including – may I add? – Camilla being with me in

Switzerland while I was skiing. I dare say there is nothing that can be done about all of this.'

Many will still cling to what they have been told. But I have no doubt that the prince is sincere in what he has told his close circle of friends.

On the wedding day itself, 29 July 1981, the world watched in awe as the 'fairytale' wedding of Charles and Lady Diana Spencer took place. Around 600,000 onlookers lined the route from the palace to St Paul's Cathedral, where they would exchange their vows. Elsewhere around the country on the hot summer's day, thousands held street parties to celebrate the wedding. Another 750 million people tuned in around the world, making it the most-watched television broadcast in history at that time. Britons enjoyed a national holiday to watch the occasion, as Lady Diana wowed the crowds outside St Paul's in her ivory taffeta, antique lace gown designed by Elizabeth and David Emanuel, before making the long walk up the red-carpeted aisle with her twenty-five-foot-long train flowing behind her.

In the congregation there was one person, Camilla Parker Bowles, by now a married woman of eight years, who probably knew even then that the chances of this marriage going the distance were limited.

Diana, still baffled by Charles's odd comment when asked whether he was in love, was probably edgy and unsure about their relationship even as she boarded the royal yacht *Britannia* for the couple's Mediterranean honeymoon. Charles was attentive to his young bride, but telephoned Camilla daily. His valet Stephen Barry said in Tina Brown's book *The Diana Chronicles*, 'If he went without his daily phone call, he would become tetchy and ill-tempered.'

Charles also received a gift from his former mistress, cufflinks with two Cs entwined like the Chanel 'C'. When Diana confronted him, he admitted Camilla had given them to him, but he did not see what was wrong with that. He loved painting in water-colours, but Diana even resented him sitting for hours at his easel. One day he returned to find she had destroyed his painting and all his materials.

It was certainly a disastrous beginning to their marriage and times would only get harder in the years to come.

CHAPTER 7

Son and Heir

Sensitivity to others, which by any definition is actually called good manners…and also, on the whole, do unto others as you'd have them do unto you, which is not a bad way of trying to operate.

**CHARLES'S RESPONSE WHEN ASKED ABOUT WHAT QUALITIES
HE HOPED HIS SONS WOULD DEVELOP**

Charles had become concerned about the fragility of Diana's mental state even before their wedding. He noticed that her behaviour was erratic and became increasingly volatile as she experienced what appeared to be uncontrollable mood swings. She had, in fact, been struggling with undiagnosed bulimia for many months by the time her honeymoon came round.

'[During the engagement] my husband put his hand on my waistline and said, "Oh, a bit chubby here, aren't we?" and that triggered off something in me,' she told her biographer Andrew Morton. 'And the Camilla thing. I was desperate, desperate. I remember the first time I made myself sick. I was so thrilled, because I thought this was the release of tension.' Her eating disorder, sadly, was to get increasingly worse and her mood swings more disruptive.

Friends said the prince was at a loss as to how to cope with it and wanted to help her. 'He was very worried about her,' said a friend. 'He started asking those close to him if they could offer any advice.' This, of course, flies in the face of the established narrative, but those close to him say Charles really did try to make his marriage work and cared deeply about his young bride. On advice, he sought professional psychiatric help through Dr Alan McGlashan, a prominent psychiatrist and eminent psychoanalyst, who was known to Charles's friend and mentor, the philosopher Laurens van der Post, and was widely respected in his field. Dr McGlashan continued to practise in his Sloane Street office until just days before his death at ninety-nine in 1997.

Charles sought help not only for his deeply troubled wife, but also for himself, to help them both cope with the inward strain of their incompatible marriage. It demonstrated that he had 'at least tried very hard to resolve their problems and even tried to save his marriage. Surely, this is something he should have been given some credit for,' said a former senior member of the Royal Household.

Dr McGlashan was brought in to treat Diana after she 'distanced herself' from the royal medics, such as the late Queen's ex-physician Sir John Batten, who also treated the princess in the early years of her marriage and painted a dire image indeed. Sir John believed Diana suffered from a 'dangerous' condition that was genetic and might be passed on to her children. His views emerged in a letter written in February 1983 by Dr McGlashan to Sir John, then head of the Queen's Medical Household, that he and his colleagues were 'plainly scared' by her symptoms and 'overawed by the possibilities of dynastic disaster'.[1]

The McGlashan letter revealed the royal doctors 'dosed her with antidepressants' and tried behavioural therapy. Only a few months after Prince William was born, Diana, then twenty-one, was also suffering from bulimia nervosa, feeling depressed and troubled by low self-esteem. In all, Diana and Dr McGlashan met eight times and the psychotherapist's assessment was vastly different to that of the royal doctors, concluding, 'She is a normal girl whose troubles were emotional, not pathological.'

Almost exactly a year after their wedding, on 9 July 1982, the Prince of Wales was overjoyed as he emerged from the Lindo Wing of St Mary's Hospital, Paddington, in north-west London, after his wife, Princess Diana, gave birth to their blue-eyed baby son. He had been at her side when the infant came into the world at 9.03 p.m., after more than thirteen hours of labour. Two minutes later, a Buckingham Palace spokeswoman reported: 'The baby weighs 7lb 1.5oz. He cried lustily. The Prince of Wales was present. We have no names which we can announce.' It later emerged that the labour had to be induced by George Pinker, the Queen's surgeon-gynaecologist, who looked after the princess throughout her pregnancy.

From the hospital the proud father rang the Queen, who was said to be 'absolutely delighted'. Queen Elizabeth, the Queen Mother, driving back to her home at Clarence House, was said to be 'overjoyed'. The news was also flashed to his brother Prince Andrew, then serving as a Royal Navy helicopter pilot in the South Atlantic task force in the Falklands, and to the rest of the Royal Family. Charles returned the next day and faced the battery of photographers, reporters and television journalists anxious to glean any snippet of information about the royal birth, but it seemed the only thing concerning the prince was the dreary wet weather.

'It's not very nice, is it,' he said, as he walked over to the battery of photographers crammed behind a barrier, poised to get the all-important picture of the infant.

'Can you tell us how the princess is?' asked one of the television journalists.

The prince, who was oddly carrying some folders and paperwork, and accompanied by his Scotland Yard personal protection officer, replied, 'She's very well.'

'And your son?'

'He's in excellent form, too,' said the prince, with the hint of a smile. 'Looking a bit more human this morning.'

Another shouted, 'When do you think your wife will be coming home, sir?'

'I hope as soon as possible,' he replied.

The media and crowd that had gathered outside did not have much longer to wait. Within a few hours and less than two days after arriving at the hospital, the Prince and Princess of Wales emerged, with their baby in Charles's arms. They appeared a perfect picture of family happiness.

Despite Diana's smiles, the princess was struggling to cope both physically and mentally. She could barely put one foot in front of the other and recalled later that she was in agony throughout the photo session and was in a hurry for it to be over. Her stitches were killing her, she said. 'It was such a strain to stand there and smile, even just for a few minutes. As soon as the car disappeared around the corner out of sight of the photographers, I burst into tears.'

Within a few minutes, after posing for pictures with the nursing staff on the steps, they were home at Apartments 8 and 9 in Kensington Palace. Diana could not wait to lock herself away with her baby and keep him from prying eyes. This public performance was all new. In the past, royal princes and their parents had been protected from such public intrusion, but this infant was different. Born into the age of modern media, with its rolling news coverage, he was the first future British monarch to have been born in hospital and not safely behind the palace's iron gates.

The new second in line to throne, a future king and direct heir to the reigning Queen, was to be named Prince William of

Wales, Buckingham Palace announced later. His parents agreed on the name after what was described later as 'a bit of an argument' between them. A compromise was reached after Diana chose William, while Charles's first choice, Arthur, went second, followed by Philip in honour of Charles's father, and Louis after the late Earl Mountbatten of Burma.

From the moment he set eyes on his son Charles was besotted, and his paternal devotion, for a short period at least, helped to heal the wounds of the Wales's failing marriage.

The prince wrote to his second cousin, Patricia Mountbatten, a close confidante and friend, and the eldest daughter of his mentor Lord Mountbatten: 'The arrival of our small son has been an astonishing experience and one that has meant more to me than I ever could have imagined. I am so thankful I was beside Diana's bedside the whole time, because I felt as though I'd shared deeply in the process of birth and as a result was rewarded by seeing a small creature who belonged to us, even though he seemed to belong to everyone else as well.'

It seems, however, that not everyone in the family was feeling as sentimental as the new father. The Queen, known for her sharp wit, joked when she met her new grandson, 'Thank heavens he hasn't ears like his father.'

The Queen and Prince Philip, both great-great-grandchildren of Queen Victoria and for whom family ancestry and bloodlines mattered, were delighted. Royal historians were having a field day too, for Diana's Spencer ancestry meant that she descended from two of Charles II's illegitimate sons, Henry Fitzroy, 1st Duke of Grafton, and Charles Lennox, 1st Duke of Richmond. It meant that the baby boy was destined to become the first blood descendant of the Stuart monarch, who restored the monarchy after Oliver Cromwell's interregnum, to accede to the throne, nearly three centuries after his death in 1685 from apoplexy with no legitimate children to inherit the crown.[2]

Despite the public perception of happiness, everything was not 'hunky-dory', as Diana would say. While Charles and Diana were both thrilled by the arrival of William, the princess began to suffer from post-partum depression. A jumble of powerful emotions and raging mood swings engulfed Diana, who was still just shy of her twenty-first birthday. She would lurch from feelings of joy to periods of dark fears and deep anxiety, often crying herself to sleep and leaving Charles desperate and bemused.

Diana had to steel herself for William's christening six weeks later on 4 August at Buckingham Palace. Privately, she was furious at the way she had been excluded from the arrangements for the future king. She later claimed that she felt shunned from William's special day. She recalled, 'Nobody asked me when it was suitable for William – eleven a.m. couldn't have been worse. Endless pictures of the Queen, Queen Mother, Charles and William. I was excluded totally that day. Everything was out of control, everything. I wasn't very well, and I just blubbed my eyes out. William started crying too. Well, he just sensed that I wasn't exactly hunky-dory.'[3]

At one point, the Queen gestured toward a visibly distressed Diana, appearing to tell her to offer the crying baby her finger to suck. The new mother obliged, and William calmed down immediately. But throughout, he screamed as soon as her finger was removed. Diana could not wait for the ordeal to be over. 'I felt desperate, because I had literally just given birth – William was only six weeks old. And it was all decided around me. Hence the ghastly pictures,' she said years later.[4]

The original plans for a royal tour to Australia by the Prince and Princess of Wales had been postponed due to her pregnancy, but the Queen and Buckingham Palace were keen to capitalise on Diana's popularity and felt she would be a big hit Down Under. They were especially delighted because the tour had been organised by the pro-monarchist Malcolm Fraser's government, before they were defeated by the republican-supporting Labour prime minister, Bob Hawke.

When Charles and Diana finally arrived in Australia on 6 March 1983, for the start of their six-week tour of Australia and New Zealand, they were joined by nine-month-old William, because Diana had refused to leave the infant behind. Upon landing in Alice Springs, William, who was affectionately dubbed 'Billy the Kid' by the Australian press, was carried down the steps of the Royal Australia Air Force Boeing 707 by his nanny, Barbara Barnes, who had looked after him since birth.

As soon as William was born, Charles had wanted to employ his own former nanny, Mabel Anderson, as his son's principal carer. She had played such a significant role in his life, he felt she would be perfect for William. Charles believed the only way to ensure that his son grew up with the traditional values that he cherished was by employing an old-fashioned British nanny. 'There were some experts very certain about how you should bring up children,' he said, 'but then, after twenty years, they said they'd been wrong. Think of all the poor people who followed their suggestions.'

However, Diana argued forcefully that Mabel was both too old and far too traditional for the job she had in mind. 'A mother's arms are so much more comforting than anyone else's,' she told her husband bluntly. Diana accepted that her position as the Princess of Wales meant she would need full-time support if she were to carry out her public duties, but she was intent on following the teachings of an altogether more modern teacher, in the shape of Dr Benjamin Spock, with whom she claimed a distant blood relationship. Spock was an influential advocate of the new permissive attitude toward childcare, and that was exactly what Diana wanted for her son.

Charles soon realised that on this subject the lady was not for turning, so he agreed to Diana's choice of Barbara Barnes. As if to draw a line under the past, she was the first royal nanny not to have at least two footmen and two housemaids to help her. 'I'm here to help the princess, not to take over,' Barbara announced tactfully. The daughter of a forestry worker, Barbara had an easy manner to which children responded, and she got on well with William and with Charles himself.

Others in the royal party for the Australian tour included former palace footman Michael Fawcett, who had been seconded to Charles and would act as butler for the couple, and chef Mervyn Wycherley. The family posed for photographers before Barnes whisked William away to the couple's base at a farm in Woomargama, Albury, a working sheep ranch where Ronald Reagan had once stayed, where Charles and Diana planned to rejoin him the following day.

The couple's press secretary was Vic Chapman, aged fifty-one, a six-foot tall, sharp-witted former press secretary to Canadian prime minister Pierre Trudeau and a former Canadian Football League player. Sensing William was a positive news story, he told the press, 'I heard Prince William cry only twice in thirty hours [during the flight].'

The decision to bring William represented a marked break with tradition, contrasting with the Queen's visit to Australia in 1954. She would never travel on a plane with Charles, in case the plane crashed, and Charles was not supposed to travel with his new son either. But bringing William was what made the visit a game-changer. A huge amount was made in the Australian press about Diana being a breath of fresh air and a modern mum.

There was a lot riding on this tour. It was a politically sensitive time, with a new wave of republicanism sweeping Australia, championed by its prime minister, Bob Hawke. Before the tour, he had flippantly dismissed the heir to the Australian throne as a 'nice young bloke'. On 6 March 1983, a mere twelve days before Charles and Diana were set to fly to the continent, a television interviewer asked Hawke if Charles would make a good king of Australia. 'I don't think we will be talking about kings of Australia forever more,' he replied. Then he said he thought people would eventually vote to have a republic.

If Charles and Diana had really been sent to save the Crown from republicanism in Australia and prevent the monarchy being dumped, they had probably arrived a little late. It had already been saved, at least for the foreseeable future, by Hawke's election victory, because, although he was anxious to assert Australia's independence, he did not believe republicanism was an urgent issue. His priority, as he made clear, was the restoration of the national economy.

Britain's travelling Fleet Street 'Royal Rat Pack'[5] were always looking for a headline-grabbing angle, and they were not going to let the truth get in the way of a good story to keep their editors happy and their expenses signed. The British red-top tabloids had already started to paint Diana as erratic. James Whitaker of the *Daily Mirror*, regarded as the doyen of the royal reporters, had run an exclusive about rumours that Diana was suffering from an eating disorder, under the headline 'Concern for Di's Health', with the strapline, 'Fears over her diet'. It may have been cynical but, not for the first time, Whitaker had got it spot on.

In Britain, meanwhile, others were concerned about Diana's staying power. Elise Taylor put it succinctly in an article for *Vogue* (November 2020):

> It's also true that the monarchy was worried about how Diana would fare. The tour was a gruelling one, by any standards:

a month long, the couple were set to cover 30,000 miles and make up to eight appearances in one day. And while Prince Charles had been doing this type of work his whole life, it was 21-year-old Diana's first overseas royal tour. 'The Queen is "terribly worried" before the tour because of Diana's youth and apparent shyness,' wrote the Press Association's royal correspondent Grania Forbes ahead of the trip.

It didn't help that the British tabloids had already started to paint her as unpredictable – the *Daily Mirror* had recently published an exploitative story about rumours of her eating disorder. While the international press waited for the couple to land in Alice Springs, Australia from London, the *Sydney Morning Herald*'s Alison Stuart recalled the reporters gossiping: 'Would she snap, would she cry, would she collapse from the heat?'

In truth, the royal tour got off to a slow start. Crowds who visited royal events in the Northern Territory were smallish, mainly consisting of mums, teachers and children, and a smattering of Union flag-waving British expatriates. But Diana was an immediate hit with the children and overall received positive press and TV coverage from the Australian media, happy to use lots of photos and footage of Charles's beautiful young bride.

Diana did indeed show signs of fatigue. She looked uncomfortably sunburnt and her eyes were downcast. Charles, sensitive to his wife's moods, apologised and said they were both still suffering from jet lag. Three days after they landed in Australia, an Associated Press reporter ungallantly described Diana as being 'red-faced and bare-legged'. So sensitive to criticism, Diana told one Australian reporter, 'I can't cope with the heat very well.'

On a visit to Ayers Rock,[6] Diana appeared uncertain. She was not nervous, just inappropriately dressed in a white dress that immediately blew open to reveal her petticoat and knees. From that moment on, Diana battled in vain to keep the dress closed, as the relentless photographers had a field day. She did not want to climb on the rock, not through fear of slipping, but because she knew when she descended it would expose her knees and petticoat to the world's press.

However, once over the jet lag, Diana began to shine. Showing her Spencer spirit, she revealed she was made of the right stuff. As the royal tour got into the swing of things, Charles and Diana thoroughly charmed the country. They danced at Sheraton Wentworth Hotel, in Sydney, the first time they had ever been filmed dancing together, with Diana donning a spectacular turquoise dress. Charles scored a goal at a polo match in Sydney and the crowd erupted into cheers. In Perth, they made headlines when Charles tenderly kissed Diana's hand in public. Back in England, 'Prince plays the gallant at royal party,' read a headline in *The Times*.

As they criss-crossed Australia wowing the crowds, William stayed with his nanny Barbara Barnes, chef Wycherley, second butler Fawcett, and his Scotland Yard protection officers at Woomargama. Charles and Diana would visit him as frequently as they could throughout their tour.

As the travelling staff's suntans improved nicely, they drew wry comments from the prince. It became a running joke that every time the royals arrived back at the hub, there would be an almighty downpour. On one occasion Charles and Diana arrived in the middle of a storm and he said, 'This is the first time I have ever had to wear a mackintosh in Australia!' Meanwhile Diana only wanted to see her son, saying, 'I must go and see little Wills.'

The six-bedroomed homestead, renovated about fifteen years

previously and owned by Gordon and Margaret Darling, boasted around 2,000 sheep and 400 cattle on the roughly 2,500-acre expanse. The local village of Woomargama was described in the press as 'a typical Australian country township', with a pub, a general store, and about ninety residents. For Diana and Charles, though, the village and the ranch served as a comfortable hub and safe home base for William, within driving distance of an airport, and roughly in between Sydney and Melbourne.

Security came in force ahead of William's arrival, with members of the New South Wales tactical response group, armed to the teeth, being installed at the gate. The airspace around the property was also secured and a helicopter was placed at the ready on the property. Chef Wycherley made sure the pantry was fully stocked with his trips to nearby Holbrook and, whenever the royal couple arrived, they asked for simple fare. Diana liked to pick on cold meats.

When Charles and Diana were away from the homestead, Nanny Barnes and William would be driven around the property every day, including near the digs occupied by the jackaroos.[7] Back at the ranch, the staff, including Michael Fawcett, were kept busy chasing after the young prince as he crawled on the carpets inside.

When Charles and Diana were in Woomargama, it was hardly a break from work. They met local children from the town's small primary school and attended a Sunday service in Holbrook at St Paul's Anglican Church, where Charles read a lesson, and practically the whole town turned out to see them. Woomargama was at the heart of the royal story for that month. Truckers passing by, for a few months at least, dubbed the town 'Windsor City'.

Diana's popularity soon started to eclipse that of Charles. Her bodyguard from the tour has since been quoted as saying that Diana's reception in Australia was akin to Beatlemania. 'The

Princess of Wales was the woman they'd come to see, and the people of the Riverland weren't disappointed,' said one of her team on the visit. She freely dispensed titbits concerning baby William's health and the weather, and jokingly enquired of an elderly citizen if she had any whisky in her picnic basket.

On 15 April, the *Melbourne Herald* published a cartoon of a map of Australia with a heart superimposed, and the caption: 'Princess Diana. A permanent imprint!' Two days later, the *Sydney Herald* echoed the same sentiment: 'Di Thrills the Queen!'. Charles on the other hand was criticised when some Australians failed to appreciate his Goonish sense of humour. He received scores of letters from disgruntled, animal-loving locals after he joked about feeding baby William on 'warm milk and minced kangaroo'.

In London, *The Times* confirmed Diana's triumph with the headline: 'The Princess who won the heart of Australia.' The story began, 'The month-long tour of Australia by the Prince and Princess of Wales, which ended yesterday when the royal couple flew to New Zealand, was an unqualified success, due in large part to the Princess. She won the heart of Australia.' The *Evening Standard* went even further: 'This tour has set Republicanism back ten years.'

Diana had delighted audiences by sharing cheerful tales about their young son. Yes, William did love his stuffed koala. But she was conscious that while praising her performance, Charles, who as future king had always been the star of the show, was uncomfortable with all the attention she was getting. In a 1995 interview with the BBC, the princess recalled that her growing popularity during the tour's royal walkabouts upset him. 'We'd be going round Australia, for instance, and all you could hear was, "Oh, she's on the other side." Now, if you're a man – like my husband – a proud man, you mind about that if you hear it every day for four weeks. You feel low about it, instead of feeling happy and sharing it.'

The visit was far from over. They still had a two-week tour of New Zealand to complete. They touched down in Auckland on 17 April and the following day 35,000 children were there to greet them at a packed Eden Park. Firstly, they had to complete a traditional Māori challenge – one of many such displays in the next few days. After that was over, the party could begin. What followed was a relentless tour, but Diana had now got into the swing of it, charming huge crowds wherever she went.

The local press praised her style at every turn. As the royal trio journeyed around the country, a demure Diana paraded an array of incredible outfits by British fashion designers, the most memorable being a pale blue, sequin-studded evening gown by David and Elizabeth Emanuel, with a diamond tiara, for a state banquet at Parliament House in Wellington.

She was a huge hit and, although there were a few protests against the monarchy during their trip, it was deemed a success. Perhaps one of the tour's most enduring moments came when ten-month-old William posed with his parents and played with a Buzzy Bee toy on the lawn of Government House in Auckland. Charles and Diana, who was wearing a long green dress with exaggerated white collar, happily accommodated the group of jovial photographers snapping away at what they believed was a happy family.

Cracks may not have been showing in Charles and Diana's relationship but, even during this 'happy family' photoshoot, a few hairline fractures emerged. Charles sat cross-legged, away from his wife and child, his arms out of reach for comfort or play, his hands in his lap instead of reaching out to his new family. Meanwhile, Diana was clearly engaged deeply with her new baby. Her focus was on William, not on the cameras, and certainly not on her husband.

On 30 April, the New Zealand tour was over and the couple boarded a plane destined for Eleuthera Island in the Bahamas for a holiday in the sunshine. Throughout the tour, Diana's new status as a global superstar had been confirmed, as she drew massive crowds wherever she went. It was the start of the Diana phenomenon and the birth of the 'People's Princess'.

The princess, however, saw it differently. Years later she recalled the tour was 'a test of endurance'. The couple, she said, were greeted by hysterical crowds in many of the cities they visited, and Diana felt 'jet lagged, anxious and sick with bulimia'. Perhaps her experiences long after the visit tainted the memory, for those on the tour with them recall the royal couple as enjoying the trip and being happy. 'I really don't remember a row, maybe once, but actually they got on very well and I think they were still in love,' said a close source.

William was a huge hit with the public. Charles and Diana understood the thirst for information and pictures and arranged several staged photocalls for the cameras and television on their return to the UK. At eighteen months, he toddled out for the 'tographers', as he called them, in the walled garden of Kensington Palace. Six months later, he returned for the sequel to celebrate his second birthday, performing for the cameras again by kicking a football and blurting out 'Daddy', to his father's and the journalists' delight.

They celebrated his second birthday with a small gathering at Kensington Palace, including the Queen. Chef Wycherley had prepared a magnificent cake in the shape of a digger – as the little prince would get terribly excited any time he saw a JCB or big truck – with two candles as the funnel and bright pink wheels, which were all edible. His fancy cakes became a theme, with Wycherley making William a Thomas the Tank Engine cake for his fourth birthday and a brilliant cake in the shape of a plane, the Queen's Flight jet, for his fifth. But soon little William's world would change forever with the arrival of a new royal baby, his younger brother, and he would no longer be the focus of attention.

CHAPTER 8

Spare

Suddenly as Harry was born, it just went bang, our marriage
– the whole thing went down the drain.[1]

PRINCESS DIANA

It was not the smartest remark for any father to make to his wife just after she had given birth. So, when the royal couple's second son arrived, and Charles jokingly said to Diana, 'Oh God, it's a boy... and he's even got red hair!',[2] her reaction was totally understandable. She did not see the funny side, and it was a catalyst to them growing even further apart. Something inside her, she said, 'closed off' at that moment.

Before the birth, Charles, had made no secret of the fact that he would have liked a daughter. During her nine-hour labour he stayed at his wife's side. He handed Diana ice cubes to suck when she was thirsty to avoid dehydration and held her hand in support as he tried to encourage her throughout the exhausting experience, although he later admitted he had dozed off a couple of times. After arriving at the Lindo Wing of St Mary's Hospital early in the morning, the couple's second son was delivered on 15 September 1984 at 4.20 p.m., weighing 6lb 14oz. Charles first telephoned the Queen with the good news, and then his father-in-law, Earl Spencer.

It should have been a moment of undiluted joy for the young family. The sad truth, however, was that despite one or two moments of shared intimacy the royal marriage, which had promised so much, was already in freefall by the autumn of 1984. Diana, at only twenty-four, felt increasingly abandoned and unwanted by the only lover she had ever known. Charles, now thirty-five, also felt imprisoned in a marriage to a woman wrecked by jealousy and mental health issues, with whom he had very little in common.

Diana later claimed that their marriage had been in 'total darkness' in between the births of their sons, and she had blotted it out because it was 'such pain'. Somehow, she said, 'Harry appeared by a miracle.'[3] Then out of nowhere, Diana admitted, the couple had become 'very, very close to each other' in the six weeks leading up to their second son's birth.

Diana had known for months that she was having a boy, but had kept it from her husband and had been mulling over a possible name. Charles's preference, if it was a boy, was Albert, after his grandfather King George VI, who adopted the name George when he became King. Eventually, Charles bowed to his wife over the name choice to keep the peace. Vic Chapman, the Canadian assistant press secretary to the Queen, who handled Charles and Diana's media relations at the time of the birth, made the announcement from the steps of the Lindo Wing. 'OK, the name is Prince Henry... they intend to call him "Prince Harry".'

The members of the press and public camped outside the hospital had to wait until the following day to see the royal baby for the first time. First William, wearing little red shorts and a white shirt, arrived with his father to meet his little brother. A short while later, royal nanny Barbara Barnes was photographed escorting William out from the Lindo Wing, while Charles stayed with Diana. Then their Scotland Yard protection officer, Sgt Alan Peters, emerged to prepare the car. Moments later Diana, wearing a red outfit and holding the sleeping baby wrapped in a white shawl, appeared on the Lindo Wing steps with Charles to pose for pictures. Unlike the birth of William, apart from a few smiles and waves the new parents did not engage with the press.

They returned to Kensington Palace after posing outside the hospital. To Diana's annoyance, as soon as they returned home Charles told her he was off to play polo at Windsor, leaving his wife alone with the two children. He did not think he was doing anything wrong, but Diana saw it as a sign of his uncaring attitude towards her. She felt abandoned.

She went to the kitchen and started picking at the selection of cold meats that chef Mervyn Wycherley had left for her in the fridge. She loved lamb cutlets and would snack on them cold. She also enjoyed caviar and foie gras.[4] On this occasion she had asked for a jug of cold custard too. By now, sadly, her bulimia was back.

Although Charles knew that Diana was deeply sensitive about the topic of Harry's sex, he brought it up again at his second son's christening, to the annoyance of Diana's mother, Frances Shand Kydd. 'We were so disappointed – we thought it would be a girl,' he told her. She was furious and reported it back to Diana.

Frances, whose acrimonious drama-filled divorce from Diana's father John Spencer after thirteen years of marriage had been finalised in 1969, was not a lady to suffer fools gladly.[5] She made it clear to her son-in-law that she found his attitude disappointing. 'Mummy snapped his head off, saying, "You should realise how lucky you are to have a child that's normal." Ever since that day the shutters have come down and that's what he does when he gets somebody answering back at him,' Diana recalled.[6] The admonishment from Frances Shand Kydd irritated Charles, and his already difficult relationship with his mother-in-law deteriorated further after that.

His lack of compatibility with Diana had been something Charles had agonised over even before their engagement. Now it had been confirmed. The fuss around Harry's arrival also seemed to upset the rather spoilt toddler, William. Until Harry's birth, he had been the sole focus of his parents' attention, as well as the coterie of staff in the Wales's household. William loved being the star attraction that his status as a future king made him. He could not even fall over without a member of the Kensington Palace staff rushing over and picking him up and dusting him down.

Harry's birth changed everything. The focus shifted to the rusty-haired baby, at least for a short while. Charles recognised his eldest son's discontent over the sudden change and felt his resentment was only to be expected. He urged his young wife not to be overly concerned, assuring her that it was normal. In truth, Charles was also pleased that his younger son Harry, initially at least, was less boisterous than William had been as a baby. He noted that Harry was 'extraordinarily good, sleeps marvellously and eats well' and that he was 'the one with the gentle nature'.

Conducted by the Archbishop of Canterbury, Dr Robert Runcie, on 21 December 1984 in St George's Chapel at Windsor Castle, Harry's baptism broke with royal tradition. Until then, most royal babies – including William – had been baptised in the Music Room at Buckingham Palace. Three-month-old Harry cried for only a couple of minutes while the archbishop performed the blessing with holy water. 'He was as quiet as a mouse throughout the rest,' said one of the choristers.

Four generations of the Royal Family attended Harry's baptism and, at the portrait session taken by Lord Snowdon that followed, there was no mistaking the pride on the Queen Mother's face as the eighty-five-year-old former Queen Consort took her fourth great-grandchild in her arms. Film footage of the christening and the party afterwards was shown on Christmas Day in the Queen's broadcast, in which William, then two and a half years old, was seen galloping through the corridors of Windsor Castle and chasing round the Archbishop of Canterbury in a game of tag with his cousins, Peter and Zara Phillips.

It was later revealed that William used to have a special name for his grandmother. After a fall at Buckingham Palace, the prince cried out for 'Gary, Gary'. When a guest asked who Gary was, the Queen stepped in and explained, 'I'm Gary. He hasn't learned to say Granny yet.'

William's overexcited behaviour and the happy smiling faces at the christening party delighted millions as they celebrated Christmas in front of their television sets, but the public relations masterstroke masked the truth. The on-screen royal smiles belied the painful truth of a 'fairytale' marriage in collapse and a Royal Family on the brink of a crisis that would rock a modern monarchy to its foundations.

Diana agonised about the best way to raise her sons. She knew they had to be made aware of royal customs that she regarded as stuffy and outmoded, but she wanted them to be free spirits just the same. Charles had his own ideas, feeling it would be best to follow the royal path of employing a governess, preferably one with experience of assisting members of the Royal Family. However, Diana stressed to Charles that she wanted their two boys to develop freely and naturally among their peers, reminding him, perhaps cruelly, that his childhood had left him an emotional wreck, withdrawn, unable to make friends easily or cope with personal criticism. How could he argue with her?

Eventually she picked a small school run by a bishop's daughter, Mrs Jane Mynors, at Chepstow Villas in Notting Hill, only a few minutes' walk from Kensington Palace. Not for the first time,

William blazed a trail for his younger brother; for where William went, Harry would inevitably follow.

In those early days, Diana relied heavily on the judgement of Nanny Barnes and was determined that her children were not going to have the same kind of upbringing she had experienced. She told friends that, as the product of a dysfunctional family, she was often left alone in her bed, frightened and confused about what was going on around her. 'A child's stability arises mainly from the affection received from their parents, and there is no substitute for affection,' she would say, when describing how she would always make sure that William and Harry came first.

When the boys went away to boarding school, she pined for them and could not wait to receive their letters, writing to them twice a week. Despite having married into the Royal Family, she was determined that when it came to her own children she would have her own way. Like many from broken homes, she did her best to give her sons as secure an environment as possible, and fortunately this was one area in which Charles truly respected her beliefs.

But Charles was a traditionalist when it came to motherhood and the duties of his wife. Although, by this time in the 1980s, society's whole attitude had changed toward what women were expected to do, Charles believed that one of the most important roles any woman could perform was to be a mother. 'Nobody should denigrate that role,' he said publicly. But even though Charles respected his wife's role as a mother, the underlying tensions between the couple surfaced almost from the moment William learned to walk.

Charles, now a father in his mid-thirties, was stepping into the political limelight more and more. Rather than shy away from controversy, he flirted with it. He was drawn to its flame, confident enough in his own position to speak out on issues that mattered to him. 'It wasn't that he was searching for recognition or anything like that,' said a former aide. 'He felt it was his duty to raise the debate on big issues. He felt it was important to challenge the politicians too, so that they would live up to what would otherwise be empty promises.'

This go-getting attitude led to clashes with the Conservative government led by Margaret Thatcher, particularly over the Tories' inner-city policies, and as a result the prince was accused of meddling in political affairs and overreaching his constitutional position. If anything, the criticism encouraged him to go further, especially regarding what he saw as the need for the rebirth of the inner cities.

Mrs Thatcher had publicly vowed to resolve the crisis of the decaying urban areas of Britain's industrial past. But she and Charles clashed over how this should be done. She believed the way to help cities prosper was by encouraging 'enterprise and civic pride' and what was needed were practical measures not imposed by governments or local councils, but in response to people's aspirations and individual efforts.

Charles wanted more than rhetoric and established his Business in the Community (BITC) to support those deprived of services. He pushed the prime minister to meet with local leaders of his outreach programme, which she eventually did, hosting a lunch at No. 10. Although, like the Queen, Charles was supposed to be non-partisan in politics, he found some of Thatcher's policies to be divisive and uncaring.

When he has been accused of jumping from one subject to the next, it has understandably exasperated Charles. For it is only when you examine all that he does in detail that the integrated and interrelated picture of his life's work becomes clearly visible. He noted in his trailblazing book *Harmony: A New Way of Looking at Our World* (written with Tony Juniper and Ian Skelly), published in 2010: 'Perhaps I should not have been surprised that so many people failed to fathom what I was doing. So many appeared to think – or were told – that I was merely leaping from one subject to another – from architecture one minute to agriculture the next – as if I spent a morning saving the rainforests, then in the afternoon jumping to help young people start new businesses.'

His infamous 'monstrous carbuncle' speech that he delivered at the 150th anniversary of the Royal Institute of British Architects (RIBA), on 30 May 1984 at a Royal Gala Evening at Hampton Court Palace, proves his point. That evening he did not hold back.

'For far too long, it seems to me,' he said, 'some planners and architects have consistently ignored the feelings and wishes of the mass of ordinary people in this country.' He went on:

> To be concerned about the way people live; about the environment they inhabit and the kind of community that is created by that environment should surely be one of the prime requirements of a really good architect... What, then, are we doing to our capital city now? What have we done to it since the bombing during the war? What are we shortly to do to one of its most famous areas – Trafalgar Square? Instead of designing an extension to the elegant facade of the National Gallery which complements it and continues the concept of columns and domes, it looks as if we may be presented with a kind of municipal fire station, complete with the sort of tower that contains the siren. I would understand better this type of high-tech approach if you demolished the whole of Trafalgar Square and started again with a single architect responsible for the entire layout, but

what is proposed is like a monstrous carbuncle on the face
of a much-loved and elegant friend.

The press inevitably zeroed in on his 'monstrous carbuncle' quote to
stir up the row with him and the architectural community further.
There is no doubt some architects were furious, and claimed it set
back hi-tech modern architecture a decade as planners would not
approve anything like it again. In his defence, most of the public
backed Charles, not the modernist architects. But if anyone had
read the full text of the speech and not relied on the headlines, they
would have seen that Charles was advocating the core principles of
the modern day.

He was once again ahead of his time – simply championing
sustainable planning in the construction industry, increased
access for those with disabilities, the importance of community
consultation and resident-led housing cooperatives, and restoring
historic street patterns and reviving traditional housing types, such
as terraces and courtyards.

Just as he was finding his voice and his public role was gaining
recognition, however, his marriage and chaotic private life was
unravelling. As a result, to his frustration, Charles increasingly
found himself a tabloid target and dismissed as a crackpot. He
was dubbed a poor father, with newspaper reporters totting up
how many days he saw his sons. Predictably, Charles returned to
the arms of his mistress, Camilla, and by 1986 Diana herself was
conducting an adulterous affair with cavalry captain (later major)
James Hewitt of the Life Guards.

Those close to Charles say he threw himself into his work,
possibly to avoid confrontations with Diana, almost becoming
a workaholic in the process. He would sometimes fall asleep at
his desk. Harry recalls, 'Countless times, late at night, Willy and

I would find him at his desk amid mountains of bulging blue post bags – his correspondence. More than once I discovered him, face on the desk, fast asleep. We'd shake his shoulders and up he'd bob, a piece of paper stuck to his forehead.'[7]

Charles would compartmentalise his life, eating dinner late before returning to his papers at his desk. Perhaps due to the lack of parenting that he experienced as a child, he lacked the tools to be a modern parent himself. He rarely joined in the play his children enjoyed with their mother or with a personal protection officer.

It was not his style and, often, he was not around or was away on business. Unlike the police team led by Inspector Ken Wharfe – Sergeant Reg Spinney, an ex-Royal Marine Commando, Sergeant Dave Sharpe and Inspector Trevor Bettles – Charles was not into the rough-and-tumble side of horseplay with his sons.

Inspector Wharfe, a long-serving protection officer in S014, the specialist department of elite armed officers charged with protecting the Royal Family, recalled that the two boys would often turn up at his bedroom at Kensington Palace (used by the Scotland Yard officer on duty). As regular as clockwork, the princes would knock at the door. 'Ken, do you want to fight?' It was not really a request or even a question: it was a statement of intent. William and Harry would pile in and they made a perfect royal tag team. 'One would go for my head and the other attack my more sensitive parts, landing punches towards my groin, which, if they connected, would make me keel over in agony,' he recalled in his best-selling memoir, *Diana: Closely Guarded Secret* (co-written by this author).

Their parents seemed to appreciate that their sons could let off steam in this way. Charles would pop his head around the door and, with a slightly quizzical look on his furrowed face, would ask, 'They're not being too much bother, are they, Ken?'

'No, sir, not at all,' he would gasp, as he recovered from another fierce royal punch.

If anyone overstepped the mark in correcting his sons, Charles, in his idiosyncratic way, would admonish the offender to let him know who was boss, albeit gently. On one occasion, when it reached Charles's ears that Inspector Wharfe had been finding fault with William's pronunciation, the prince stepped in. As a youngster, William spoke with that slightly clipped, upper-class English accent. Wharfe persisted in correcting the way he said 'out' like 'eight', but the young boy insisted he was right, because his father always said it that way.

'Ken, I understand you have been giving William elocution lessons,' he said, his tone just a little critical. Wharfe had clearly overstepped the mark and, in his own gentlemanly way, the prince was letting him know. 'When Diana found out about my telling-off, she thought it was hilarious,' Wharfe said, and she urged him to retell the story acting out all the voices.

Charles did insist that his sons display good manners in his presence. When meeting people, they would offer a handshake and look them in the eye. He also insisted on the boys writing thank-you notes. One of the more charming aspects for visitors to Kensington Palace or Highgrove was when the boys came downstairs in their dressing gowns to say goodnight, although one of the few people not to be immediately bowled over by the young princes was Sir Bob Geldof. He had come to Kensington Palace to discuss African famine with Charles, when William sauntered in. Unsurprisingly, the dapper youngster was taken aback by the Irishman's appearance.

'He's all dirty. He's got scruffy hair and wet shoes,' William remarked.

Not one to stand on ceremony, Sir Bob retorted, 'Shut up, you horrible little boy. Your hair's scruffy, too.'

'No, it's not. My mother brushed it!' he chipped back.[8]

Charles would defer disciplining his children to nursery staff. Sadly, by this time the relationship between Nanny Barnes and her employers had begun to unravel, mirroring the disintegration of feelings between Diana and her husband. The princess wrongly saw the dedicated servant as a rival for her sons' affections.

The final straw came when Charles was shown photographs taken when the nanny had flown to the West Indies before Christmas 1986 for the sixtieth birthday party of her former employer, Lord Glenconner, on his private island, Mustique. She was seen enjoying herself in the company of such fellow revellers as Princess Margaret and Jerry Hall. Charles had old-fashioned views about staff knowing their places and, inevitably, on 15 January 1987, it was announced that Barbara Barnes would be leaving.

The statement was timed to coincide with William's first day at his new school. 'I thought no one would notice,' Diana said later, 'but I was wrong, wasn't I?' The British press did not miss a trick. Sensing a story, the tabloid editors elevated the news of Barbara's departure to page one, and relegated William's arrival at his new pre-preparatory school to the inside pages.

Charles and Diana's strained relationship deteriorated further over issues such as spending time with their children. Michael Shea, the Queen's former press secretary, said, 'The only arguments they had were over the children.'[9] It was, of course, untrue. Their arguments were volatile and often fuelled by Diana's jealousy over Charles's infidelity with Camilla Parker Bowles. William and Harry reacted to the problems in their parents' marriage in their own way. William was always described as being 'forceful', his brother as 'sweet and a little reserved and shy'.

At Mrs Mynors' school in Notting Hill, Harry would sometimes hide in the playground and refuse to join the other children in their games, but, as he grew older and his mischievous character came to the fore, he became more disruptive. 'Harry's the naughty one, just like me,' his mother would say, with a sparkle in her eye. Harry also developed a passion for animals and the countryside, and he started to echo his father's famous belief in talking to plants. 'Harry loves animals and plants,' Charles remarked. 'I tell him all about them and say that they have feelings, too, and mustn't be hurt.' By contrast, William became more introverted, observed his maternal uncle Charles, now the ninth Earl Spencer. 'He is quite formal and stiff.'

From a very early age, Harry understood he was in the shadow of his older brother, aware of the imbalance in the roles they would be destined for as adults in the Royal Family. He was the Spare, after all. Harry loved his 'beloved' brother, but William was also famously his 'arch nemesis'.[10] Tensions over the drastic differences in their roles blew up during an argument when they were only young. One day Harry, just six, made an odd outburst, and Ken Wharfe was surprised by what he heard. 'Diana would always take the two boys to Highgrove. On one occasion Diana was driving, I was sat in the front, William and Harry in the back. "You'll be king, I won't," said Harry, "so, I can do what I want!" The princess and I just looked at each other, a little shocked by what he said.'

Harry could easily have felt hurt as William was given precedence. It is true that senior members of the family and even some of the staff seemed to show William deference. The Queen Mother used to put a seat next to her and call for William to sit on it, and he would also go to Clarence House to see her, without Harry. His brother, however, seemed to revel in the freedom he knew that William would never have. He was far more mischievous than William, who would often tell tales on Harry to his nanny or police officer.

Harry's nanny Olga Powell felt the best way to deal with his naughtiness was to impose strict rules. Olga took no nonsense from the boys. She would occasionally give them a smack. 'When he was a little older, I remember one of her classic phrases to Harry was, "Harry, I love you, but I don't like you," because he was a nuisance. He was vibrant. But she was strong with him, and I think children like that because they know where they stand,' said Inspector Wharfe.

Charles, of course, loved his sons but, sadly, by this time he had fallen out of love with their mother. It was better, he felt, to let Diana have her own way with the children, largely to avoid clashing with her. He would be the first to admit he was not necessarily the most attentive father, but on weekends off he would often go looking for his sons to keep an eye on them, and he was always in tune when their exuberance had gone too far and would appear on the scene out of the blue.

Harry loved it when Charles played with them and bemoaned the fact that he was an older dad, which he felt 'created problems' and 'placed barriers' between him and his sons. Harry claims in *Spare* that Charles became 'more sedentary, more habitual', somebody who 'liked his routines'. He recalls one fun occasion when Charles chased his sons all over Sandringham, making up 'wonderful games', such as one where he wrapped them up in blankets, like hot dogs, until the boys screamed with 'helpless laughter', and then yanked on the blankets so they shot out the other side. But such laughs were few and far between, according to Harry, because Charles did not have the 'enthusiasm – the puff'.[11]

On one occasion Harry burrowed himself into a huge haystack and was struggling for breath before being found in some distress by his protection officer. Another time, Harry caused a major ruckus when he disappeared again on a hot summer's day. He had crawled into one of Charles's giant urns as it was cooler inside, and he could not hear the increasingly desperate staff and parents calling his name.

By the mid-1980s, Charles and Diana were effectively living separate lives, apart from the occasional joint public appearance. Diana, however, had not given up on trying to woo her husband back. In one final attempt, she staged a surprise for his birthday in December 1985 by performing a special routine alongside the ballet dancer Wayne Sleep, at a private event at the Royal Opera House for a select group of VIPs, the Friends of Covent Garden.

The magnificent auditorium fell silent when the princess suddenly walked onto the stage to join Wayne Sleep. What they did not know was that Diana had been secretly rehearsing with the diminutive 5ft 2in ballet dancer for weeks. Diana, who towered above him at 5ft 10in, performed a dance to Billy Joel's hit song 'Uptown Girl'.

Sleep recalled, 'The audience gasped when Diana appeared, as if they'd all taken one huge breath. The routine had a bit of everything: jazz, ballet, even a kick line. At one point, I pirouetted, and she pushed me down; then I carried her across the stage. I remember thinking, don't drop the future Queen of England. She loved it, but was most thrilled we'd kept it secret from Charles, and our rehearsals away from the paparazzi.'[12]

The audience loved it, but Charles clearly did not, although he smiled from the box and applauded. Sleep joined Charles and Diana for a small reception afterwards and the prince behaved rather coolly to them both. The dance may have failed to win Charles's approval, but it gave the princess a sense of freedom. She wrote a letter to Sleep a few days later, saying, 'Now I understand the buzz you get from performing.'

At this time of mutual estrangement, Charles and Diana reached an understanding that during the week the prince rarely went to

Kensington Palace and they used Highgrove at weekends almost on a rota basis, neither being there when the other was. It meant that James Hewitt, who was Diana's lover by this time, became a frequent visitor to both residences. He would be assigned his own room, but would stay the night with Diana, although he took care that his arrivals and departures were not seen by the press.

Hewitt would even join in the play fights that the protection officers had with William and Harry around the garden pool at Highgrove. Diana would burst out laughing when she was thrown into the pool fully clothed. Of course, her sons did not know then that their parents were involved in adulterous relationships; James was simply another avuncular chap on the scene.

Not everyone believed in the almost saintly status that the press liked to paint of Diana, as the beautiful doting mother and neglected wife. Many on the staff grew tired of her mood swings and temper tantrums. She would rage at them about her husband's affair, yet not see herself as the hypocrite whom the staff saw, given that she was having an affair herself, with Hewitt. The boys' care was often left to staff, too.

One of the police team, who found Diana extremely difficult to deal with, regarded her as a Machiavellian manipulator. Another member of the security detail was so frustrated by her hypocrisy that he discharged all his bullets into a tree in a garden of a large landowning family where the Wales's were staying. 'That should wake them up,' he said to a shocked police colleague, who urged him to reload quickly to avoid a backlash, and say nothing about the incident. Before leaving, the same officer, whom I have chosen not to identify, remarked to his replacement, 'Good luck, you're going to need it. If these kids [Princes William and Harry] were brought up on a council estate somewhere in south London, they'd have been taken into care by now.'

CHAPTER 9

Taking Sides

What Kind of Father Are You?

THE HEADLINE IN THE *SUN* AFTER PRINCE CHARLES
WENT TO THE ROYAL OPERA HOUSE WHILE WILLIAM
UNDERWENT MAJOR SURGERY

When they stepped out in public together at home or overseas, Charles and Diana created an incredible vibe. It seemed to those who operated in their slipstream – the palace hierarchy, their respective staffs and royal journalists – that as the public face of the Royal Family, they were unsurpassable. But those on the inside knew this great pretence could not go on indefinitely. The sham marriage was about to implode.

The sudden departure of nanny Barbara Barnes and Diana's increased royal workload meant she needed extra help with the boys in the nursery. She hired another two nannies, Ruth Wallace, from her Kensington Palace neighbours, Prince and Princess Michael of Kent, and Jessie Webb, who had worked for the interior decorator Nina Campbell for fifteen years.

The whole childcare operation was presided over by the senior nanny at Kensington Palace, the indomitable Olga Powell, who had worked her way up from under-nanny. All three were strict disciplinarians and did their best to curb the boys' overexcited behaviour. William tended to toe the line, but Harry proved a handful. Both boys used to play Jessie up, telling her she was too fat, and she sometimes asked the protection officers to step in.

Harry was hyperactive and struggled to focus when he was in the classroom, too. He compensated by being a joker. There were too many distractions at school and his teachers were always reprimanding him. If he was getting out of control in her charge, Jessie would sandwich him up against the wall with her frame, saying it was the only way she could gain control. The two brothers would often roam around Highgrove like a couple of street urchins.

'They would think nothing of relieving themselves from the top of the giant haystack in the garden when they were so inclined, much to the annoyance of their father, who caught them in the act on occasion and gave them a dressing-down. But he was ignored,' said Inspector Wharfe.

In fairness, it was an emotionally challenging time for both William and Harry, who sensed the tension between their parents. When his mother locked herself in the bathroom to cry uncontrollably, William tried to help by pushing tissues under the bathroom door. Although the prince and princess tried to keep their unhappiness from the children, and conducted their extramarital romances in private, Highgrove would become a marital battleground on the rare occasions they stayed there at the same time. Charles refused to concede an inch of ground to his demanding wife – as heir to the British throne, he genuinely believed that his birthright decreed he did not have to. If that meant upsetting his beautiful princess, then so be it.

Charles would arrange to meet his friends, after promising a special dinner with Diana. Her reaction was understandable and often volatile. His friends were not her friends, she would say, after he revealed that their private plans had been scrapped because he was entertaining some of his circle. Unmoved, Charles would rejoin his party, explain that the princess had retired with a headache, and continue as if nothing had happened. Such scenes were commonplace in a marriage that was by now doomed.

Charles and Diana spent weekends at Highgrove, but it was very rare for them to have an entire weekend there alone together. Visits by Charles's ex-girlfriends were common too. In any event, the house was full of guests; if it was not Sarah Keswick, wife of the merchant banker 'Chips' Keswick, it would be the Duchess of York or any number of other acquaintances. Charles appeared to relish the arrival of his friends at Highgrove, perhaps because their presence meant that he did not have to spend too long alone with his wife, whose behaviour he found tiresome and exhausting.

Summer weekends were also dominated by Charles's polo commitments. Inevitably, his passion would lead to more rows between them, as Diana found polo both recklessly dangerous and mind-numbingly dull – except when she was watching James Hewitt, that is. The press added to the problem. Even when the princess did bow to pressure and take her sons to the polo field to watch their father play, the photographers focused on her. The only time they showed any interest in Charles was if she was with him, or he took a tumble and fell off his pony and injured himself. If Diana did support him and her photograph was in the newspapers the next day, he would accuse her of playing up to the cameras. 'Quite the glamour girl,' he would say disdainfully.[1]

In the end she gave up, feeling she could not win – she was criticised if she attended a match, and damned if she did not. When Charles adopted this stance, however, Diana would fly into a rage without warning, whereupon he would usually wander off to tend to his beloved garden, desperate to avoid further confrontation. 'If only I was as important as your garden. Go on, talk to your plants,' she would goad him.[2]

By the mid-1980s, the relationship had reached an all-time low. By now they were hardly speaking to each other but, when they were together, Diana still seemed to revel in antagonising her husband. In return, he would barely acknowledge her existence. Inevitably, Charles turned for solace to his mistress Camilla, whose own marriage was now a sham as Andrew Parker Bowles had returned again to his philandering ways, and Diana turned to James Hewitt, conducting their trysts away from prying eyes at his mother's home, Sheiling Cottage, in Dorset.

Diana knew she wanted more from life, however. Her affair with Hewitt, while passionate, felt shallow. Over time she began to see less and less of the charming tank commander, and even began to find excuses not to be with him.

'She became fixated by Mrs Parker Bowles and conveniently seemed to ignore her own infidelity, and would explode with rage about Charles's relationship, no matter how discreetly he behaved, which in fairness he did,' said Inspector Ken Wharfe, who would accompany the princess on her visits to James Hewitt's mother's cottage. 'I have to say that hypocrisy of this nature was her métier,' he said.[3] Diana, oddly, still saw no contradiction in her behaviour.

In March 1988, the prince and princess returned to his favoured ski resort, Klosters in Switzerland, for a holiday with a group of friends including the Duchess of York, Charles and Patti Palmer-Tomkinson, and the prince's close friend Major Hugh Lindsay, a former equerry to the Queen. On 10 March, the group, which did not include Diana or the Duchess of York that day, as Sarah was pregnant with Princess Beatrice, went out skiing on Gotschnagrat Mountain, led by local guide Bruno Sprecher.

What happened next left one of the ski party dead and another seriously injured. Charles, who felt revitalised by skiing in the Alps and had been going to Klosters for a decade, escaped death by inches. He recalled the details of the 'terrifying' accident in a 1994 ITV documentary. He had been skiing off-piste with a group of five on the Wang run, a challenging path that had just been reopened after bad weather, when an avalanche struck. Charles, who was not hurt in the incident, joined other members of the party in a frantic bid to dig out Major Lindsay, who was caught in the cascade of tons of freshly fallen snow.

Diana and Sarah, back in the chalet, were informed by an aide about the accident and had an agonising wait. Charles recounted in the documentary, 'The next thing I heard was Bruno's voice shouting "Jump!". This vast roaring, I have never forgotten the sound of it, this mass of snow and vast blocks crashing down past us. I realised then that Patti and Hugh obviously hadn't made it and they weren't with us. I have never seen anything so terrifying in my life. This staggering maelstrom went past with vast clouds of snow. And I kept thinking, my God, the horror that they've gone down with this lot, that they must be dead, there's no way they could survive it.'

Major Lindsay and Patti Palmer-Tomkinson had been swept over a precipice. Luckily Bruno had located Patti, who miraculously was still alive, but unconscious and blue. 'Poor old Hugh was dead,' Charles said. 'He'd obviously been hit by something on the way down.' Charles described how he sat with Patti in a hole talking to her and encouraging her. He told her, 'Patti, you're going to be all right and the helicopter is coming, and we're going to get you out of here.' Gradually, he said, she started to 'mumble and mutter'.

Contrary to newspapers reports, he said he did not 'panic', but did what needed to be done. 'That's what I hope we did,' he said. Lindsay and Palmer-Tomkinson were helicoptered to a hospital in the nearby town of Davos, but Hugh Lindsay was pronounced dead on arrival. Patti, who had severe injuries to both of her legs and her lungs, made a full recovery.

The incident proved another marker in the failing Charles and Diana marriage, as it marked the day that Diana finally hardened her heart against her husband. Without evidence, she blamed Charles, who was a very experienced skier, for what she saw as his recklessness in leading the group down such a dangerous route, despite an investigation finding that he could not be charged with Lindsay's death or Mrs Palmer-Tomkinson's injuries. Indeed, the whole group was determined to be at fault, since an avalanche warning had apparently been issued that day and they had willingly followed.

Upon landing at RAF Northolt in west London after their ski trip, the couple immediately separated. Charles returned to Highgrove, while Diana stayed to comfort Major Lindsay's pregnant widow, Sarah, who worked in the palace press office. Charles and Diana attended Lindsay's funeral a week after he died, accompanied by Queen Elizabeth, Prince Andrew and the Duchess of York, and Sarah Lindsay later revealed how Diana supported her for years afterwards.

'She looked after me, supported me and encouraged me. She was amazing. She knew that Sunday evening was a lonely time for me, and she rang me every week for three years. She was just thoughtful and kind and knew the bad moments. She was always there when I wanted her.' Diana gave Sarah Lindsay her personal telephone number and told her she could always ring her at any time, and she remained close to Sarah, who remarried and became Sarah Horsley after giving birth to baby Alice. For years afterwards, Charles was penitent over the tragedy. He became Alice's godfather and later wrote in a letter that, 'I still find it hard to understand why I survived, and he didn't.'[4]

Taking Sides

By the beginning of 1989, battle lines had been drawn up between the two camps and the Wales's household was not a place for the fainthearted. To the outside world, everything in the royal garden was rosy. But the flowers had died and the petals long since fallen – all that was left were sharp, uncompromising thorns.

The more astute commentators outside royal circles already sensed that something was very wrong with Charles and Diana's relationship. Without naming their respective lovers, even broadsheet newspapers such as the *Sunday Times* had printed articles surmising that Diana, like royal wives throughout history, had accepted the time-honoured royal option of a cool and arranged marriage, in which the husband, at least, could largely behave as he wished, provided he was discreet and attended to his royal duties.

In effect, they were saying that she had settled for a business relationship, but they were wrong. For Diana, partly schooled as she was in the romantic novels of her step-grandmother, Barbara Cartland, had never stopped believing in the Holy Grail of true love. To her, there was no reason why her husband should behave so coolly and, arguably, even cruelly towards her. Perhaps the romantic princess was right, but the realists among her inner circle cautioned her that to strive for that ideal must inevitably lead to disappointment and pain.

By now Fleet Street's love affair with Diana was also beginning to wane, just as the spice was starting to go out of her liaison with Major James Hewitt. But although, privately, the royal couple remained at loggerheads, they continued the charade in public. Their official visit to Hungary was to be one of their last great acts of togetherness. Amazingly, the press seemed to swallow the palace spin and focused on how well Charles and Diana appeared to be getting on in the beautiful city of Budapest, whose people had been liberated from communist authoritarianism.

Diana, the consummate actress, could put on a show. As Charles's feelings for her reached freezing point, she threw herself into supporting good causes and, for the journalists who wrote about her, 'Caring Di' became the go-to phrase in their reports.

In March 1989, Charles and Diana visited Dubai in the United Arab Emirates, while tension was growing in the Gulf region because of the threat by the president of Iraq, Saddam Hussein, to 'reclaim' Iraq's southern neighbour, Kuwait. Prime minister Margaret Thatcher asked Charles to reconsider playing polo while on the visit, which he had originally agreed to do, after MI6 warned of assassination threats against him by fanatical Iranians.[5]

Eventually Charles, who enjoyed a close affinity with the Gulf states' rulers such as his host, Dubai's ruler, Sheikh Rashid al-Maktoum, reluctantly withdrew from the match. A decision that annoyed his hosts, who accused the British government of overreacting, with Dubai's minister of protocol, Humaid Bin Drai, remarking angrily, 'Your prince was perfectly safe with us.'

Diana's decision to reinvent her public image had worked. The press was back on side. So when she embarked on her most ambitious mission to date, to help rid the world of the prejudice about AIDS, it was seen as a risky but bold move. At that time, little was known about the deadly disease, so the move worried the Queen and her advisers, who felt that the princess should steer clear of controversy. In their eyes, becoming the champion of AIDS sufferers was one step too far, and might backfire on the House of Windsor.

During an audience with the Queen, Diana was told by Her Majesty that although she admired her courage in confronting and publicising the AIDS issue, she thought her daughter-in-law was misguided. The Queen was only trying to protect Diana and the monarchy. After all, her stance on AIDS had led one acid-penned press critic to label her the patron saint of sodomy. Diana emerged from the meeting distraught and had to be consoled by Ken Wharfe, who warned her that she might have been losing her perspective on the issue. 'She was not in the mood to listen,' he said. 'In her anger and frustration, she was determined to play the victim.'

Despite the palace's attitude, Diana could not be knocked from her course. She deserves every credit for her work, but it reached a point at which no one, not even the monarch, could soften her approach, even when there were good reasons for doing so.

Perhaps the most dramatic moment in the Charles/Diana/Camilla love triangle came in February 1989, when Diana personally challenged the lovers face to face. The clash, a confrontation witnessed by Ken Wharfe, happened at a fortieth birthday party for Camilla's sister, Annabel Elliot, hosted by Lady Annabel Goldsmith at her house on Ham Common, on the south-western outskirts of London. Charles was shocked when Diana, who knew Camilla would be there, announced that she would be joining him. The guests too were surprised when the royal couple arrived together.

Once dinner had finished, Charles and Camilla quietly slipped away together and the princess found them locked in conversation in the basement children's play area of the house. As soon as they saw Diana they leapt to their feet, perhaps acknowledging their guilt. Despite Diana urging him to stay, Inspector Wharfe withdrew from the room and waited for her at the basement stairs, staying as close as possible without intruding.

When she emerged from the room, she was elated. She confided to Ken Wharfe afterwards that she had asked Camilla if she wanted to sit down. She said she had then asked her what exactly was going on between her and Charles. Diana herself takes up the story: 'It wasn't a fight – calm, deathly calm – and I said to Camilla, "I'm sorry I'm in the way, I obviously am in the way, and it must be hell for both of you, but I do know what is going on. Don't treat me like an idiot.'"

Camilla responded coolly that she did not know what Diana's issue she was, as she had her sons. Charles, who must have found it excruciating, said nothing. A few seconds later, Diana composed herself and returned to the party, where the clash of the two women was already being discussed. The prince and Camilla returned to the party a few minutes later, still shaken, as much by Diana's resolve as by her decision to confront them. For the rest of the time at the party they circulated separately, as though nothing had happened.

The journey back to Kensington Palace was tense, Diana repeating, 'How could you have done this to me? It was so humiliating. How could you?' Charles remained silent. Diana was distraught. What infuriated her was her husband's readiness to humble her publicly without apparent remorse. After that moment, Camilla became 'the Rottweiler' – Diana's nickname from then on replacing her usual euphemisms such as 'that woman' and 'his lady'.

More importantly, Diana now knew, once and for all, that her marriage was finally over.

CHAPTER 10

An Unfortunate Year

*1992 is not a year on which I shall look back with undiluted
pleasure. In the words of one of my more sympathetic
correspondents, it has turned out to be an 'Annus Horribilis'.
I suspect that I am not alone in thinking it so.*

HER MAJESTY THE QUEEN

By 1992, Charles and Diana's marriage was not the only royal union
in freefall. Buckingham Palace formally announced the Duke and
Duchess of York's separation on 18 March 1992. Then a few weeks
later, Princess Anne, who had separated from her husband Captain
Mark Phillips in 1989, filed for a divorce, which was finalised on
23 April.[1]

Bizarrely, it gave Charles and Diana hope that they could also
escape their sham marriage. But although the Queen had sanctioned
another royal divorce, that did not mean she would allow her direct
heir to end his marriage, too, given that it would have repercussions
for the monarchy they both served. In fact, both the Queen and
Prince Philip pulled out all the stops to counsel the couple against
divorce and to work harder at their marriage.

Philip played a pivotal role in trying to save the Wales's marriage.
He enjoyed an easy rapport with Diana at the start. Claims that
she 'hated' Philip are not true. Their relationship had begun well;
they would chat at family functions and he helped her to conquer

her shyness. As Charles and Diana's marriage crumbled, Philip tried his best to help, writing to his daughter-in-law in warm and encouraging correspondence, signing off with the word, 'Pa'. In those letters he repeatedly questioned his eldest son's affair with Camilla, and said he was wrong to risk everything for his mistress. Diana felt vindicated, but by now it was too late.

In a letter from Philip to Diana, made public at the High Court in London during the inquest into her death, Philip wrote to the princess that he and the Queen totally disapproved of Charles's affair. He wrote:

> Charles was silly to risk everything with Camilla for a man in his position. We never dreamt he might feel like leaving you for her. I cannot imagine anyone in their right mind leaving you for Camilla. Such a prospect never even entered our heads... I will always do my utmost to help you and Charles to the best of my ability.
> With fondest love, Pa.

Diana wrote back:

> Dearest Pa,
> I was so pleased to receive your letter, and particularly so, to read, that you are desperately anxious to help. I am very grateful to you for sending me such an honest and heartfelt letter. I hope you will read mine in the same spirit.
> With fondest love, from Diana.

Despite the state of their relationship, duty to the Crown still mattered to both Charles and Diana. A joint tour of India had been in the diary for many months and was due to start in February.

Diana knew that their relationship would come under the media microscope, but she no longer cared who knew – press or public – how far the marriage had sunk. Before the trip, the *Sun* published an exclusive front-page story revealing that she would be visiting, by herself, the Taj Mahal, the great marble mausoleum near Agra, under the headline: 'Di to Visit Taj Mahal on Her Own'. Built in the seventeenth century by Shah Jahan in memory of his favourite wife, it is regarded as the world's greatest monument to love.

The article quoted Charles, who, in accordance with the tradition that surrounds the Taj Mahal, had said during a previous visit in 1980 that he would return with the woman he loved. Could there ever be a more significant statement about the state of the royal marriage? Despite the headlines, Charles did not change his schedule. After their arrival in India, he insisted that he would attend a business function in Delhi, 200 miles away, on the day when Diana went to the Taj Mahal alone. Everyone could see the symbolism of this decision. The newspapers turned on Charles. The *Daily Express* editorial criticised his PR blunder, publishing a photograph of Diana in front of the Taj Mahal under the headline: 'Temple of Loneliness'.

After the Taj Mahal visit, the tour began to unravel, reaching a head on Valentine's Day in Jaipur, capital of Rajasthan. Charles had played very well in an exhibition polo match, scoring a hat-trick, and afterwards Diana was supposed to present the cup to her husband along with a kiss. Diana, however, was in no mood to be used in a palace PR stunt.

After a pitch invasion, the police finally got control and the prize presentation could go ahead. But when Charles approached the rostrum and puckered up to kiss his wife on the lips, she deliberately turned her head to the side, forcing him to air kiss and, worse, humiliating him in front of the world's press. Charles was furious at what he saw as her petulance. Diana had made him look a fool but did not care; she was not going to pander to him or his PR advisers. The following day, the *Sun* published a front-page photograph by Arthur Edwards under the headline: 'The Kiss that Missed!'

The prince and princess, who had separate hotel suites wherever they were staying, hardly spoke to each other during the rest of the tour. As Diana and her entourage headed for Calcutta to see at first hand the work of Mother Teresa, Charles, still seething over his humiliation, flew instead to the Himalayan kingdom of Nepal for a solo visit. After the couple returned from the Indian subcontinent, nothing would ever be the same in the royal world again. Accepting the inevitable, Charles took the first steps for a legal separation.

Kept in the dark about the marriage crisis, William and Harry had been desperate for their parents to take them skiing. Charles had promised to arrange it, but Diana, who had vowed after the avalanche in Klosters that she would never return to the Swiss resort he favoured, was against a 'happy family' trip and made excuses. Charles made it equally clear that he would do exactly what he wanted and that, if she did not care to join him in Klosters, that was her prerogative.

Her decision to take her sons to Lech, Austria, instead, understandably irritated him, as he was hoping to watch his two boys, then aged nine and seven, learn how to ski. If he wanted to see William and Harry, he would have to go to them, which he did. Diana would have preferred it if he had stayed away, but in March 1992 she was not about to stop their sons from seeing their father, whom they adored.

Until his arrival at the five-star Hotel Arlberg, everything had gone well. The owners, the Schneider family, treated their royal guests impeccably. Without a press officer on hand, Diana's police

Left: Princess Elizabeth and Lieutenant Philip Mountbatten RN on the day their betrothal was announced on 9 July 1947. Born Prince Philip of Greece, Philip asked King George VI for his daughter's hand in marriage in 1946. The king consented but insisted that the public announcement be made after Elizabeth's 21st birthday, in April 1947. The royal couple married on 20 November 1947 in a ceremony at Westminster Abbey.

Right: Proud mother Princess Elizabeth cradles Prince Charles at his baptism on 15 December 1948 in the Music Room of Buckingham Palace. The little prince, who is pictured wearing the famous Honiton Lace Gown, was then second in line to the throne. He was born a little over a month earlier at 9.14 p.m. on 14 November 1948, at Buckingham Palace, weighing 7lb and 6oz.

Above: Prince Charles held aloft by his father Prince Philip, Duke of Edinburgh, alongside his mother Princess Elizabeth and baby Princess Anne, in August 1951. Anne was born a year earlier on 15 August 1950 at their new home, Clarence House. Charles and Anne shared a close bond from an early age and they relied on each other for company when their busy parents were away on overseas tours or carrying out royal duties.

Right: Prince Charles pictured being pushed around Green Park in his pram by one of his nannies on his second birthday, 14 November 1950.

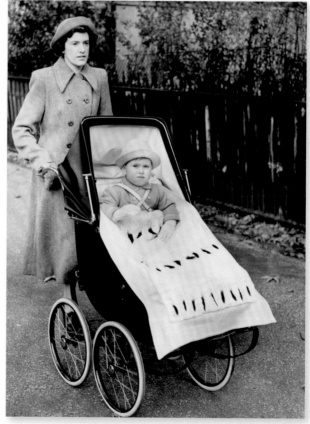

Left: The Queen pictured with her growing family. There is a decade between the birth of Princess Anne and Prince Andrew, who was born on 19 February 1960. On 8 February 1960, eleven days before Andrew's birth, the Queen declared that she had adopted the surname 'Mountbatten-Windsor' as the name for all her descendants who did not enjoy the title of His or Her Royal Highness.

Right: A charming photograph of Prince Charles and his sister by the Queen's cousin, the celebrated photographer Patrick Anson, 5th Earl of Lichfield. In his practice he was known as Patrick Lichfield. By the time their youngest brother Prince Edward was born in 1964, Anne was thirteen and Charles was fifteen. The two have remained close into adulthood.

Left: The Queen and Prince Philip's family was complete with the birth of their fourth child, Prince Edward, on 10 March 1964. By then, the Queen had become more comfortable in her role and what was expected of her. She had learned to manage her time more effectively and to ensure that she left space in the schedule for her family, too. Elizabeth spent more time playing with her two younger children and once a week, Edward and Andrew's nanny was given the night off and Elizabeth would take over.

Left: Prince Charles shakes hand with his headmaster Robert Chew on his first day at his boarding school Gordonstoun on 1 May 1962, watched by old boy Prince Philip. Charles found aspects of his school life difficult and had to contend with early morning runs, cold showers, and relentless bullying. He alluded to the German prisoner-of-war camp Colditz Castle when he called the Scottish school 'Colditz in Kilts'.

Prince Charles enjoyed his time at Aberystwyth University where he was tutored in Welsh language by Dr Edward Millward, who was founder of the Welsh Language Society. He spent time at the language laboratory in The Old College Building. He said his time there made an 'enormous difference' to his understanding not only of the language, but the way Wales worked and its sense of real community.

Left: The Prince of Wales at his investiture at Caernarfon Castle, 1 July 1969, flanked by his proud parents. The event, which had a UK television audience of 19 million, was a carefully choreographed by Lord Snowdon, Princess Margaret's husband, who ensured there would be more than a nod to the epoch and towards the future.

Right: At his investiture as Prince of Wales, Charles was invested with the Insignia of his Principality and the Earldom of Chester: a sword, coronet, mantle, gold ring and gold rod. He acquitted himself well as he gave his formal response: 'I, Charles, Prince of Wales, do become your liege man of life and limb and of earthly worship and faith and truth I will bear unto you to live and die against all manner of folks.'

Left: After graduating from Trinity College, Cambridge, in 1970, Charles trained as a jet pilot at Royal Air Force Cranwell, before enrolling in the Britannia Royal Naval College for a six-week course of study. He began his Royal Navy service on the guided missile destroyer HMS *Norfolk* on 5 November 1971. The prince later qualified as a helicopter pilot and joined the 845 Naval Air Squadron aboard the aircraft carrier HMS *Hermes*. In February 1976, Charles commanded the coastal minehunter HMS *Bronington*. He was promoted to the rank of Commander and ended active service in the Royal Navy in 1977.

Left: Prince Charles first met the love of his life, the then Camilla Shand, in 1971 and they started of a brief, but nonetheless passionate love affair. They resumed that affair after she married Andrew Parker Bowles and again after his marriage to Princess Diana had 'irretrievably broken down'. He told the Queen her position in his life was 'non-negotiable' and the two eventually married on 9 April 2005, when she became HRH The Duchess of Cornwall.

Right: Prince Charles met singer and Hollywood actress Barbra Streisand in 1974 when visiting the set of the film *Funny Lady*. He said he was dazzled by her 'effervescent talent and unique vitality', and Streisand was equally as effusive about Charles, saying she loved spending some time with him at Highgrove. When he came to see her show she said on stage, 'You know, if I played my cards right, I could have wound up being the first Jewish princess!'

Left: On 6 February 1981, Charles proposed to Lady Diana Spencer and she agreed to marry him. Asked if they were in love during their engagement interview, the prince followed up Diana's quick 'of course' with that infamous line, 'Whatever "in love" means'. Even before their relationship disintegrated, Charles was deeply unsure about the marriage as he believed they were incompatible and he wanted to call off the wedding. The wedding, described by the Archbishop of Canterbury, Robert Runcie, who officiated at the ceremony, as the 'stuff of which fairytales are made', went ahead on 29 July 1981.

A global television audience of 750 million in seventy-four countries watched the wedding of Prince Charles and Lady Diana Spencer, with around 600,000 onlookers lining the route from the palace to St Paul's Cathedral, where they exchanged their vows.

Almost exactly a year after their marriage, on 9 July 1982, the Prince of Wales was overjoyed as he emerged from the Lindo Wing of St Mary's Hospital, with Princess Diana, after she had given birth to their blue-eyed baby son, Prince William. The proud father rang the Queen from the hospital, who was said to be 'absolutely delighted'. Despite Diana's smiles, the princess was struggling to cope both physically and mentally. She could barely put one foot in front of the other and later recalled that she was in agony throughout the photo session and was in a hurry for it to be over.

Right: One of the most enduring moments of the tour of New Zealand in April 1983 came when, in a 'happy family' photoshoot with accredited photographers, baby Prince William played with his parents on the lawn of Government House in Auckland.

Left: Princess Diana and Prince Charles pose outside the Lindo Wing after the birth of Prince Harry on 15 September 1984. By this point the couple's marriage was distinctly rocky. Diana had known for months that she was having a boy but had kept it from her husband. When they returned to Kensington Palace, Charles told her he was off to play polo at Windsor. Diana saw it as a sign of his uncaring attitude towards her and later said she felt abandoned.

Right: Diana poses with her sons, smartly dressed in their Wetherby School uniforms, on Prince Harry's first day at school in 1989.

team had arranged unofficial photocalls at the foot of the main ski-lift in exchange for privacy of sorts. Charles and his entourage arrived late, after snowdrifts blocked the Arlberg Pass, the only route into the village. He knew he would not be welcome in her private suite, so his staff had asked Hannes Schneider to find him another room in the hotel, which was difficult as it was fully booked.

A small room was made available, but unfortunately it did not have a refrigerator for his Martini mix. Inspector Tony Parker had to raise the issue with Herr Schneider, whose go-to phrase in English was, 'No Problem.' Twenty minutes later he arrived back at the hotel, having carried a mini fridge through the snowstorm. He gave his stock response again when the prince said he hoped he had not been too much trouble.

As destiny would have it, Charles never did get to see his sons ski that year in Lech. On 29 March, news reached the princess's head of protection in Lech, Ken Wharfe, that Diana's father, Earl Spencer, had died at the Brompton Hospital in South Kensington, after years of ill health. When Wharfe went to tell Charles's private secretary, Commander Richard Aylard, he presumed the prince would want to break the news to his wife himself. Charles, however, felt it would come better from Inspector Wharfe, as he had a good working relationship with her and 'knew her better than anyone'.[2]

Charles recognised that his wife would be inconsolable, and he was equally aware that he would bear the brunt of her grief and frustration, and she might lash out. When she was told the news, the princess was calm at first, but soon broke down in tears. She had not expected her father's death, as nobody ever does, however much they may have readied themselves for the possibility.

When Inspector Wharfe broached the subject of what to do next, Diana made it clear that she wanted to return to her family as soon as possible, but without her husband. That could not happen, as Charles needed to save face, and he relied on the experienced officer to resolve it.

'I told her that this was not open for discussion. She had to go with it,' Wharfe said. He tried to comfort her and also reminded Diana of her father's lifetime of loyalty to the Crown.[3] 'I told her that her late father would not have wanted this. He was a loyal man; he would not have wanted his death turned into a media circus, and it seemed to strike a chord with her, and thankfully she agreed to do it.'

When the royal party left Lech by car for Zurich airport the following morning, with Inspector Tony Parker at the wheel, Ken Wharfe in the passenger seat, and the royal couple in the back seat, it was a crisp, clear day, with a beautiful blue sky and wonderful powder snow sprinkled on the slopes. 'The tension in the car was electric. I looked in the mirror in time to see the princess's eyes rise heavenwards in a gesture of exasperation at comments made by the prince. Perhaps wanting to break the ice, he said, "Look at all that powder, it's such a shame we have to go so soon."' There was an icy silence for the rest of the two-hour journey, said Wharfe.[4]

At the airport, they boarded the Bae 146 of the Queen's Flight that was waiting for them, while the media, who were out in force, scribbled notes and the photographers' flashguns fired. Nothing was said during the entire flight. The princess did not want to speak to her husband, and he did not dare even to try starting a conversation.

It was soon apparent that the clever PR spin had worked. The next day it was reported that Charles was at Diana's side in her hour of need. Yet as soon as they arrived at Kensington Palace they went their separate ways – he to Highgrove, as Diana went to pay her respects to her father. At the earl's funeral, two days later, the atmosphere between the royal couple had deteriorated yet further. Charles attended the funeral against his wife's wishes, arriving by helicopter.

By the summer of 1992, the year of the Queen's infamous *annus horribilis* speech, the Royal Family seemed hell-bent on self-destruction. The Duke and Duchess of York had separated after the infamous toe-sucking incident, in which intimate photographs of the Duchess with her Texan 'financial adviser', John Bryan, had graced the front pages of the British tabloids. The Princess Royal was divorced from Mark Phillips and was now having an affair with the Queen's former equerry, Commander Tim Laurence (whom she would later marry), while Prince Edward was making headline news by bizarrely announcing, 'I'm not gay!' without, it seems, having been asked the question. Above all, the marriage of the Prince and Princess of Wales had been exposed as a sham.

By the time the royal couple returned to Britain from a cruise aboard billionaire John Latsis's yacht, the marriage was on the verge of collapse. A tape of an intimate telephone conversation made on New Year's Eve 1989 between Diana and her new lover James Gilbey, a wealthy car dealer, was then released to the press. Coming as it did so soon after the row over Andrew Morton's devastating book, *Diana: Her True Story*, it proved to be one scandal too many. Diana's critical comments about the Royal Family were the catalyst for her exit from the House of Windsor.

On 25 August 1992, the editor of the *Sun*, Kelvin MacKenzie, published transcripts of the illegally recorded conversation after the existence of the tapes was mentioned in America's top-selling magazine, the *National Enquirer*. 'Dianagate' or 'Squidgygate', as the scandal came to be called, effectively exploded the myth of Diana as the innocent, perfect princess.

The *Sun* even put an extract from the tapes on a premium telephone number, so that readers could call and listen to

Diana's unmistakable voice. Throughout the conversation, Diana described life with her husband as 'real, real torture' and spoke of her frustration and resentment towards the Royal Family. She also spoke of her fears of becoming pregnant with her lover's child. Gilbey called her 'darling' fifty-three times, and 'Squidgy' fourteen times. In one exchange, he says, 'Oh, Squidgy, I love you. Love you. Love you.'[5]

At one point during her conversation with Gilbey, Diana says, 'I was very bad at lunch and I nearly started blubbing. I just felt really sad and empty and thought, bloody hell, after all I've done for that fucking family, it is so desperate.' Diana also told Gilbey how the Queen Mother had given her a strange look at lunch. 'It's not hatred, it's a sort of interest and pity.' It was devastating for Diana.

Nobody knows who made the original recordings of the conversations and why. They were picked up by amateur radio hams using basic scanners, but they were being transmitted regularly at different times to ensure the conversation was heard, knowing that it would eventually end up in the hands of the media. There are at least two sets of Diana tapes in existence, recordings of the same conversation made on different days by different radio buffs.

A full investigation was carried out by the internal security services, the results of which were never made public. They identified all those involved, but for legal reasons I cannot expand further, nor is it necessary to do so. It does, however, lend credence to Diana's belief, so often dismissed, that the Establishment was out to destroy her and her reputation. In the end, the 'Dianagate' scandal was a pretty tawdry, if not squalid, affair, which reflected little credit on most of those concerned.

Diana was determined to upstage her husband on their next and, as it transpired, their last overseas tour together, to South Korea. Whether it was flirting with a good-looking army officer or storming ahead of Charles as he courteously greeted people in the line-up at the opera, her behaviour demonstrated at every turn that she no longer cared whether he was with her or not. Charles, ever the diplomat when on duty, was beginning to lose his patience.

Journalists covering the tour, tired of being fobbed off with lies from palace officials about the marriage, were not prepared to take it anymore either. Peter Westmacott,[6] who had been seconded from the Foreign Office to act as deputy private secretary to Charles, was their first victim. Pressed by veteran *Daily Mirror* royal reporter James Whitaker about the state of the marriage, he let slip, 'Of course there are problems.'

This conversation was overheard by Simon McCoy, the royal reporter for Sky TV, who went on air with the story. Without naming Westmacott, McCoy said a senior official had for the first time admitted that the marriage was on the rocks. The following day the *Sun* named Westmacott as the whistleblower.

The next to come under attack from a relentless royal press pack was the palace press secretary, Dickie Arbiter. The newshounds, having tasted blood, told him that if he could not tell them where and when Charles and Diana's next official overseas visit would be, they would write that South Korea was to be the last and that the marriage was over. Dickie promised to get back to them. Naturally, he could not. The reporters rightly ran their story. It was time, Diana said, for her to spread her wings.

Charles felt trapped. His personal life was impacting his mental health and he was desperate to resolve it and move on. In a private letter written on 8 November 1992, on the flight back to Britain after the ill-fated trip to South Korea, he despaired about the media interest in his fracturing marriage: 'I feel so unsuited to the ghastly business of human intrigue and general nastiness… I don't know what will happen from now on, but I dread it.'[7]

Speculation about Charles's relationship with the married Camilla Parker Bowles intensified in November, when rumours surfaced about a lurid conversation between the two lovers. Just over a month later, on 9 December 1992, the prime minister John Major got to his feet in the House of Commons and from the dispatch box announced the formal separation of the Prince and Princess of Wales. Bizarrely, he said there was no reason why Diana should not be crowned Queen in due course. Both Charles and Diana knew that would never happen.

The boys spent Christmas Day at Sandringham with their father, who had taken on his old nanny, Mabel Anderson. 'It's just like old times,' the Queen is said to have remarked. But when they joined Diana, it was very different. She whisked them off to the Caribbean for sea and sun, quite a contrast to a bleak, flat Norfolk. For Diana, the difference was more than merely symbolic. She was determined that the boys would grow up in an emotionally healthier environment than she had done herself. Subsequent holidays abroad were spent without their father, who would prefer they enjoyed traditional royal holidays at home on the Queen's estates.

Within weeks, in early 1993, the heat was on Charles when a tape of an intimate late-night conversation with his married lover, recorded in December 1989, was released. It was published by the *People* newspaper under the headline: 'Charles and Camilla – The Tape'. Their six-minute conversation took place as Charles was preparing to address Oxford University on the teaching of English in school. The conversation soon became sexual, with Charles referring to her tampons and wanting to live 'inside her trousers'. It was branded 'sick' by Diana, who felt vindicated.

Camilla too felt hurt and was left exposed, as her marriage to Andrew was now in tatters. At a private meeting, Camilla's father, the war hero Major Bruce Shand, whom Charles greatly admired, reproached the prince, leaving him humbled and in tears.

In 1994, two years after his separation from Diana, Charles agreed to take part in a television documentary fronted by Jonathan Dimbleby to accompany the broadcaster's biography of the prince and to mark twenty-five years since his investiture as Prince of Wales. *Charles: The Private Man, the Public Role* aired on 29 June and was a sympathetic assessment of Charles's achievements, but is only remembered for the interview conducted at Highgrove in which he confirmed that he had been unfaithful to Diana.

Charles, knowing the repercussions, looked uncomfortable when he was directly asked by Dimbleby if he had been 'faithful and honourable' when he was married. His response was not spontaneous, as he knew it was coming. 'Yes, absolutely,' he said, but was then pushed further. 'And you were?' Charles replied, 'Yes, until it became irretrievably broken down, us both having tried.'[8] It emerged later that this was the second version of the interview, after Charles had been convinced to admit to the affair.

In a documentary exploring the origins of Diana's *Panorama* interview, it was revealed that Charles did not initially intend to confess to his affair with Camilla Parker Bowles, but was persuaded it would be best if he did, as Jonathan Dimbleby would ensure it came out in a more considerate manner. Sir Max Hastings, former editor of the *Daily Telegraph*, said, 'Somebody convinced him, "Look, sir, this is going to come out sooner or later, wouldn't it be better if it comes out in a sympathetic form, in sympathetic hands."'

Prince Philip was infuriated by his son's indiscretion. The rest of Charles's family were deeply shocked that he had been so open and left himself so exposed. It put Camilla in an impossible position, too. She was labelled a 'marriage wrecker', a temptress and worse. Camilla remained silent, but some friends and family did not.

Simon and Caroline Parker Bowles, her brother and sister-in-law, accused Charles of blaming everyone but himself for his marriage break-up, saying his revelations had left Camilla 'in a heap'. Simon, who owned Green's Restaurant and Oyster Bar in Mayfair, London, went further, stating, 'The Prince of Wales does not have our sympathy at the moment.' Historian Dr David Starkey, however, stressed there were no constitutional implications, as throughout history there had been kings who were divorced or separated, and even a few who had boyfriends.

The same day the documentary was televised, with Charles's admission of his infidelities, Diana stepped out at *Vanity Fair*'s annual fundraiser in the Serpentine Gallery wearing a sexy black dress designed by Christina Stambolian, afterwards forever known as her revenge dress. The next day, the *Sun* was in no doubt whose side they were on. Their headline read: 'The Thrilla He Left to Woo Camilla'. The prince's adultery confession signalled the end of Camilla's marriage to Andrew Parker Bowles, too. She filed for divorce the following year, by which time they had been living apart for more than two years. The pair said in a statement, 'There is little of common interest between us.'⁹

Charles agreed to support his mistress, which he did both emotionally and financially. To him, Camilla's role in his life was 'non-negotiable',¹⁰ but she was now seen as the 'most hated woman in Britain' and had to lie low.

Charles recognised that he would have to step up as a father now that he and Diana were separated. However, his work schedule was relentless and he knew early on that he needed support when his sons stayed with him. He turned to Alexandra 'Tiggy' Legge-Bourke, whom he appointed as a companion to his two sons.

Tiggy was like a big sister and accompanied them on the ski slopes in Klosters, or on yachts during summer cruises with their father. 'I give the princes what they need – fresh air, a rifle and a horse,' she remarked. The boys liked her, but her presence infuriated a jealous Diana.

Unfortunately, the innocent Tiggy found herself cruelly dragged into the mudslinging of the royal marriage crisis. It turned ugly when the BBC television reporter Martin Bashir, who had his own agenda, spread false claims against her to help secure his infamous interview with Diana on the *Panorama* programme. At one meeting, the mendacious Bashir produced an extraordinary fake dossier of smears about the Prince of Wales and other royals, calculated to feed Diana's paranoia. They included the shocking and totally false claim that Charles was 'in love' with Tiggy and that the two were planning a holiday together. [11]

As absurd as this sounded, Diana believed it. In fact, she became so obsessed with the idea that Miss Legge-Bourke was pregnant by Charles – and had lost the baby – that she confronted her about it at a Christmas party for palace staff on 14 December 1995, at the Lanesborough Hotel in London. Tiggy was left utterly shocked and embarrassed. She even threatened legal action and Sir Robert (now Lord) Fellowes, the Queen's private secretary and Diana's brother-in-law, launched an internal inquiry, which showed that Diana's claims were groundless.[12]

William showed his sensitivity, aged fourteen, when he asked his parents not to attend Eton's Fourth of June celebrations, as he felt the circus entailed by their presence, with all the accompanying press and security, would spoil the annual parents' day for his fellow pupils. Instead, he asked Tiggy to attend in their place, which upset Diana and surprised Charles.

When *Panorama* aired on 20 November 1995, 22.8 million

people tuned in to watch Diana's interview, in which she said her estranged husband was not suited to the 'top job' of King and their relationship had failed because 'there were three of us in this marriage', a devastating swipe at Charles and Camilla's adultery. Her purpose in taking part was simple – to inflict serious and lasting damage to Charles's reputation – and she achieved it. It also led to calls from senior Establishment figures for the Crown to skip a generation to Prince William after the Queen's death.

Years later, on 20 May 2021, William revealed his 'indescribable sadness' at the BBC's failings in airing the *Panorama* interview, which he said had exacerbated his mother Diana's 'fear, paranoia and isolation'. He said he was in no doubt that Martin Bashir's web of deceit 'substantially influenced' what his late mother said and 'was a major contribution to making his parents' relationship worse.'[13]

His deeply personal recorded statement followed the damning findings of an independent report by the former Master of the Rolls, Lord Dyson, in May 2021. Lord Dyson had carried out a six-month investigation into the scandal and ruled that Martin Bashir had faked documents and 'deceived and induced him [her brother, Earl Spencer] to arrange a meeting with Princess Diana.'

It is easier to analyse and evaluate situations when we are looking back on them, and many believe that such was Diana's determination she would have found a media outlet to vent her frustrations no matter what. Nonetheless, Diana's actions were an affront to the institution of monarchy and forced the Queen's hand. Finally, she bowed to Charles's wishes and instructed him to start divorce proceedings, which he did. The Queen also requested that Diana and Charles make their separation official shortly after the *Panorama* interview.

Buckingham Palace released a statement on 21 December 1995,

saying the Queen had written to Charles and Diana urging them to divorce, which they agreed to do. When the divorce was finalised, it emerged that the princess would be stripped of her royal title, Her Royal Highness. She would now be known as Diana, Princess of Wales until she remarried. It was agreed the couple would have shared custody of their boys and she received a lump sum settlement of £17m (equivalent to about £33m in 2022), as well as £400,000 per year (about £800,000 today).

The couple signed a confidentiality agreement that prohibited them from discussing the details of the divorce or their married life. The fairy tale had ended years before, but at least the nightmare could now start to be over. When William learnt that his mother had been stripped of her title, he was upset. He threw his arms around her and exclaimed, 'Don't worry, Mummy. I'll give it back to you one day, when I'm king.'

Sadly, it is a promise he will never be able to keep.

CHAPTER 11

Death in Paris

*I feel like everyone else in this country today, utterly
devastated... She was the people's princess, and that's how
she will stay, how she will remain in our hearts and in our
memories, forever.*

**PRIME MINISTER TONY BLAIR ON PRINCESS DIANA
AFTER LEARNING OF HER DEATH**

What happened next rocked the monarchy to its foundations and
raised questions about Charles's fitness to be king. Even senior
Establishment figures began to doubt Charles's suitability to reign.

On 31 August 1997, his ex-wife Diana, Princess of Wales,
was killed in a car crash in the Pont d'Alma tunnel in Paris. She
was being driven in a speeding Mercedes by Henri Paul, whose
judgement was impaired through drinking alcohol and who had
tried to outrun several foreign paparazzi who were following them
on mopeds. Those who died in the crash – Diana, her new boyfriend
Dodi Fayed and Paul – were not wearing seatbelts. Her bodyguard
Trevor Rees-Jones, who suffered serious injuries and memory loss,
was not wearing one either, but he survived.

Diana survived the crash but was in critical condition. The
princess suffered serious chest injuries as well as concussion, a
broken arm and a cut thigh, and was treated at the scene by Dr
Jean-Marc Martino for almost forty minutes before the ambulance

set off for the hospital. He instructed the ambulance driver Michel Massebeuf to drive slowly in an attempt to try to save the dying princess. She was taken to the city's Pitié Salpêtrière hospital, where a young duty general surgeon, MonSef Dahman, led a two-hour operation to save her life, but he and his team were unable to get Diana's heart to beat properly and she never regained consciousness. Diana finally succumbed to her injuries at 4.53 a.m.

At around 1 a.m., 800 miles away in the Scottish Highlands, Charles had been woken and told by telephone that there had been a crash in Paris involving his ex-wife. Her companion Dodi, he was told, was dead and Diana was seriously injured. A few hours later came the call with the shocking confirmation that Diana had also died. Racked with grief, Charles broke down and wept. He went to see the Queen, who advised him against waking his sons, counselling that it was best to let them sleep.

Dreading having to tell them the devastating news, Charles went for a walk alone. Only hours earlier William and Harry had spoken to Diana, albeit briefly, and now she was gone. 'Harry and I were running around, playing with our cousins [Peter and Zara] and having a very good time,'[1] William recalled twenty years later. They had kept the telephone call brief so they could return to playing – something they deeply regret to this day.

Charles returned at around 7 a.m. and his eldest son, William, was already awake. Charles went to his room and broke the news, then hugged his son. Both then turned their thoughts to Harry, still asleep in the bedroom next door.

In his book *Spare*, Harry remembers how Charles sat down on his bed, put his hand on his knee and said, 'Darling boy, Mummy's been in a car crash.' Still in shock himself, his father said there had been complications. 'They tried, darling boy. She didn't make it.' As Harry has always maintained, however, his father was not good at showing emotions or being intimate face-to-face, so he did not hug his younger son. Harry then remained in his room alone until the piper began to play at 9 a.m. For a while, he pretended that his mother had faked her own death to escape the media attention and was hiding in a Paris flat.[2] But the reality and manner of her death has clearly affected both of her sons deeply ever since.

The Queen believed the boys needed to be shielded from the media frenzy, which they both acknowledged later meant a great deal to them. Speaking twenty years later, in 2017, William explained, 'At the time, my grandmother wanted to protect her two grandsons, and my father as well.' He was thankful they were given 'the privacy to mourn – to collect our thoughts'.

In an interview with Alastair Campbell for *GQ* magazine, William admitted he had locked his grief inside for many years. 'I am in a better place about it than I have been for a long time, where I can talk about her more openly, talk about her more honestly, and I can remember her better, and publicly talk about her better. It has taken me almost twenty years to get to that stage. I still find it difficult now, because at the time it was so raw. And, it is not like most people's grief, because everyone else knows about it, everyone knows the story, everyone knows her.'

Unfairly, there was intense opprobrium by the public towards Charles and even the Queen over their perceived lack of emotion and aloofness after the death. Overnight, the Royal Family in Balmoral, where William and Harry were holidaying, were cast as the villains of the story, and Diana was elevated to the status of saintly victim. The facts did not seem to matter anymore.

On the morning of the funeral, 6 September 1997, a great calm fell over central London. Hundreds of thousands of mourners took to the streets to pay their respects, lining the route along which the princess's coffin would be borne on a gun carriage from Kensington

Palace to Westminster Abbey. Everywhere her famous face was to be seen on the thousands of newspaper and magazine special editions being sold on the streets. It appeared as if the nation had come to a complete halt. Around the world, more than two billion people sat and watched the sombre event unfold.

Prince Philip had told William he would regret it later if he did not walk behind Diana's coffin, and the duke joined William and Harry, Charles, and Diana's brother, Earl Spencer, on the long, solemn procession to the Abbey, where 1,900 invited guests waited within its spectacular Gothic interior. As the bells of Big Ben tolled eleven, the funeral cortège reached the west door. Then eight Welsh Guardsmen, bare-headed, their faces taut with strain, carried the quarter-ton coffin on their shoulders as they slow-marched the length of the nave. Harry sobbed when the coffin passed him and, as his tears flowed, Charles pulled him closer and his elder brother William laid a comforting hand on his shoulder.

The Prince of Wales looked traumatised as the music of 'Libera Me' played, and he then had to endure the eulogy of Diana's brother Charles Spencer, the content of which reportedly angered the Queen. Suddenly a sound like a distant downpour of heavy rain swept into the abbey, rolling on and on until it reached the altar. It was not rain, but the noise of people clapping outside after hearing Earl Spencer's no-holds-barred address on loudspeakers. Many respected Earl Spencer for his courage. William and Harry joined in the applause and so too, generously, did Charles, but the Queen, the Duke of Edinburgh and the Queen Mother sat unmoved in stony-faced silence.

England's rose was gone. She was a woman of great courage, generosity and warmth, but also a complicated, troubled woman prone to bouts of depression. That said, she had certainly made the people of the world sit up and take notice of her during her thirty-six years on the planet. From now on, Diana's early, tragic death meant that her legacy would be viewed through rose-tinted glasses. Charles's reputation, in contrast, was at rock bottom, and he knew it would be an uphill battle to improve it. He also understood that his plans to step out into the limelight with Camilla would have to be put on hold. The public simply would not accept it. Moreover, he would have to devote himself to his new role as a single father and protect his sons.

Charles showed a great strength and compassion as a single father, which many of his critics had believed him to be incapable of doing. Perhaps it was guilt, knowing his devotion to his work had cost him precious bonding time with his sons. His feelings towards his late wife softened, as he saw how Diana's devotion to them had paid off and they had seemingly grown into loving, confident boys. Charles realised that he now had to step up, too.

He wanted to ensure that his two sons could cope with the expectations of their birth right, but recognised that they should have time to be boys and also needed their father more than ever. Charles cancelled all his immediate engagements to focus on his sons. Diana's past accusations of his being an absent father echoed in his mind. If he had been a poor husband before, now that she was gone he was not going to fail her again as guardian to the sons they both cherished. Charles threw himself into the role of devoted single dad, although Harry now questions his father's suitability for parenthood, saying that Charles had an air of 'never being quite ready' for it, while at the same time he admits, 'To be fair, he tried.'[3]

Charles also listened more to his sons' views and began, tentatively, to embrace a more modern way of life, their generation's way. In an interview with Tom Bradby on ITV in January 2023, Harry would relate the moment when he finally told his father about the extent of his mental health issues over dinner at Highgrove.

When he had finished, Charles said softly, 'I suppose it's my fault. I should have got you the help you needed years ago.' Harry assured his father it was not his fault, but said he appreciated the apology.[4]

In August 1997, Charles took Harry with him on an official royal tour to South Africa, where Charles met Nelson Mandela, and both father and son met the Spice Girls. Harry later said the trip helped him to 'get away from it all' following Diana's death, although he now dismisses it as purely a royal PR exercise.

There was no great ambition behind Charles's next joint overseas trip with his two sons. It was a skiing holiday in Canada, where they could bond and relax, just seven months after Diana's death. However, several royal engagements had been scheduled soon after their arrival at Vancouver airport, on 24 March 1998, before the three princes headed by helicopter to the resort of Whistler, in British Columbia, to enjoy four days on the slopes.

Nobody knew quite what the public would make of the beleaguered trio, especially as Charles was being thought by many as somehow culpable for Diana's death, yet any mention of William and Harry prompted outpourings of public sympathy. The two boys had largely been shielded from public scrutiny since their mother's funeral, when William, much taller, had seemed more mature than Harry, then thirteen, who appeared to be heartbreakingly vulnerable. Three months short of his sixteenth birthday, however, William was still painfully shy, and possessed of all the awkward self-awareness of the teenage years.

Crowds had waited for hours for the royal visit and went wild, jostling against police barricades. Among them were many teenage girls keen to see William. They screamed and waved banners in a display that would have unsettled the most seasoned public performer. William had never experienced anything like it before and, although he tried to hide his discomfort, it was obvious he hated it. When he arrived at the Pacific Space Centre, a crowd of around five thousand was there to greet him. He did his best, spending ten minutes shaking hands, but he looked close to tears and clearly could not wait to escape. Inside, he had a meltdown, and told his father he did not want to go on with the public appearances.

Charles managed to persuade his son to reconsider, much to the relief of his newly installed PR man, Mark Bolland. Later, it fell to Mr Bolland to try to restrain the overheated press, telling them he would appreciate it if the coverage was 'calmer and cooler'.

Back in Britain, he also found unlikely allies among various doom-mongering commentators, who argued that William and Harry were being overexposed far too soon after Diana's death. A *Daily Express* columnist wrote, 'Would Diana, if she were alive today, want her elder son to start carrying out royal duties at such a tender age?' Yet again, Charles was blamed for exploiting his sons for positive publicity.

It was a challenging conundrum for Charles and his aides. After all, how they could visit a realm where Charles would one day be king and not connect with the public? Moreover, how could they control, never mind quash, the outpouring of affection for William? The genie was out of the bottle and not even an accomplished media fixer like Mark Bolland could put it back and seal up the stopper.

Either way, in Canada, Charles's calming words seemed to have the desired impact on William. When the three princes were presented with scarlet 'Roots' branded caps – worn by the country's Winter Olympics team – William showed his father that the caps should be worn back to front, delighting the photographers. Then they headed for the slopes of Whistler for a welcome four-day skiing holiday together as guests of Charles's friend, the Canadian billionaire Galen Weston and his wife, Hilary, who was then Ontario's lieutenant-governor. They stayed in a chalet there owned by friends of the Westons.

It had been a close call but, although William proved a media triumph, Harry was more of a concern. The cheeky little boy had become introverted and depressed in the wake of his mother's death. Unlike William, who vowed privately to make his mother proud of him, Harry's tears still flowed in private moments. The media fascination with Diana hurt them both. Every time another photograph of her appeared on the front pages, the pain returned. They grew protective of their much-maligned father too and were upset by what they saw as unfair criticism of him.

A year after Diana's death, the two boys decided to do something about it and issued a personal statement, calling for an end to the public mourning and what had been called the 'Diana industry' – the commercial exploitation of their mother, with even her own recently established Memorial Fund using her signature on margarine tubs. After liaising with Charles, the princes issued a statement in which they insisted Diana would want people to move on. 'She would have known that constant reminders of her death can create nothing but pain to those she left behind,' they said.

They were also distressed by the references to conspiracy theories surrounding their mother's death emanating from Mohamed Al-Fayed and his team. Fayed's spokesman hit back, saying the Egyptian businessman could not rest until he knew the full truth about how his son Dodi had died in Paris.

It was not until eleven years after Diana's death that the inquest jury finally and definitively decided that she and Dodi Fayed had been unlawfully killed by a combination of the driving of their Mercedes by their chauffeur Henri Paul, who also died in the crash, and the behaviour of the vehicles following – the posse of paparazzi photographers who had been dogging their final journey. Years later, Harry admitted in his memoir that he had asked to be driven though the Pont d'Alma tunnel at 65mph – the exact speed the police stated Diana's car was travelling at the time it collided with a solid pillar.

According to Harry, both sons wanted an official inquiry into Diana's death reopened and members of the paparazzi put behind bars, but they were talked out of doing so by 'the powers that be'.[5] At least with the final inquest verdict they had a partial victory and some blame was attributed to the paparazzi who had chased the Mercedes into the tunnel. After the jury had deliberated for twenty-two hours, its forewoman told the coroner Lord Justice Scott Baker that the deaths had been caused by 'grossly negligent driving'. As nobody is found guilty or innocent at an inquest, however, no criminal or civil liability was ever determined. The six-month hearing, which had cost the taxpayer £6.5m and heard from 278 witnesses, was to be the last word on the death of Princess Diana.

Five years after the traumatic events of 1997 and the dent that Diana's death made on the reputation of Charles and the Royal Family, the nation would unite once again to celebrate Her Majesty the Queen's fifty years on the throne. But the Golden Jubilee year got off to a sad start.

On 9 February 2002, Charles's 'darling aunt', Princess Margaret, died peacefully in her sleep at King Edward VII's Hospital after suffering a stroke. Charles remains close to her son Lord Snowdon, who regularly accompanies him to his private nature retreat in the Zalán Valley in Transylvania, Romania, and in a televised address he called 'Margot' a 'free spirit who lived life to the full' and was 'vital, beautiful and talented'. A few weeks later, on 30 March 2002, Charles was devastated again on the death of Queen Elizabeth, the Queen Mother, whose condition had deteriorated rapidly after a bad fall, at the age of 101. He said, 'She was quite simply the most magical grandmother you could possibly have, and I was utterly devoted to her.'

Her passing came at a low point in Charles's life, as many speculated that he might never be king, something that he explained to NBC News interviewer Brian Williams was not something he spent too much time on. 'You think about it a bit, but it's much better not to. If it comes to it, regrettably it comes as a result of the death of your parent, which is not so nice, to say the least.' His mother was then seventy-six, and stepping down had not crossed the Queen's mind. She made that clear to the 103rd Archbishop of Canterbury, Dr George Carey, when he went to see her after his resignation that year. 'That's something I can't do.'

Still clearly in mourning for both her mother and her sister, on 2 May 2002 the Queen embarked on her nationwide Golden Jubilee tour, starting at Falmouth, in Cornwall, to the sound of a twenty-one-gun salute and rousing cheers from flag-waving children. Over the next three months, she and Prince Philip criss-crossed the nation, travelling as widely as possible across England, Scotland, Wales and Northern Ireland.

The focal point of the celebrations was the Golden Jubilee weekend of 1–4 June, when street parties and parades were held across the country. On Monday, 3 June, a crowd of over a million people converged on The Mall to watch on giant screens the Party at the Palace, an evening pop concert in the grounds of Buckingham Palace, featuring superstar acts including Sir Paul McCartney, Elton John and the Beach Boys' former lead singer Brian Wilson. The monarch and other royals were joined by 12,000 guests and the concert was televised around the world. The enduring image will be of the rock group Queen's lead guitarist, Brian May, playing 'God Save the Queen' from the roof of the palace.

Inevitably it was left to Charles to pay his mother the ultimate tribute, when he called her 'Your Majesty... Mummy' from the stage after the pop concert. With her standing next to him, he said, 'I don't think that any of us will ever forget this evening. It really has been a wonderful celebration of some of the best of British musical talent. Well, nearly all British... nearly all British.' He went on to say what everyone present was thinking:

> You have embodied something vital in our lives – continuity. You have been a beacon of tradition and stability in the midst of profound, sometimes perilous change. Fifty years ago, at nearly four years of age, I would probably have been playing in the sandpit in the garden just behind this stage. But now you have generously invited everyone in for a thoroughly memorable party... and we probably frightened the poor old geese into the bargain. So, Your Majesty, we are all deeply grateful to you and, in the words of the non-politically-correct second verse of the national anthem, you have defended our laws and certainly given us cause to shout with heartened voice, 'God Save the Queen'.

Despite reams of paper in books devoted to the apparent frostiness of their relationship, especially while Charles was a boy growing up, when the Queen's public duty meant she had to put some motherly duties second, the prince cared deeply for, loved, and respected his mother, and he showed it with his heartfelt words.

The next day, following a national service of thanksgiving at St Paul's Cathedral with a congregation of 2,500, including senior politicians and forty-seven members of the Royal Family, the

Queen attended a special lunch in the Guildhall. In a speech, Her Majesty said she was both 'overwhelmed and deeply moved' by the public's response to her jubilee, and made clear how vital the support of her family had been during her fifty-year reign.

'The Duke of Edinburgh has made an invaluable contribution to my life over these past fifty years, as he has to so many charities and organisations,' she said, as guests applauded. 'We both of us have a special place in our hearts for our children. I want to express my admiration for the Prince of Wales and for all he has achieved for this country. Our children, and all my family, have given me such love and unstinting help over the years and especially in recent months,' she added, referring to the recent deaths of her mother and sister.

A 'river of gold' then paved the Queen's journey along The Mall as 400 children waving gold-coloured streamers ran alongside the open-topped Range Rover carrying the Queen and Prince Philip to the royal box on the Queen Victoria Memorial. It took the Prince of Wales and his sons almost half an hour to walk from St James's Palace to their seats, as they stopped and chatted to spectators along the way. There the Royal Family and their guests watched the jubilee parade, as a procession of around 20,000 people marched cheerfully past them, including floats, choirs, representatives of all the services, and children from all fifty-four nations in the Commonwealth wearing their national costumes.

A truly memorable day ended with the Queen and the Royal Family appearing on the balcony of Buckingham Palace, as Concorde and the RAF Red Arrows flew overhead. A poll in the *Mail on Sunday* said the Queen was now the most respected figure in Britain, showing that her popularity had recovered after Diana's death five years earlier.

Camilla, who watched on from the royal box, was by now

publicly as well as in private an integral part of Charles's life. She had sustained him and assuaged his loneliness, but also knew when he wanted to be alone to focus on his work. When on the public stage, their closeness made them a redoubtable couple. During the jubilee Camilla was at the heart of the celebrations, watching alongside the Queen and other senior royals. Although she did not sit next to Charles in the royal box, being relegated off to the side with Princess Anne, the fact that the Queen had invited her to attend was interpreted as a significant step forward in Charles's campaign to gain acceptance for her.

It had taken time and astute PR management for Camilla to reach this position. Mark Bolland had worked hard, through a carefully managed campaign dubbed 'Operation Mrs PB', to secure enough public acceptance of Camilla as Charles's partner that a royal marriage between them would be possible. He employed all the dark arts of public relations and even used Princes William and Harry, claiming they had met Camilla and got on with her, when this was not the case.[6]

To the Machiavellian courtier – officially Charles's deputy private secretary – the ends justified the means. When Bolland had taken the helm in 1996 as Charles's spin doctor in chief, Princess Diana was still alive and universally adored. For many, after Charles confessed to adultery on television, Camilla was public enemy No. 1, irredeemably the other woman. Diana's death would make Bolland's task considerably tougher, for the princess and her legacy cast a long shadow.

Mark Bolland's masterstroke was the couple's first public appearance together on 28 January 1999, when Charles and Camilla stepped out as a couple after a birthday party for Camilla's sister, Annabel Elliot, at London's Ritz Hotel. Around 150 photographers were present to capture the pair leaving together.

The sharp-witted PR man had handled another tricky issue with aplomb, too. In January 2002, the now defunct *News of the World* broke the story that seventeen-year-old Harry's cannabis use and underage drinking was out of control. The newspaper's royal editor Clive Goodman's scoop, 'Harry's Drugs Shame', caused a sensation.

He wrote that Harry, whose father and brother were away from Highgrove at the time, frequented the Rattlebone Inn in Sherston, and got drunk. Harry had then been banned for calling the French chef 'a fucking frog'. Goodman also claimed that Harry had invited friends back to Highgrove for further drinking and cannabis-smoking sessions. It was the latter, in a converted basement at Highgrove he called 'Club H', which led to him being caught when staff could smell cannabis. Harry maintains in his book that it was 'Lies, all lies.' He claimed that he did not smoke weed there and the facts of the story are all wrong. Bizarrely, however, he does admit to taking cocaine and magic mushrooms as well as cannabis, on one occasion 'a shopping bag full', which allowed him to see 'the truth'.[7]

Mark Bolland moved fast. The *News of the World* claimed they had evidence that Harry was a 'drug addict'. When confronted, Harry said he had done only 'basic teenage stuff'. Bolland negotiated a story with the newspaper bosses that Harry now describes as having spun him 'right under the bus' but showed Charles in a good light, bolstering his father's 'sagging reputation'.[8] It related to what was perceived to be his father's non-confrontational approach to the problem in arranging for Harry to visit the Featherstone Lodge rehabilitation unit, which won praise from various drugs organisations.

Peter Martin, chief executive of Addaction, a drug and alcohol treatment agency, agreed and said, 'It seems that the Prince of

Wales has acted with deep sensitivity and very quickly, which is exactly what is needed.' Charles even won praise from the prime minister, Tony Blair, whose eldest son Euan was once caught underage drinking. Blair told Sir David Frost on the BBC, 'I know this myself. I think the way that Prince Charles and the Royal Family have handled it is absolutely right and they have done it in a very responsible and, as you would expect, in a very sensitive way.'

After the public backlash to the story, the director of the Press Complaints Commission, Guy Black (later Lord Black, and Bolland's partner), stressed that it did not mean the press could now freely intrude on Harry's private life. However, he accepted the story, stating, 'It is important to underline that this was an exceptional matter of public interest.'

Clarence House, however, now wanted to shut it down quickly. They issued a blunt statement: 'This is a serious matter which was resolved within the family and is now in the past and closed.' This infuriated Harry, who felt he had been used to make his father look good. In fact, he claims that he had visited the suburban rehab centre months earlier with his aide Mark Dyer, whom he called 'Marko', as part of his charity work.

William is said to have sympathised with his brother over the whole affair, in what Harry would later dub the 'public sacrifice of the Spare'.[9]

CHAPTER 12

Dissident at Heart

*He [Prince Charles] would readily embrace the political
aspects of any contentious issue he was interested in...
He often referred to himself as a dissident working against
the prevailing political consensus.*

**MARK BOLLAND, DEPUTY PRIVATE SECRETARY
TO THE PRINCE OF WALES 1997–2002**

A British monarch's residual powers – the so-called royal prerogative
– are mostly exercised through the government of the day. These
include the power to enact legislation, to award honours on the
advice of the prime minister, to sign treaties and, crucially, to declare
war. But would King Charles, given his deeply held convictions,
simply have rubber-stamped a decision to invade Iraq on prime
minister Tony Blair's say-so, as the late Queen Elizabeth did?

Indeed, would Sir Tony, as he is now,[1] have been so hawkish
if his king and commander-in-chief of the British armed forces
had kicked back and insisted that Blair disclose and discuss the
so-called irrefutable intelligence that Iraq's dictator Saddam
Hussein had weapons of mass destruction? After all, it is a British
prime minister's constitutional responsibility to tell the monarch
what is happening and the monarch's constitutional duty to probe
and to ask questions about what they are being told.

It is supposition, of course, as we do not know what stance the late Queen took with Blair, and what he told her. Like Her late Majesty, ultimately King Charles would have had to acquiesce eventually to remain politically neutral, as he must. That said, given his deep knowledge and extensive and high-level contacts in the Gulf states, and the esteem in which he is held in in the Arab world, it is hard to imagine Charles would have remained silent, and that Blair would have had an easy ride.

Charles was not alone in his grave reservations about sending in the troops in what was being called an 'illegal war', as the offensive did not have United Nations backing. Kofi Annan, the United Nations secretary-general, stated clearly in September 2004 that he believed the US-led, UK-backed invasion of Iraq was an illegal act that contravened the UN Charter, and any decision should have been made by the Security Council, not unilaterally. Blair's government responded by saying the attorney general made the 'legal basis... clear at the time'.[2]

Sources close to Charles, however, believe that while as monarch he would have had no choice but to allow Blair to pursue his agenda, he would undoubtedly have voiced 'his strongest possible objections' on the war. 'He most certainly would have advised the prime minister to think again and warned against British military intervention,' said an informed source. His advice to Blair, senior sources confirmed, would have been to heed the warnings of experienced Arab leaders in the region, rulers with whom Charles had built up a good rapport and working relationships over many years.

As Prince of Wales, Charles's desire to be seen as a pioneer and a shaper of ideas, and to enjoy growing political influence, was a source of serious concern to his advisers. Several said that the prince actively engaged in contentious issues because it raised the debate on a subject that would otherwise be swept under the carpet. His former deputy private secretary, Mark Bolland, said he 'tried to dampen down the prince's behaviour in making public his thoughts and views on a whole range of issues.'

In a statement that was released to the media as the prince began a High Court case against the *Mail on Sunday* (for publishing comments allegedly made in his journal about China's regime), Bolland wrote: 'The Prince's expressions of his views have often been regarded with concern by politicians because we would be contacted by them – and on their behalf. Private secretaries to government ministers would often let us know their views and, typically, how concerned they were.'

Bolland's remarks may be tainted by his abrupt departure from Charles's household after seven years in 2003, with little credit, particularly after his important work such as the successful 'Operation Mrs PB'. The former senior aide's assessment should not be taken lightly, however, as he did have the prince's ear at a crucial time. But Charles knew his role as heir was very different from being monarch.

When asked by documentary film-maker John Bridcut whether his public campaigning would continue once he was king, the prince replied categorically, 'No, it won't. I'm not that stupid. I do realise that it is a separate exercise being sovereign. So of course, I understand entirely how that should operate.'[3] Told by the interviewer that 'some people' had accused him of 'meddling', the prince laughed before replying drily, 'Really? You don't say!'

He continued, 'I always wonder what meddling is. I mean, I always thought it was motivating, but I've always been intrigued: if it's meddling to worry about the inner cities as I did forty years ago and what was happening or not happening there, the conditions in which people were living... if that's meddling, I'm very proud of it.'

Charles was clear that in his view his interventions had been within the parameters of his role as heir. 'I've tried to make sure whatever I've done has been non-party political,' he said. He went on to emphasise the fundamental difference between being an heir and being a king. 'Clearly, I won't be able to do the same things I've done, you know, as heir, so of course you operate within the constitutional parameters. But it's a different function. I think people have forgotten that the two are very different.'

Asked whether he could continue to use his 'convening power', which sees him gather experts together to make progress on his chosen issues, the prince added, 'Well, you never know, but you could only do it with the agreement of ministers. That's how it works.'

Privately, however, those close to him[4] have said that Charles was 'diametrically opposed' to the Blair–Bush Iraq War strategy, and more in line with Labour's canny former foreign secretary, the late Robin Cook, who had tried to pursue an ethical foreign policy during his tenure from 1997. Cook was subsequently demoted to Leader of the House in 2001 and effectively forced to quit the government in March two years later, saying, 'I cannot support a war without international agreement or domestic support.'

Cook's words in the House of Commons echoed what Charles had been telling his friends, including leading politicians, in private. 'I can say without any doubt that those weekly meetings would have been tough going for the PM,' an ex-household source reiterated. 'As king, he would have been given access to all the state papers and would have insisted on seeing the so-called proof that Saddam had weapons of mass destruction ready to use. Blair would not have had an easy ride.'

Today, as the King, Charles is a respected figure in the Gulf states and Middle East, not least for his sympathetic speeches about

Islam when Prince of Wales. Like Tony Blair, he has studied the Koran in depth, and he started learning Arabic in 2012, although he admitted that he struggled and eventually gave up.[5] When corresponding with Arab leaders, he always signs his name in Arabic, another show of respect and a small nod to respecting the other culture.

Back then Charles considered that, by shackling Britain to the flawed Bush administration, Tony Blair had missed a golden opportunity to forge an alternative consensus, one that both secured the crucial support of Arab leaders and embraced their unique understanding of the often troubled region. Among friends, Charles was less than complimentary about the Labour prime minister – and US President George W. Bush, for that matter. He castigated them over their role in Operation Iraqi Freedom, the 2003 military invasion of Iraq.

In fairness to him, his views did not come with hindsight. He made his position clear to influential people at the time. He told political figures and those in his trusted circle that he regarded the Bush administration as 'terrifying', and pilloried what he believed was Blair's lack of perspicacity. He thought Blair had behaved like Bush's 'poodle'.

With a heavy dollop of irony, he scornfully dubbed the premier 'our magnificent leader' whenever talking about him in private, and derided him for ignoring the wealth of sound intelligence available to him that contradicted the American view. He also told friends that Blair should have listened to Arab leaders about how to act over Iraq. After all, Western-style democracy in Iraq, the prince felt, was and always will be a 'pipe dream'.

When given the chance, Charles would point out why the delicate differences in culture in the region were so crucial to understand. It was a region, he would stress, still dominated by tribal loyalties. So, marching in carrying a banner for Western-style democracy was futile, in his view. One of Charles's circle of friends, who was fully aware of his views, said, 'The prince was wise enough to foresee that. Why weren't the politicians of the day? It was as if they had. Perhaps it didn't suit their or the government's hawkish agenda at the time.'

In Charles's view, the only way to achieve anything resembling a proper democracy in Iraq and for the West to have stood any chance of winning the so-called 'war on terror' was by dealing with the 'real toxin' infecting the whole world: the Israel–Palestine question. To this day, privately, he maintains that the West must focus on education and resisting what he believes is a 'terrible distortion' of Islam and how it is perceived in the West. Only then – when the wider world embraces the true Islam, combined with a serious collaborative effort to find a workable solution to the Israel–Palestine question – will, in his opinion, the rage that drives the war on terror start to wane.

'I have heard him [Charles] say time and again, "Remove the poison and you remove the cause of so much of the terrorism,"' a source close to the King said, adding that it was his core belief on the issue.

A regular and welcome visitor to the Gulf states, Saudi Arabia and Jordan during his time as Prince of Wales, Charles has always enjoyed a close personal relationship with the ruling houses, who include some of the world's last remaining absolute monarchies, many of which have come under scrutiny for human rights abuses in their country. This may seem controversial to some, but whenever he visits the region, Charles sees part of his role as being to make these rulers, so often ignored by the superpower USA, feel how valued they are to Britain and the importance of that long-standing relationship.

Since the 2011 Arab Spring uprisings, Charles has held nearly a hundred meetings with eight Middle Eastern states whose power and control were briefly threatened by the protests. He believes that the best way to improve human rights in these countries is through dialogue at the highest level. He knows how to speak to such rulers, and when to adopt a table-thumping stance, through mutual respect.

Over the last decade, Charles has also played a crucial role in advancing £14.5bn worth of British arms exports to these Middle Eastern monarchies. But he is understood to have made it clear to UK ministers that he no longer wants to use his royal connections to assist in selling arms on behalf of British companies to the Gulf states.

The King's Arab sympathies have sometimes caused him to be unfairly accused of being anti-Jewish and anti-American. Perhaps that is one reason why, when he was Prince of Wales, it was his son William, then the Duke of Cambridge, who was chosen by the Queen and the Foreign Office to make the historic first official royal visit to Israel and the occupied Palestinian West Bank, in June 2017. William would have consulted his father before making the visit, but surely Prince Charles, as heir, should have been the one to go?

Positive headlines flowed from the moment William touched down in the region. He was predictably dubbed 'peacemaker' in the headlines and there is little doubt he should be lauded for his deft diplomacy. Inevitably, he found himself being drawn into the complex politics of the region when Israel's president asked him to act as a peace envoy and to take a message of hope to the Palestinian premier.

British officials immediately stepped in and insisted that was not William's role, but hoped his landmark visit to the Jewish state and the occupied Palestinian West Bank would act as a catalyst, highlighting the need to kick-start a long-stalled peace process in the world's most intractable dispute. In fact, William's visit sparked a call for peace from Israel to Palestine's president Mahmoud Abbas and placed the second in line to the throne into the role of statesman.

Charles's well-known public views on Islam and his Arab friendships probably disqualified him from the role of peacemaker in Israel. He has, after all, never shied away from espousing his views and they could have been thrown back in his face. But when he was Prince of Wales, Charles was very careful about what he said publicly in his speeches. His addresses always came with many last-minute edits.

Privately, Charles disagrees with the bans imposed in France and Belgium on Muslim women covering their faces with burqas and niqabs, seeing it as 'an infringement of human rights', which criminalises women rather than challenging the custom. He has also expressed sympathy for Palestinians living under Israeli occupation.

But anti-Jewish? That is certainly not his position. Charles has an excellent relationship with the British Jewish community and was the first member of the Royal Family to attend the installation of the chief rabbi Ephraim Mirvis in 2013. In fact, the chief rabbi, whom Charles knighted in his first New Year Honours list in recognition of his interfaith initiatives, is scheduled not only to attend the coronation with his wife Valerie in London on Saturday, 6 May 2023, but to spend the night before it at Clarence House, the King's residence.[6]

To this day, however, Charles strongly believes a solution can be achieved only by listening to and acting upon the advice of powerful Muslim figures. He came under fire in November 2017, when his views were revealed publicly in a letter that he had penned in 1986 to his friend and mentor, Laurens van der Post:

'I now appreciate that Arabs and Jews were all a Semitic people originally,' he wrote, 'and it is the influx of foreign, European Jews (especially from Poland, they say) which has helped to cause the great problems. I know there are so many complex issues, but how can there ever be an end to terrorism unless the causes are eliminated? Surely some US president has to have the courage to stand up and take on the Jewish lobby in the US? I must be naive, I suppose!'

The letter, found in a public archive, was written on 24 November 1986, following an official visit the 38-year-old Charles had made to Saudi Arabia, Bahrain and Qatar with his then wife, Princess Diana.

He wrote that the tour was 'fascinating' and that he had learned a lot about the Middle Eastern and Arab outlook. He added in the letter, 'Tried to read bit of Koran on way out and it gave me some insight into the way they [Arabs] think and operate. Don't think they could understand us through reading Bible though.'

Clarence House rather lamely said in a statement that the opinions expressed in the 1986 letter were 'not the prince's own views', but instead reflected the opinions of those he met on his trip. It certainly did not read like that. Charles's lack of trust of America is a recurring theme. He is not only critical of their lack of a coherent Middle East policy but was deeply concerned by the US's refusal to sign up to any international convention on climate change – a stance made even worse by President Donald Trump when he was in the White House.

Charles is also 'horrified' by US agri-industrial activities: the appalling animal welfare and environmental consequences of the cattle-feed-lot system. He believes the vast industrial-scale output of chemical-dependent and government-subsidised corn, which leads to economic surplus and is then turned into every conceivable form of fast food, is leading to an ever-growing health crisis in the

USA. This is through obesity-related problems, not to mention the rapidly increasing rates of diabetes, which makes his 'hair stand on end', as does the huge lobbying power of the gigantic corporations and fast-food companies.

Today, as King, behind closed doors, Charles will undoubtedly use his personal relationships with the Arab leaders in the Gulf for the greater good. I was one of the few journalists who accompanied the prince and the duchess on their tour of the Gulf states in November 2016, including, controversially, to Bahrain, which has been widely criticised for human rights abuses. The visit undoubtedly left many influential figures, both in the region and at home, feeling better about Britain and its place in the world.

One area he will not be drawn into – in such a lucrative potential marketplace – is marketing weaponry. This is despite his previous forays into this area. In Jonathan Dimbleby's 1994 documentary, Charles defended his appearance at the Dubai arms fair on the basis that he was boosting British trade, arguing without much conviction that the arms would likely be used as a deterrent, and that if the UK did not sell them someone else would. Since then, he has made a complete volte-face, and heaven help the royal aide who suggests slipping in such an engagement these days!

The photographs from that tour – of a smiling Charles sword-dancing in Oman or shopping in a Bahraini souk with the Duchess of Cornwall – told some of the story, but certainly not all. For, as the world tried to come to terms with the fallout after Donald Trump's victory in the US presidential election, Charles had once again been in the heart of the Muslim world, sent on behalf of the Foreign Office to strengthen and reinforce Britain's relationships with Oman, the United Arab Emirates and Bahrain.

The seven-day visit encompassed fifty engagements, four cities, five flights, numerous helicopter rides and serious talks with the most influential leaders and heads of state. It was seen as a requisite overseas visit by Charles, the Queen and the Foreign and Commonwealth Office and, from my ringside seat, its impact was palpable on so many levels. For, if you looked only at the images printed in newspapers and published online, the subtle diplomatic, business and cultural benefits could easily be missed. There is a much bigger picture at play here – the trip was a serious and complex undertaking, crucial for Britain's interests in the area.

This was his fourth visit to the region in four years, at the request of the British government, promoting the UK's partnership in the region in key areas such as religious tolerance, military cooperation, supporting women in leadership, creating youth opportunities, preserving cultural heritage and wildlife conservation.

During his visit, he opened a new welfare block at Britain's naval base in Manama, Bahrain, met sailors on board HMS *Middleton*, and visited a plant built on land gifted by the government, which uses wastewater-treatment technology deployed by Bluewater Bio. The award-winning British firm is a global specialist in technologies for cost-efficient, environmentally friendly water and wastewater treatment.

Charles and Camilla's trip to Bahrain was the final leg of a tour on which they both embraced subjects close to their hearts – and some unusual photocalls. Their first stop, Oman, produced headline-grabbing photographs of Prince Charles wielding a three-foot sword in a ceremonial dance held to welcome the couple to the country. The prince also saw at first hand the impact of conservation work on the tiny island of Bu Tinah, where he raced along in a dune buggy and took a boat tour to see important marine and coastal ecosystems.

A long-time champion of the need for environmental and business sustainability, Charles also made a powerful address to business leaders in Dubai in which he warned that there was a 'very real risk' of a climate-change disaster. He told them, 'We are facing what I believe is perhaps the greatest challenge ever faced by our economy and society. I have been finding the struggle somewhat exhausting and frustrating over the past twenty-five to thirty years to overcome the deniers and sceptics. If we are honest, we know all too clearly that we can't go on as we are.'

Indeed, ever since his youth, Charles has built a reputation for his so-called 'interventions'; but he has a different take on it. 'I don't see why politicians and others should think they have the monopoly of wisdom,' he told his biographer Jonathan Dimbleby when asked about his involvement in politics.

In 2015, the question of Charles one day becoming an 'interfering' king had flared up again with the conclusion of the so-called 'black spider memos' case after ten years of legal wrangling. The term, which he dislikes, refers to the private letters and memos written by the prince to British government ministers and politicians over many years. They were controversial due to the Prince of Wales's position as the heir to a monarch, who by convention remains politically neutral.

These letters were written by hand before being sent to be typed, but after they were returned for the prince to sign, he often underlined text and added exclamation marks in flowing black or red ink. It was these additions and his distinctive, spirally handwriting that gave his letters their nickname.

The case came at the end of a long saga involving attempts by the *Guardian* journalist Rob Evans to obtain the secret letters and memos between Charles and government ministers. Evans wanted to show that through such correspondence, the heir to the throne was seeking to shape government policy.

The attorney general Dominic Grieve had challenged the

disclosure of the letters, warning that the release 'would be seriously damaging to his [Charles's] role as future monarch because, if he forfeits his position of political neutrality as heir to the throne, he cannot easily recover it when he is king.'

The correspondence was finally published by the Cabinet Office in May 2015, after an independent tribunal upheld an earlier Supreme Court decision and ordered it to be released.

The *Guardian*, of course, recorded this as a triumph for press freedom. They claimed that the publication of twenty-seven letters after a decade-long legal battle showed the heir to the throne petitioning ministers on subjects from the Iraq war to alternative therapies.

Once made public, however, the letters turned out to be rather dull. The areas covered and the content were predictable, involving subjects close to Charles's heart. They confirmed his interest in a wide range of areas, including architecture and, rather whimsically, the plight of the Patagonian toothfish.

He also urged the prime minister, Tony Blair, to replace Lynx military helicopters, complaining that delaying their replacement was 'one more example where our armed forces are being asked to do an extremely challenging job (particularly in Iraq) without the necessary resources.' Blair responded that replacement would be a priority for spending.

Charles further urged the health secretary, John Reid, to expedite redevelopment at a hospital site in Sunderland in which the prince's architecture charity was involved, saying 'chickens will come home to roost' in Reid's department if action was not taken.[7] The letters and their responses showed that ministers valued his intervention and acted as a result. Tony Blair replied to him in one letter, 'I always value and look forward to your views – but perhaps particularly on agricultural topics.' More importantly, it showed that as the UK's constitutional arrangements remain 'unwritten', the nature of the British constitution creates scope for discord as to what principles mean and how they relate to each other. The furore died down quickly.

Despite the 'black spider' revelations, insiders say Charles was aware of all the parameters of the job of monarch and now that he is King he will not upset the constitutional apple cart to pursue his own agenda. Like the late Queen, when he was heir Charles was kept up to date with all government plans, and he regularly held audiences with ministers, which was within the remit of his role. In fact, the prince was confused by newspaper reports ahead of US president Donald Trump's visit to Britain in July 2018 that he would 'rant' at him, metaphorically thrust a copy of his book on climate change into his hand, and demand he act on it. When he read this, Charles was genuinely baffled. 'Why would they think that?' he asked of a close aide.

It is not how Charles, then as Prince of Wales and now as King, behaves and it infuriates him that people try to second-guess him.

CHAPTER 13

Home and Dry

*They have overcome Becher's Brook and the Chair and all kinds
of other terrible obstacles... and I'm very proud and wish them
well. My son is home and dry with the woman he loves.*

**QUEEN ELIZABETH COMPARING CHARLES AND CAMILLA'S
RELATIONSHIP TO THE GRAND NATIONAL, WHICH TOOK PLACE
ON THE SAME DAY AS THEIR WEDDING**

When I broke the world-exclusive story of the royal engagement of
the Prince of Wales and Camilla in the *London Evening Standard*
on 10 February 2005 – and, according to the prince's biographer
and friend Jonathan Dimbleby, 'bounced' Clarence House into
issuing a formal announcement – the courtiers were ill-prepared.
The wording of the statement that was released, long after the
Evening Standard had broken the scoop, was simple enough. 'It is
with great pleasure that the marriage of HRH the Prince of Wales
and Camilla Parker Bowles is announced. It will take place on
Friday 8 April,' the statement said.

My inside source had been spot on and we were both elated
and relieved. In the weeks that followed, the extent to which my
newspaper scoop had caught Charles's team off guard was woefully
apparent, as it marked the start of a torrid time for Clarence House
officials, whose grasp of the finer and legal points of this royal
wedding was exposed as being tenuous at best.

It was clear to everyone that Camilla, the love of Charles's life, was not only his lover but his soulmate and companion. What was not expected, only seven years after Diana's death, was that Charles felt the public would back his wedding to the woman Diana publicly blamed for wrecking her marriage.

His sons were not happy either. According to Harry, the two boys urged him not to marry Camilla, fearing that she would be their 'wicked stepmother', but Charles made it clear he was going ahead anyway.[1]

The prince had earlier laid down a marker, not only to the public, but to the grey-suited mandarins at the palace and to the Queen herself, that he would not wait any longer. He still felt aggrieved at the way his 'darling Camilla' was being treated, and made it abundantly clear that he would not accept it.

He bemoaned what he felt was an unfair portrayal in the media of the woman he loved. He reportedly told respected BBC journalist Gavin Hewitt in a 1998 interview discussing their relationship,[2] 'I thought the British people were supposed to be compassionate. I don't see much of it.' He went on, 'All my life people have been telling me what to do. I'm tired of it. My private life has become an industry. People are making money out of it. I just want some peace.'

Charles resolved that the only way he could get that peace was through bold and decisive action, and he took the plunge. The next step was marriage.

It started well enough. The ring, £100,000 worth of platinum and diamonds, had been a gift from the Queen. It was a 1930s Art Deco design, a central square-cut diamond with three smaller diamonds, and was one of her favourites. When asked how she felt, Camilla said she was just coming down to earth.

Prime minister Tony Blair sent congratulations on behalf of

the government, and the Queen and the Duke of Edinburgh issued a statement saying they were 'very happy' and had given the couple their 'warmest wishes'. The Archbishop of Canterbury, Rowan Williams, was pleased, too, that they had taken 'this important step'. He said, 'These arrangements have my strong support and are consistent with Church of England guidelines concerning remarriage, which the Prince of Wales fully accepts as a committed Anglican and as prospective Supreme Governor of the Church of England.'

But soon critical newspaper headlines followed. The legality of the marriage was called into question, and the impossibility of a church wedding threatened to turn Camilla into the House of Windsor's first 'town-hall bride'. For a while in the early spring of 2005, barely a day passed without the revelation of some apparent monumental oversight or error by Charles's usually meticulous private secretary, Sir Michael Peat, and his team.

Perhaps the most embarrassing was their failure to appreciate that the Marriage Act now permitted weddings to be formalised in 'approved premises'. This meant that if Windsor Castle was given a licence to host the civil wedding for the royal couple, anyone could apply to marry at the Queen's residence.

While Charles's office struggled to control the situation, they were also forced to address one key question they might rather have ignored: what did William and Harry think about their father marrying the woman who ostensibly helped break up their mother's marriage?

William gave his blessing, saying that both he and Harry were 'delighted' at their father's happiness. Privately, their mood was more of acceptance of a fait accompli rather than undiluted joy at the prospect of having Camilla, a woman their late mother loathed with a passion, as their stepmother. Publicly, Harry was more effusive and helped to seal Camilla's acceptance by describing her as a 'wonderful woman and she's made our father very, very happy, which is the most important thing.' He went on, 'William and I love her to bits.'

Charles, William and Harry faced down the press when the question was put to them in public at a prearranged photocall only seven weeks before the wedding, while the boys were enjoying a skiing holiday with their father in his favourite resort of Klosters, in Switzerland. Charles knew the question was coming, as it had all been cleared with his communications team – but the impertinence!

'Your Royal Highnesses,' began the seasoned BBC broadcaster Nicholas Witchell, shouting from behind the barrier separating the royals from the media. 'It's eight days now to the wedding.'

'You've heard of it, have you?' Prince Charles interrupted, with a forced smile.

Caught a little off guard, the unfortunate Witchell continued, 'Can I ask how you are feeling and how, in particular, Princes William and Harry are feeling at the prospect of the wedding?'

'Very happy,' replied Prince William immediately. 'It'll be a good day.'

'And Prince Charles, how are you feeling?' asked Witchell, after a second or two of silence.

'It's a very nice thought, isn't it?' said Prince Charles, eventually, without a smile, then added a little sarcastically, 'I'm very glad you've heard of it, anyway.'

With that, he turned his head slightly away and, in a very quiet aside aimed solely at his sons, added, 'Bloody people. I can't bear that man. He's so awful. He really is.'

With most of the journalists unaware that they had been the subject of Charles's fit of pique, or even what exactly had been said, the questioning continued in good humour, with William telling the press pack he was looking forward to his role as witness at the wedding. 'Very much so. As long as I don't lose the rings, it will be all right,' he joked.

Charles, who had not seen the microphones in the snow before he spoke so loosely, was unaware that his curmudgeonly remarks had been picked up. It was a gaffe more befitting of his father, Prince Philip, than the usually media-savvy and careful Prince Charles.

It proved another low point in Charles's relationship with the British press. During the collapse of his marriage to Diana, he had grown to loathe the cynicism of the tabloids for the blatant commercialisation of his personal misery. 'We must realise that certain sections of the media have now proved to their own satisfaction that sensationalised royal stories are one of the best ways of selling newspapers in a recession,' he wrote in a memo to the Queen's private secretary on 23 October 1992, only weeks before his separation from Diana. In the intervening years, nothing had happened for him to change his damning opinion.

Eventually, the location for the wedding was changed to the Guildhall in the heart of Windsor, which meant that neither the Queen nor Prince Philip would attend, although they did go to the Service of Prayer and Dedication afterwards at St George's Chapel, conducted by the Archbishop of Canterbury, who had denied them a church wedding as it would be unacceptable to religious leaders, even though he could have granted it.[3] The ceremony date was also changed to 9 April 2005, to allow Charles to attend the funeral of Pope John Paul II, who had died aged eighty-four in Rome.

Charles and Camilla used the wedding as an opportunity to repent the sins of their past deeds, as each had been involved in the break-up of the other's marriage. The couple chose the sternest possible prayer of penitence from the 1662 Book of Common Prayer to be read by themselves and their guests at the blessing of their marriage.

The prayer read: 'We acknowledge and bewail our manifold sins and wickedness, which we, from time to time, most grievously have committed, by thought, word and deed, against thy Divine Majesty, provoking most justly thy wrath and indignation against us. We do earnestly repent and are heartily sorry for these misdoings.'

Charles gave a touching speech at the reception, hosted by the Queen, in which he thanked 'my dear mama' for footing the bill, and 'my darling Camilla, who has stood with me through thick and thin and whose precious optimism and humour have seen me through'. The duchess, looking serene in an Anna Valentine dress with a golden headpiece by milliner Philip Treacy, emerged triumphant.

It was the Queen, however, who had the last word. She compared the happy couple's relationship to the Grand National, which showed that Camilla was embraced by the family and she had finally got her man. She began by saying she had two important announcements to make. The first was that Hedgehunter had won the race at Aintree; the second was that, here at Windsor, she was delighted to be welcoming her son and his bride to the 'winners' enclosure'.

Many cheered, others were close to tears. For the prince, that day brought an end to his long life of loneliness. His soulmate was at long last at his side. They still had a long way to go to win over the people, but, as far as the palace and the prince were concerned, it was a triumph.

Camilla's father, Major Bruce Shand, aged eighty-eight and ailing, had stalled going to the doctor until after the wedding. He was desperate to see his daughter, so often maligned, be remarried and it mattered a great deal to him that Charles should do the right thing by her. When he finally sought medical help, four days later, Major Shand was diagnosed with pancreatic cancer – and died fourteen months later.

When I had revealed the couple's plans to marry, my inside source was adamant that other key areas such as titles had been discussed well in advance of going public. The source said that Charles categorically intended his wife to be his Queen Consort when he became King.

'There was no doubt in his mind at the time about that and I honestly don't think anything has changed. In fact, he hardened his resolve that this must be the case. For there to be any other outcome would be, in his view, to lessen his role as king. His marriage to Camilla is legal. She happens to be his second wife. That was it. After all, all Henry VIII's six wives were made his Queen Consort.'

Clarence House created speculation about the duchess and her future role. Charles's office always insisted that the duchess would be styled 'Princess Consort' when the time came, indicating that she would eschew the title of 'Queen Consort' normally expected for the wife of a king. However, a redesign of the couple's official website saw the explicit statement about this role quietly removed, leading to reports that she could be given the title of 'Queen' when the Prince of Wales acceded to the throne.

When they wed, Clarence House issued what it described as a clarification of sorts about the future title of Camilla. The official wedding announcement said, 'It is intended that Mrs Parker Bowles should use the title HRH the Princess Consort when the Prince of Wales accedes to the throne.' The big word in this statement was of course 'intended'. What Clarence House was in fact doing was buying time for a hostile public to warm to Camilla.

My inside source of the story was correct, too, that Camilla, when married, would not take the title HRH the Princess of Wales, even though it was her right to do so, as it would be insensitive and cause undue hostility bearing in mind Diana, Princess of Wales. She used the title HRH the Duchess of Cornwall instead, as the prince was Duke of Cornwall, which did not reduce her royal rank. It was a title of convenience.

Since then, the duchess – now the Queen Consort – through hard work and the fact that time heals has cemented her place in the Royal Family. Queen Elizabeth marked her official ninetieth birthday by tidying up plans for her death and elevating the duchess to her most senior advisory body, the Privy Council.

It was, as ever, all done very quietly. But it is unprecedented in modern times for a royal wife not in direct line to the throne to be a member of the Privy Council – the cornerstone of the constitutional monarchy, enacting Acts of Parliament and advising the sovereign on the use of powers that do not formally go through Parliament. It also showed the esteem in which the Queen held Camilla, and reflected the Royal Household's efforts to prepare the public for a smooth succession.

Perhaps sensing she was coming to the end of her life, the Queen gave her daughter-in-law the ultimate seal of approval. On Accession Day, 6 February 2022, seventy years after she succeeded her father, Queen Elizabeth issued a significant written message in which she said it was her 'sincere wish' that Camilla would have that title, Queen Consort, and be thus crowned and anointed at her son's coronation, 'in the fullness of time'. It came a month after she had signalled her strong approval by making Camilla a Royal Lady of the Most Noble Order of the Garter, in recognition of her contribution to the monarchy.[4]

It was clever housekeeping too, ensuring the transition of the Crown to her son as the King, when it came, was as seamless as

Left: Princess Diana presents a trophy to cavalry officer, Major James Hewitt, at the inter-regimental polo championship in 1989. Diana enjoyed a five-year illicit affair with Hewitt which ended in 1991. During her infamous BBC Panorama interview in 1995, Diana admitted that she 'loved' and 'adored' Hewitt and had been devastated by his betrayal when he wrote a kiss-and-tell book.

Right: The Prince and Princess of Wales on their official four-day visit to Hungary in May 1990. This was to be one of their last great acts of togetherness. Amazingly, the press seemed to swallow the palace spin and focused on how well Charles and Diana appeared to be getting on in the beautiful city of Budapest.

Left: The Princess of Wales was instrumental in trying to stop the stigma against HIV/AIDS. On 9 April 1989, she opened a new AIDS ward at the Middlesex Hospital in London, and was photographed shaking hands with an HIV positive male patient without wearing gloves. At the time, many incorrectly believed people could 'catch' HIV through touch, so her actions were seen as ground-breaking and helped allay the fears of the public.

On their joint tour of India in February 1992, Princess Diana posed in front of the world's greatest monument to love, the Taj Mahal in Jaipur. Instead of joining her Prince Charles attended a business function in Delhi. The photograph was published under the headline: 'Temple of Loneliness'. On 9 December 1992, the prime minister John Major got to his feet in the House of Commons and from the dispatch box announced the formal separation of the Prince and Princess of Wales.

On 31 August 1997, Diana, Princess of Wales, was killed in a car crash in the Alma tunnel in Paris. On the morning of the funeral at Westminster Abbey, thousands of mourners lined the route along which the princess's coffin would be borne on a gun carriage. Prince Philip reportedly told Prince William he would regret it later if he did not walk behind Diana's coffin, and so the duke joined William and Harry, Charles, and Diana's brother, Earl Spencer, on the procession to the Abbey.

Charles and Camilla, on a visit to Bahrain bazaar in November 2016.

The King believes in and actively promotes interfaith dialogue. He enjoys close relations with religious leaders and is pictured here with Britain's Chief Rabbi, Ephraim Mirvis, who was knighted in recognition of his interfaith initiatives and work with the Jewish community.

Charles and Camilla used the wedding on 9 April 2005 to repent the sins of their past deeds, as each had been involved in the break-up of the other's marriage. The couple chose the sternest possible prayer of penitence from the 1662 Book of Common Prayer to be read by themselves and their guests at the blessing of their marriage. Camilla, who decided to use the title HRH The Duchess of Cornwall, looked serene in an Anna Valentine dress with a golden headpiece by milliner Philip Treacy.

The wedding of the Duke and Duchess of Cambridge (now the Prince and Princess of Wales) on 29 April 2011, brought an estimated £2 billion to the UK economy and was watched by an audience of 26.3 million throughout the country. It was also a global media sensation that provided a massive boost to brand Britain.

Left: The Queen's Diamond Jubilee was a unique and special event, marking Elizabeth II's sixty years on the throne and showing British royal pomp and pageantry at it best. Four days of celebratory events culminated with an appearance by the Queen on the palace balcony before a cheering crowd, as a flypast by Second World War aircraft and the Red Arrows thundered overhead. Charles was loudly cheered when he publicly thanked Her Majesty for her inspirational 'selfless duty and service'.

Right: Prince William and Catherine acquitted themselves well during the 2012 London Olympics, when they appeared in Team GB T-shirts to shout encouragement to the athletes. They were photographed celebrating a Team GB gold when cyclists Sir Chris Hoy and his team-mates pedaled to victory at the Velodrome. On 3 December 2012, William and Catherine capped what had been a wonderful Diamond Jubilee year by announcing that they were expecting their first child.

Left: The author of this book, Robert Jobson, shares a lighter moment during a conversation with the Duchess of Cornwall at a reception in Australia in November 2012.

Charles inspects a royal honour guard in Brisbane, April 2018. Charles and Camilla were in Australia to open the Gold Coast Commonwealth Games. In February 2023, the country's Reserve Bank announced that King Charles III will not replace Queen Elizabeth II on Australia's new $5 banknotes. Australian Prime Minister, Anthony Albanese, has indicated he will seek to hold a referendum on whether his country should become a republic.

Prince Harry and Meghan Markle, the new Duke and Duchess of Sussex, wed at St George's Chapel on 19 May 2018. In January 2020, the Sussexes decided they wanted to step back as senior members of the Royal Family and start a new life, at first in Canada and eventually California, away from the palace and the press, and even the Royal Family. They have agreed not to use their HRH titles but keep their designations as the Duke and Duchess of Sussex.

Four days of festivities for the Queen's Platinum Jubilee kicked off in June 2022. The Queen was joined by working members of the royal family to watch the special RAF flypast at Buckingham Palace. Elizabeth II was joined by Prince Charles, the Duchess of Cornwall, Prince William, the Duchess of Cambridge and their children Prince George, Princess Charlotte and Prince Louis. The spectacle saw seventy planes fly overhead, culminating with the iconic Red Arrows filling the sky with red, white and blue smoke.

At 11 a.m. on 19 September 2022, Queen Elizabeth II's state funeral was held at Westminster Abbey. After the poignant service, the coffin was conveyed from London to Windsor and along the Long Walk to the Castle. The final, private service was held in St George's Chapel, which would be the Queen's final resting place, where she is buried alongside her parents and husband.

Right: King Charles was formally proclaimed monarch at an accession council in an ancient ceremony at St James's Palace, which was televised for the first time. He was pictured signing the proclamation flanked by the Queen Consort and his son William, the new Prince of Wales, who both signed the document after the King.

Left and below: During his televised Christmas message, Charles spoke about the 'great anxiety and hardship' experienced by many trying to 'pay their bills and keep their families fed and warm'. The King and Queen Consort have carried out many engagements across the country during the first months of his reign. He cares very deeply about the people he serves, and the world and environment we live in, today and in the future.

Left: The author with the man himself, King Charles III.

possible. It had been quite a journey for Camilla. 'I feel very, very honoured and very touched,' she said, when asked of her thoughts on the special title granted by the Queen.

The main reason that the Queen wanted Camilla (as well as William) included as Privy Councillors was so they could be part of the Accession Council, which handled the succession to the throne after her death. The Queen wanted Camilla to be beside Charles when he formally succeeded her as monarch, in the ceremony held at St James's Palace within twenty-four hours of the death of a sovereign.

To have denied Camilla her rightful status would have been a PR own goal, like insisting a president's wife should not be allowed the role and title of 'First Lady' – and the late Queen was wise enough to see it and sort it out before her death. After all, the new Queen Consort was impeccable when representing the Crown at home and abroad or supporting her husband.

Queen Camilla has endured years of scrutiny. She was among the most unpopular people in Britain after her affair with Charles was blamed for ending his marriage with Diana. Talking to *Vogue* for their July 2022 issue, Camilla said: 'It's not easy... I was scrutinised for such a long time that you just have to find a way to live with it. Nobody likes to be looked at all the time and, you know, criticised... but I think in the end, I sort of rise above it and get on with it. You've got to get on with life.'

She had gone further in an interview with the *Mail on Sunday*'s *You* Magazine in 2017, saying, 'It was horrid. It was a deeply unpleasant time, and I wouldn't want to put my worst enemy through it.'

Yet, Camilla has earned her stripes through the love and loyalty she has shown the King and by devotion to duty to the Crown. When the time came in his first speech as King, Charles

III confirmed his wife as his Queen. 'In recognition of her own loyal public service since our marriage seventeen years ago, she becomes my Queen Consort,' he said. 'I know she will bring to the demands of her new role the steadfast devotion to duty on which I have come to rely so much.'

CHAPTER 14

Defender of the Faith

Britain has the proudest tradition of accommodating new communities. Over recent centuries we have seen how, first Protestants, then Jews, then Muslims, Sikhs and Hindus, have enhanced... the whole of society.

FROM AN ARTICLE IN THE *DAILY MIRROR* BY HRH CHARLES, PRINCE OF WALES IN THE AFTERMATH OF THE TERRORIST ATTACKS ON LONDON

On 7 July 2005, four suicide bombers with rucksacks full of explosives attacked central London, killing 52 people and injuring 784 others. It became known as the 7/7 attacks – the UK's 9/11 – the worst single terrorist atrocity on British soil. Three of the murderers, Mohammad Sidique Khan, Shehzad Tanweer and Hasib Hussain, travelled from Leeds in a rented car to join Germaine Lindsay in Luton before heading to London by train. They said their goodbyes at King's Cross and went on to detonate three devices at around 8.50 a.m. on the London Underground, in the vicinity of Aldgate, Edgware Road and Russell Square stations. The fourth device exploded at 9.47 a.m. on a double-decker bus in Tavistock Square.

All four bombers were radicalised UK citizens – so-called home-grown terrorists. Predictably, it led to British-born Muslims being 'securitised' and increasingly becoming viewed as a security threat by politicians, the media and many non-Muslims. In the aftermath of the bombings, Islamophobia in the UK began to rise, and police reported an increase in hate crimes directed at British Muslims.

The willingness of Charles to embrace and work alongside other faiths during his time as Prince of Wales has bizarrely been seen as a weakness by his more blinkered critics, rather than something to be lauded. Indeed, he has even been dubbed a 'secret' Muslim. Soundbites plucked from long, detailed speeches were taken out of context and made headlines, claiming to show his 'conversion'. In a speech titled 'Islam and the West' at the Oxford Centre for Islamic Studies on 27 October 1993, Charles said, 'Islam can teach us today a way of understanding and living in the world which Christianity itself is poorer for having lost.'

This was widely quoted as proof that he had abandoned his Christian faith. Despite the hostile atmosphere in the aftermath of the terrorist attacks on London, the prince decided to enter the debate by penning an article published in the *Daily Mirror*. Charles risked a backlash, but he stuck to his guns, when he wrote:

> News of the breakthrough in the police investigation has now switched media attention from the victims to the perpetrators of this monstrous crime. Inevitably, people will be asking how it might be that young men brought up in this country can set out to cause such grief and mayhem among their fellow citizens...
>
> Although the facts are not yet clear, it is difficult to escape the conclusion that some deeply evil influence has been brought to bear on these impressionable young minds. We seem to be seeing a cycle, from Bali to Baghdad, from New York to London, of willing recruits sacrificing their young lives to slaughter innocent people in some inhuman cause...

Some may think this cause is Islam. It is anything but. It is a perversion of traditional Islam. As I understand it, Islam preaches humanity, tolerance, and a sense of community, as do Christianity, Judaism and all the great faiths. It is for this reason that so many Muslims have been quick to condemn these and other atrocities. They are right to say that these acts have nothing to do with any true faith. Those who claim to have murdered in the name of Islam have no care for the lives they have so brutally destroyed. Offended by the good relations between faiths and cultures, the extremists seek to break up the communities that make up our modern, multicultural society.

Charles was simply reflecting his long-held belief in the article. But given the possible backlash and his constitutional position, to some people it was a controversial stance, and could even be interpreted as goading those who disagreed with him. His critics inevitably focused on the negatives. After all, before putting pen to paper, he was fully aware of the criticism he had faced in the early 1990s, a time of extremist militant Islamic factions. Back then, to his credit, Charles was quick to point out, 'Extremism is no more the monopoly of Islam than it is the monopoly of other religions, including Christianity.' He caused more controversy when he said on 20 June 1994 of Christianity, 'It has no right to challenge Islam or any other religion. It is merely a Western face of God.'

In his speech at Oxford in 1993, he was even more supportive, calling on the West to recognise Islam as a part of its culture. 'Medieval Islam was a religion of remarkable tolerance for its time,' he said, 'allowing Jews and Christians the right to practise their inherited beliefs, and setting an example which was not, unfortunately, copied for many centuries in the West.' He continued, 'The surprise, ladies and gentlemen, is the extent to which Islam has been a part of Europe for so long, first in Spain, then in the Balkans, and the extent to which it has contributed so much towards the civilisation which we all too often think of, wrongly, as entirely Western.'

After making the controversial address, he became patron of the Oxford Centre for Islamic Studies. His speech 'Islam and the West' was reprinted in newspapers across the Middle East and earned him widespread praise in countries where Islam was the predominant religion. But an ability to see what is good in another religion does not make him a convert.

In a 1997 *Middle East Quarterly* article entitled 'Prince Charles of Arabia', Ronni L. Gordon and David M. Stillman examined 'evidence' that Charles had secretly converted to Islam. They sifted through his public statements, identifying some where the prince in their view defended Islamic law, praised the status of Muslim women and, apparently, saw in Islam a solution for Britain's ailments. Their conclusion was fudged, but put on the record that, 'Should Charles persist in his admiration of Islam and defamation of his own culture,' his accession to the throne would usher in a 'different kind of monarchy'.

That, of course, goes without saying. The key word in this conclusion is 'should'. Charles has long faced criticism over his acceptance of other faiths and willingness to embrace and understand other views and beliefs. But this is something for which he should be praised rather than seen as having a failing.

Throughout his life Charles has always been a natural adapter, a broad-centred man, deeply aware of others and their needs. He sees the commonality between different faiths as a positive, not a negative. His religious life began conventionally enough. He was less than a month old when Geoffrey Fisher, then the Archbishop of Canterbury, christened him in the Music Room at Buckingham Palace on 15 December 1948. His mother, then Princess Elizabeth, chose the first hymn to reflect the sacred significance of the event: 'Holy, Holy, Holy.'

Twenty years later, however, as an undergraduate student at Cambridge, he began writing to Mervyn Stockwood, the Bishop of Southwark, who refused to dismiss 'psychic happenings' and believed that the miracles of Jesus demonstrated 'the Saviour's oneness with nature'. Later, in his twenties, Charles grew close to Laurens van der Post, the South African-born writer and explorer, whom he would later ask to become one of Prince William's godparents. Van der Post introduced him to mysticism and encouraged him 'to see the old world of the spirit'. Charles was captivated by his adviser's history of bushmen in the Kalahari Desert and travelled with him to spend a week in the Aberdare Mountains in Kenya. The friendship left a lasting impression on Charles's faith. He once spoke up for respecting the natural world for the glory of God.

The King is also an admirer of the Orthodox Church and used to make regular spiritual retreats to stay in the monasteries of Mount Athos, the Greek republic run by two thousand monks. Officially, he went there because he was interested in the architecture and spirituality of Athos. Of course, there is a family connection, too: his paternal grandmother, Princess Alice of Battenberg,[1] was an Orthodox nun, and Charles has also incorporated Byzantine icons in the Sanctuary, a simple chapel in the grounds at his country estate Highgrove. It is a very important place for him, where he goes to pray and to meditate.

His interest in eastern Orthodox Christianity even led to more speculation in some quarters about his faith. After one of his visits to Mount Athos, an Athonite monk was quoted in one newspaper declaring that there is no question that he is Orthodox in his heart. Those close to Charles, though, have dismissed claims that he was a convert to Orthodoxy. The King may be naturally more high church but, like successive English (and later British) monarchs since Henry VIII, he is known by the title Defender of the Faith – *Fidei Defensor* – and is Supreme Governor of the Church of England.[2] He is a practising Anglican.

Indeed, those close to him say it is because he has read and thought so deeply about his own Christian heritage, and is so firmly rooted in it, that he is able to engage with other religions. During his visits around the country, he has always made sure he reaches out to all faiths, visiting Sikh, Muslim, Hindu and Jewish, as well as Christian, communities.

The truth is that, far from it disturbing him – as Prince of Wales – most of the time he enjoyed the controversy. After all, it encourages debate. He has always seen himself as a freethinker, working against an established consensus. As King, however, he will let his actions speak and will say less. At his coronation, he will take an oath, promising to rule according to law, to exercise justice with mercy and to maintain the Church of England, and, under a canopy of golden cloth, he will be anointed with holy oil, blessed and consecrated by the Archbishop of Canterbury, Justin Welby.

The King's belief in interfaith dialogue has long been on his agenda. His opinion is that talking openly and honestly can only help to strengthen communities and understanding and that different faiths have 'a great deal in common' with Christianity. 'The future surely lies in rediscovering the universal truths that dwell at the heart of these religions,' he has said. He told his biographer Jonathan Dimbleby in 1994, 'When you begin to look at what… [they] are saying, you find that so much of the wisdom that is represented within these religions coincides.'[3]

Clearly, our Supreme Governor of the Church of England plans to interpret the role a little differently. 'He is an individual who wants to chart new territory, and that will be very interesting indeed,' said Lord Carey, the former Archbishop of Canterbury. 'He is very outspoken.' Over the last four decades, this has become obvious. As Prince of Wales, he tested the boundaries of his public role by attending Catholic masses, and his private spiritual enquiry has been frequent fodder for satirists, forcing him to deny using Ouija boards and 'dabbling in the occult'.

Such caricatures serve only to distort the King and his position. 'All I have ever wanted to do is build bridges that span these chasms,' Charles explained. But his bid to build bridges has left some confused and encouraged his critics wrongly to point an accusatory finger, suggesting a lack of commitment to being a Christian and to the Church of England. They could not be further from the truth.

Much of the doubt about the King's faith stems from his admission of adultery during his marriage to Diana, Princess of Wales, and the bitter divorce that followed. His detractors seem conveniently to ignore the fact that he remained 'faithful and honourable' in the marriage until, in his view, it had 'irretrievably broken down, us both having tried'. The preferred Charles narrative forgets that there was wrongdoing on both sides. It also appears to be driven by him apparently telling his biographer Dimbleby that he wanted to be seen as a 'Defender of Faith' rather than 'Defender of *the* Faith' on his accession.

Back then, Dimbleby said that Charles was planning this symbolic change when he became King to reflect Britain's multicultural society. Understandably, it caused a furore, particularly among senior Anglicans and several politicians. Changing years of established tradition over this title would mean Charles having to overcome huge obstacles, including Parliament agreeing to amend the 1953 Royal Titles Act, which came into law after changes were made for the Queen's coronation. While it is a praiseworthy concept, it must also be remembered that the coronation of the monarch remains an Anglican ceremony, and any change to that would require legislation.

Britain's foremost constitutional expert, the political scientist and historian Professor Sir Vernon Bogdanor, has speculated that after the coronation at Westminster Abbey, it is plausible that a second service could be held for other denominations and faiths, such as Muslims and Hindus. 'It would be a way of the new King showing their importance in the country,' said Professor Bogdanor.

As sovereign, King Charles wants to show that he is a monarch for all his subjects, irrespective of their religious beliefs. In the planning for his shorter, less flamboyant coronation on 6 May 2023, he made sure that religious leaders from different faiths were present. But a wholesale change to the service would mean him having to get permission to rewrite nearly 500 years of tradition, which was never going to happen. Dimbleby's book led to a predictable response, with several MPs publicly reminding the future king that he would be playing a dangerous game, as Britain is a Christian country.

'It's our heritage and we should defend it,' came the message from several senior parliamentarians. The message was clear: 'Don't tinker with a state occasion without clearing it with us – the eyes, ears and voice of the people and your future subjects – first.'

Since then, Charles's position on the wording to be used at his coronation has evolved. It has been made clear to this author that the King will 'absolutely 100 per cent' swear to be named as 'Defender of *the* Faith' when he is crowned. But he will also demonstrate through action that he believes wholeheartedly in the importance of his connecting with all faiths of the subjects over whom he will reign. Other faith leaders, therefore, will be present at the coronation ceremony.

In 2015, in an interview with BBC Radio 2, Charles clarified his position, saying his views had been misinterpreted. He said, 'As I tried to describe, I mind about the inclusion of other people's faiths and their freedom to worship in this country. And it's always seemed to me that, while at the same time being Defender of the Faith, you can also be protector of faiths.' He pointed out that Queen Elizabeth had said her role was 'not to defend Anglicanism to the exclusion of other religions. Instead, the Church [of England] has a duty to protect the free practice of all faiths in this country. I think in that sense she was confirming what I was really trying to say – perhaps not very well – all those years ago.'

King Charles, in his inaugural address, said his own Anglican faith was 'deeply rooted'. Significantly, however, he also said that Britain had become a society of 'many cultures and many faiths' during his mother's long reign.[4] So, while the British monarchy during Charles's reign will remain anchored in Christianity, the new King has made it clear that he feels a responsibility to defend all faiths and will champion the right to religious freedoms, beliefs and practice of all subjects, not just Anglicans.

There is no doubt that Charles's faith is all-encompassing. His appreciation of other religions comes from his wealth of study and discussions over many years. In these difficult times when some British Muslims blame Islamophobia (and vice versa) for the rise in fundamentalism and the terror that flows from blinkered views, the King remains one of the foremost Western faith leaders, who continues to call for more dialogue between faiths and a better understanding of Islam.

As Prince of Wales, he earned widespread respect as an international envoy representing the Queen around the world, and as an independent thinker. As a result of his tireless work in this area and his speeches, he is still held in high standing in the Muslim world. He has shown that he understands and respects both sides and has worked to find common ground in contentious religious disputes. That will not change, close sources say, now he is King.

To Charles, being monarch has nothing to do with power – he believes his role is to lead. It is up to others whether they choose to follow.

CHAPTER 15

New Beginnings

*I'm thrilled. They have been practising long enough. It makes
me feel very old.*

**REMARK BY CHARLES TO THE PRESS WHEN ASKED FOR
HIS REACTION TO WILLIAM AND CATHERINE'S ENGAGEMENT,
NOVEMBER 2010**

Looking nervous, biting his bottom lip, he waited his turn along
with thirty fellow Geography students from St Andrews University.
They all hovered by the side of the stage in Younger Hall as
the Dean of Arts, Professor Christopher Smith, called out the
students' names. 'William Wales,' he said from the lectern, before
the prince stepped forward watched by his proud father, Charles,
his stepmother, Camilla, and his grandparents, the Queen and
Prince Philip.

'I have thoroughly enjoyed my time at St Andrews and I shall be
very sad to leave. I just want to say a big thank-you to everyone who
has made my time here so enjoyable,' he said in a statement issued
by the palace press officer on his graduation day, 23 June 2005.
William, who had secured a 2:1 in Geography, added significantly,
'I have been able to lead as normal a student life as I could have
hoped for and I am very grateful to everyone, particularly the locals,
who have helped make this happen.'

As he was able to enjoy a normal student life, the prince had also been able to fall in love and live with a beautiful young woman, who would later become his wife. Seated five rows in front of William, and graduating eighty people ahead of him, was Catherine Elizabeth Middleton. Wearing high heels and a short black skirt above her knees, and a white blouse beneath her black gown, Catherine had an aura about her. When she was called to the stage to be capped with the red and black hood by the vice-chancellor and then collected her 2:1 degree certificate in Art History, she caught William's eye. She flashed him a broad smile as she returned to her seat. He could not take his eyes off her.

'Today is a very special day,' William said, in the statement issued after the graduation ceremony. 'I am delighted I can share it with my family, particularly my grandmother, who has made such an effort to come, having been under the weather.' He then introduced Catherine's parents, Michael and Carole, to his father as well as the Queen and the Duke of Edinburgh.

Before the graduates disbanded along North Street and into St Salvator's Quad to meet up with their proud families, degree certificates in hand, they were addressed by Dr Brian Lang, the vice-chancellor of St Andrews. 'You will have made lifelong friends,' he said. 'I say this every year to all new graduates: you may have met your husband or wife. Our title as the "Top matchmaking university in Britain" signifies so much that is good about St Andrews, so we can rely on you to go forth and multiply.'

Dr Lang's words were met with laughter, of course, but there must have been a few couples in the auditorium that day who prickled slightly at his words and wondered if they referred to them – perhaps William and Catherine were among them. She had become an integral part of William's life ever since she caught his eye romantically when she strutted down a catwalk wearing a transparent dress, at a student charity fashion show. They soon realised they shared the same interests, and started spending more time together as their relationship blossomed. She played a key role in William overcoming his wobble in April 2002, and him changing courses, after he considered quitting university.

William later admitted he had been 'daunted' by the university experience. He discussed the matter with his father, spelling out his desire to abandon the four-year course altogether. Charles, who had become a much better listener to both his sons' concerns since Diana's death, was sympathetic at first, but understandably concerned about the wider implications. He asked his private office to devise a strategy that would enable William to withdraw from the university should it prove necessary, but they were concerned about the fallout in the media that would follow.

It was only then that Charles strongly advised his son to 'stick with it', as first-term insecurities were normal and it took most students going up to university time to settle in. It was solid fatherly advice that William mulled over before deciding he had to go back. He later conceded there had been a problem and that his father had been a big help. 'We chatted a lot and in the end we both realised – I definitely realised – that I had to come back.'

On his return, he switched courses from Art History to major in Geography and immediately felt happier and more confident. His social life began to look up, too, and his relationship with Catherine began to flourish with the privacy they enjoyed due to the deal that Charles had struck with the media through the Press Complaints Commission.

The young couple had both enjoyed relative freedom from the press as undergraduates, but they knew their lives were about to change dramatically after graduation, not least because the privacy deal expired once William had finished full-time education. They may have been through a few rocky patches during their student relationship, but the trials that lay ahead would test their commitment to each other to the limit.

In 2006, along with her family, Catherine watched William graduate from Sandhurst Military Academy after completing his forty-four-week training course, as he was commissioned as an Army officer in the Household Cavalry (Blues and Royals). The couple would split up briefly in 2007 before reuniting several weeks later, and Catherine was with William again when he received his wings from Charles at a graduation ceremony at RAF Cranwell, after he had spent four months learning to fly both Tucanos and Squirrel helicopters. It seemed, however, that her career had been put on hold for him. She would unfairly be dubbed 'Waity Katie' in the media, since she had been waiting so long for a marriage proposal.

When the time came, they were both twenty-eight, and his proposal was truly romantic. At a remote spot beside a shimmering Lake Alice in Kenya, against the backdrop of a snowy Mount Kenya during a private break in late October 2010, William got down on one knee and presented his bride-to-be with the sapphire and diamond engagement ring that had belonged to his late mother.[1]

William initially even kept his big news from the Queen and his father, as he and Catherine excitedly made their secret plans for a future together. On 15 November, he telephoned the Queen to tell her the good news. She was delighted. Charles, too, was happy, although the Prince of Wales's public reaction that his son and future daughter-in-law had 'practised long enough' was a classic illustration of his whimsical sense of humour. Later, on 23 November, the palace announced that the wedding would take place on Friday, 29 April 2011 at Westminster Abbey, an event that at last eclipsed the terrible sadness of William's late mother Diana's funeral there in 1997.

The couple seemed unflappable as they delivered their vows to each other and as William placed the band of Welsh gold on Catherine's finger. The Queen concurred. 'It was amazing,' she said, as she left the abbey.

'Are you happy?' Catherine asked her husband as she climbed into the open-topped 1902 State Landau to return to the palace. 'It was amazing, amazing,' replied William, the newly ennobled Duke of Cambridge. 'I am so proud you're my wife.' They were totally at one with each other, and represented a young, fresh reboot for the institution of monarchy.

The next day, the newly-weds dressed casually before flying off in a helicopter on the shortest of breaks. Their honeymoon was put on hold, because William had to return to RAF duties as a search-and-rescue pilot only a few days later. The couple sent a message of thanks to the nation for their support on the 'most wonderful day of our lives' and the new Duchess of Cambridge said with characteristic humility, 'I am glad the weather held off. We had a great day.'

The wedding of the Duke and Duchess of Cambridge brought an estimated £2 billion to the UK economy. It was also a huge global media event that drew millions of viewers and provided a massive boost to Brand Britain. Public support and media attention were repeated the following year for the Diamond Jubilee celebrations, marking the milestone of Queen Elizabeth's sixty years on the throne.

Prince Philip had hoped to be at his wife's side throughout the four days of events, but the Thames River Pageant held on Sunday, 3 June – a flotilla of 1,000 boats from across the Commonwealth – contributed to a worsening of Philip's health. In freezing rain, he had stood on the deck of the royal barge for the duration, refusing to sit in one of the rather gaudy gilded thrones provided for them; Philip choosing to stand meant the Queen had to stand too.

Afterwards, royal doctors insisted he took no further active part in the celebrations, and he was later admitted to King Edward VII's Hospital in London, where he was treated for a bladder infection.

The next day was the Diamond Jubilee Concert in front of Buckingham Palace, organised by Gary Barlow of Take That and featuring musical acts from each decade of the Queen's sixty-year reign. At the close of the concert, Charles stepped up to the microphone to deliver a heartfelt tribute to his mother, who looked every inch a diamond Queen in Swarovski crystals and an elegant cocktail dress of gold lamé.

His opening word, 'Mummy', earned him rapturous applause from the crowd. He then warmed his audience up by making a joke about the terrible weather for Sunday's Thames Diamond Jubilee Pageant: 'If I may say so, thank God it turned out fine!' It was when he made a poignant reference to the Duke of Edinburgh, in hospital only a few miles away, that Her Majesty's stiff upper lip for once appeared to weaken, if only for a moment:

> Your Majesty, millions, we are told, dream of having tea with you. Quite a lot nearly had a picnic with you in the garden of Buckingham Palace. The only sad thing about this evening is that my father could not be here with us because, unfortunately, he was taken unwell. But, ladies and gentlemen, if we shout loud enough, he might just hear us in hospital and get better.

Spontaneous cheers and applause broke out and Charles spoke for everyone when, turning to his mother, he added:

> Your Majesty, a Diamond Jubilee is a unique and special event. Some of us have had the joy of celebrating three

jubilees with you, and I have the medals to prove it. We are now celebrating the life and service of a very special person over the last sixty years. I was three when my grandfather George VI died and suddenly, unexpectedly, you and my father's lives were irrevocably changed when you were only twenty-five. So as a nation this is our opportunity to thank you and my father for always being there for us. For inspiring us with your selfless duty and service, and for making us proud to be British.

It was a timely and brilliant performance by the heir to the throne, who won plaudits in newspaper editorials the following day.

Four days of celebratory events culminated with an appearance by the Queen on the palace balcony before a cheering crowd, as a fly-past by Second World War aircraft and the Red Arrows thundered overhead. Significantly, it was not witnessed by the usual extended Royal Family. For the first time, the sovereign was joined by only five family members: the Prince of Wales, the Duchess of Cornwall, the Duke and Duchess of Cambridge, and Prince Harry, in what was a conscious decision to show the shape of things to come.

Prince Philip was back alongside the Queen for the London 2012 Olympic Games in July, but his enforced absence at most of the staged events for the Jubilee had focused minds at the palace. It was clear to the Queen and her family that it was unreasonable to expect Philip to keep up the same pace at the age of ninety-one. It had also become obvious to Charles and senior palace aides that both his parents would need to slow down, and the younger generation take up the slack.

There was talk of Charles adopting a 'Shadow King' role, enabling his mother to spend more time with her husband privately. But officially, the palace pushed back on the idea. 'There is no question of Her Majesty abdicating her responsibilities,' one senior member of the Royal Household insisted. 'It's more about sharing the workload and being more selective of the duties she undertakes. Her Majesty and the Duke of Edinburgh worked tirelessly throughout the Diamond Jubilee. Perhaps too much was expected of them.'

The aide went on, 'The Queen is remarkably fit, but she appreciates that when she is on duty the duke, as her liegeman, believes it is his duty to be at her side. The difficulty is persuading him that any of his sons can step in for him to accompany Her Majesty and that that would be acceptable. If the Duke does not agree to that, the only solution is for Her Majesty to do fewer engagements and for the younger members of the family to represent her at the others.'

The younger generation had already acquitted themselves well during the London Olympics, when they appeared in Team GB T-shirts to shout encouragement to our athletes. Now they would become far more visible. Despite his PR slip in Las Vegas – when pictures were published by the *Sun* that showed him standing naked in front of a nude woman, ahead of him being deployed to Afghanistan – royal advisers had high hopes for Prince Harry, too. They felt he could have a key role to play with the 'Firm', as they called it, following his successful Jubilee visits to Jamaica and Brazil earlier that year.

On 3 December 2012, William and Catherine capped what had been a wonderful Diamond Jubilee year by announcing that they were expecting their first child. The news apparently caught even the Queen and the Prince of Wales by surprise. William had wanted to keep the pregnancy secret so badly that they had kept even their closest family members in the dark. He had to break the news to his grandmother, father and brother in hurried telephone calls only minutes before making the announcement to the world, after his wife was taken to hospital suffering from acute morning sickness.

Charles seemed to capture the mood perfectly. When asked about the pregnancy as he was boarding HMS *Belfast* in London to cross over to the S.A. *Agulhas*, where he was meeting Sir Ranulph Fiennes to wish him well on his latest Antarctic exhibition, he told reporters, 'I'm thrilled, marvellous. A very nice thought of grandfatherhood at my old age, if I may say so. So that's splendid. And I'm very glad my daughter-in-law is getting better, thank goodness.' The Archbishop of Canterbury, who married the couple, said, 'The whole nation will want to join in celebrating this wonderful news. We wish the Duchess the best of health and happiness in the months ahead.'

Britain was in the grip of a heatwave when the time came for the royal baby to come into the world. On a couple of days in mid-July, temperatures hit 90°F (32°C). At 7.14 p.m. on 23 July 2013, twenty-seven hours after the birth, an exhausted but beaming Duchess of Cambridge emerged through the door with her proud husband, William, who could hardly keep his eyes off his son and heir as he stood at her side. In her arms, Catherine showed off their 8lb 6oz bundle of joy, amid tumultuous cheers from hundreds of well-wishers and hospital staff crammed into every vantage point. Simultaneously, television transmitted the picture-perfect image of our 'New Royal Family' to hundreds of millions of fans around the world.

The Queen made the short journey from Buckingham Palace to Kensington Palace in a dark-green Bentley to meet her great-grandson for the first time and to give her blessing to the couple, who had called the boy George in honour of her late father. William later opened his heart about the joy of becoming a father in an interview on camera at Kensington Palace with CNN correspondent Max Foster on 12 August. He spoke about wanting to be hands-on as a parent:

'He does like to keep having his nappy changed, and I did the first nappy, yeah. A badge of honour, exactly. I wasn't allowed to get away with that. I had every midwife staring at me, saying, "You do it. You do it." He's growing quite quickly actually. But he's a little fighter. He kind of, he wriggles around quite a lot. And he doesn't want to go to sleep that much, which is a little bit of a problem.'

Never one to miss an opportunity, the prince also used the interview, which he knew would generate widespread coverage, to highlight one of his great passions, saving endangered species in Africa, and spoke of how he would like his son to follow in his footsteps. William is patron of the conservation charity Tusk and he said he wanted his son to experience the same Africa that he saw as a boy and a young man, and to give his son a passion for preserving the rarest animals, as Prince Charles had encouraged in him.

George's christening ceremony was relatively low key, given his status. Three months after his birth, once Her Majesty had returned from her annual summer at Balmoral, the third in line to the throne was baptised at the Chapel Royal in St James's Palace by the Archbishop of Canterbury, Justin Welby. The intimate service on 23 October had a congregation of just twenty-two, as the small size of the chapel meant that numbers on the guest list had to be kept to a minimum.

It was in stark contrast with William's own christening at Buckingham Palace in 1982. Then, a large crowd had gathered outside the palace and the Queen Mother had appeared on the balcony before the ceremony. For George, it was a closed event. Photographer Jason Bell was selected to take the historic photographs at Clarence House, including one of the three direct heirs, Princes Charles, William and George, the first time such a picture had been taken since 1899, when an eighty-year-old Queen Victoria posed with her direct successors, Edward VII, George V and Edward VIII. This time, the Queen, then eighty-seven, was pictured with her son the Prince of Wales, sixty-four, her grandson the Duke of Cambridge, thirty-one, and three-month-old great-grandson Prince George.

The Queen's subtle move to take a step back in 2013 undoubtedly had deeper and more far-reaching consequences for the heir to the heir, Prince William – still serving as an RAF search-and-rescue pilot for the first half of that year – and his then-pregnant wife. It meant he would need to rethink any ideas for a longer-term military career if he had to become a full-time royal to fill the void.

When Prince Philip was taken ill and hospitalised again a few weeks later – advised by his medical team to spend six days in Aberdeen Royal Infirmary while on his annual Balmoral holiday – the Queen took the opportunity to discuss how to handle this important reshaping of the monarchy with Charles. The transition was imperceptibly gradual and tightly managed. The British like their Royal Family, even if they come across as a little dull, to appear calm, always composed and in control. The Queen backed it up with real action.

The palace revealed she was poised to quit long-haul overseas travel so that she could 'pace herself' for her future role as monarch. Her last long-haul flight, as it turned out, was to Perth, Australia, in 2011 for the Commonwealth summit. Her last state visits were to France in 2014, her fifth time, which coincided with the seventieth anniversary of the D-Day landings on 6 June, when the Queen participated in official commemorations in Normandy before travelling on to Paris at the invitation of the French president François Hollande; and to Germany the following year, again for the fifth time, at the invitation of the President of the Federal Republic of Germany, Joachim Gauck, when she visited Berlin, Frankfurt and Celle.

Queen Elizabeth II surpassed her great-great-grandmother Queen Victoria's record as the longest-reigning British monarch on 9 September 2015. When the moment to mark that record came, she did so with her customary humility. She ruled out any staged major celebration and, once she had delivered her speech acknowledging the milestone, it was straight back to the opening of the £294m Scottish Borders Railway, accompanied by Prince Philip and Scotland's first minister Nicola Sturgeon, leader of the Scottish National Party.

The historic milestone was reached a few hours later, at 5.30 p.m. At that precise moment, Elizabeth II had reigned for 23,226 days, 16 hours and about 30 minutes. The British prime minister, David Cameron, described her service as monarch as 'truly humbling'.

After the Queen was hospitalised in 2013, suffering from gastroenteritis, she showed her determination to manage her workload appropriately in her twilight years. Her decision to ask Charles to go to Colombo, Sri Lanka, in November to represent her at the Commonwealth Heads of Government Meeting was also a smart move. From then on, he would be expected to step in whenever the Queen needed him to represent her on future long-haul trips, just as he and other royals had done during the Diamond Jubilee year. It seemed that not only had the Diamond Jubilee celebrations been a crowning moment for the Queen, they might also have been her final great public display of pomp and pageantry.

Now it was time to give the next generation their chance, and, for Charles, there was no better place to showcase his skills than among Commonwealth leaders at the three-day summit. Charles told them the Queen had a deep affection for the 'family of nations' and he held the same sentiment. He spoke too of his faith in the Commonwealth to help cure the world's troubles.

'Each one of us is here because of the hope and trust we place in the Commonwealth to bring that "touch of healing" to our troubles and deliver the very best future for our people,' he said, as he declared a summit of the organisation's leaders open. It was the kind of vision and leadership expected of a future head of the Commonwealth.

Charles has been a vocal and active supporter of the Commonwealth for more than forty years. He shows his support through official visits, military links, charitable activities, and other special events. On 4 April 2018 in Brisbane, he opened the Commonwealth Games and then toured Australia before flying back for the full Commonwealth Heads of Government Meeting later that month in London and Windsor.

As I discovered in my conversation with him on the royal flight back from Vanuatu to Australia, he is deeply passionate about the organisation that represents 2.3 billion people and fifty-four independent countries – a third of the world's population. 'I have long had an instinctive sense of the value of the Commonwealth,' he said, and has spoken of the 'pivotal role' the Commonwealth must play in safeguarding our planet.

Since 1969, the prince has visited forty-four Commonwealth countries. He led the charge for member island states that face being wiped out by a rise in sea levels with his Blue Economy initiative. In growing the Blue Economy, he hopes to combat poverty and accelerate prosperity in these under-threat regions. But still, some said he was not passionate about it. Ahead of the 2018 London summit, *soi-disant* royal pundits on BBC's *Today* wrongly claimed that Charles was not all that keen on the job, as the Commonwealth did not mean as much to him as it did to his mother. He was understandably irritated by the comments.

The issue for Charles and for the monarchy was that the position of head of the Commonwealth is not enshrined in the constitution of the voluntary association of member nations. The role is symbolic, with no formal powers. In her final years, the Queen had worked hard behind the scenes to ensure that Charles succeeded her as head of the Commonwealth on her passing. It was a responsibility she had cherished – perhaps her greatest legacy – but, unlike the British Crown, it was not one that Charles would inherit automatically. Nonetheless, there was little doubt, after years of distinguished service, that few were better qualified for the albeit titular role.

The Queen left nothing to chance. On 19 April 2018, as she spoke at the official opening of the Commonwealth Heads of Government Meeting at Buckingham Palace, she made a heartfelt address spelling out for the first time her hopes for the future of the Commonwealth and offering her unadulterated support to her son in the role. 'It is my sincere wish that the Commonwealth will continue to offer stability and continuity for future generations and will decide that one day the Prince of Wales should carry on the important work started by my father in 1949,' she told the leaders gathered.

There is little doubt that the Queen's public words galvanised the world leaders into pushing through the decision. 'We are certain that, when he will be called upon to do so, he will provide solid and passionate leadership for our Commonwealth,' Joseph Muscat, the prime minister of Malta, said of the prince in the same ceremony. Later that day, Malcolm Turnbull, the Australian prime minister, confirmed that his country 'strongly supports the continuation of the king or queen of the United Kingdom as the head of the Commonwealth… Prince Charles in time will succeed his mother,' he stated unequivocally.

Speaking to the media, Justin Trudeau, the Canadian prime minister, said, 'I very much agree with the wishes of Her Majesty that the Prince of Wales be the next head of the Commonwealth.' While Ralph Regenvanu, the foreign minister of the Pacific state of Vanuatu, disclosed, 'We see it almost naturally that it should be the British Royal Family, because it is the Commonwealth after all.'

The next day, Charles took another step closer to the chalice when Commonwealth leaders backed the Queen's 'sincere wish' to recognise that her heir, the Prince of Wales, would one day succeed her as the next head of the Commonwealth. Theresa May, then the British prime minister, announced the decision after private deliberations among Commonwealth leaders at Windsor Castle.

When the formal announcement was made, Charles was typically self-effacing. He responded by saying, 'I am deeply touched and honoured by the decision of Commonwealth heads of state and government that I should succeed the Queen, in due course, as head of the Commonwealth. Meanwhile, I will continue to support Her Majesty in every possible way, in the service of our unique family of nations.'

Commonwealth presidents and prime ministers then met to finalise plans for the future of the association, confirming that the decision to make a hereditary appointment was a one-off. The ruling did not apply to Charles's direct heirs, William and George, who will not be automatically in line to hold the office. They decided it would remain a non-hereditary position.

A year later, in March 2019, Charles backed his words with action when he embarked on a major tour of Caribbean Commonwealth realms, as well as a historic visit to communist Cuba, the first by a British royal. Speaking at an open-air event in St Lucia on the first stop of his twelve-day tour, Charles said the Commonwealth was 'as vital as ever'. This was of course a thinly veiled reference to Britain's post-Brexit prospects.

He also made an impassioned plea to the entire Commonwealth to use its power to tackle worldwide problems such as climate change. 'The Commonwealth has been a cornerstone of my life for as long as I can remember and, through all the unprecedented global challenges of these past seven decades, it seems to me that the Commonwealth remains as vital today as it has ever been,' he said. Here were two clear cornerstones of his future reign.

For Charles, being head of the Commonwealth is not about applauding past successes but galvanising the modern Commonwealth to play a vital role in building bridges between countries, fairer societies within them, and a more secure world around them. It is a fundamental feature of his life.

As head, those close to him say he hopes his role will enable member states not only to revitalise the bonds with each other, but also to give the Commonwealth a 'renewed relevance to all citizens', finding practical solutions to their problems and giving life to their aspirations. That way, he believes, the Commonwealth will be a cornerstone for the lives of future generations.

CHAPTER 16

H and M

*This is a great love story… She sacrificed everything that
she ever knew, the freedom that she had, to join me in my
world. And then, pretty soon after that, I ended up sacrificing
everything that I knew to join her in her world.*[1]

**PRINCE HARRY DESCRIBING HIS RELATIONSHIP
WITH HIS WIFE MEGHAN**

Meghan Markle, an actress on the USA Network series *Suits*, looked
bemused when the interviewer asked her whom she would prefer to
go on a date with, Prince William or Prince Harry. The question
seemed to have blindsided the actress, who starred as paralegal
Rachel Zane in the hit series. 'I don't know,' she said, laughing.
It was only when the interviewer suggested Harry that Meghan
replied, 'Harry? Sure.'

Fast forward to the *Harry & Meghan* Netflix documentary
released in December 2022, where Meghan is sitting on a sofa
reviewing the footage. 'Honey, I'm sorry,' she says. 'I, of course,
choose you.'

Harry notes that the clip was recorded less than a year before the
two met. 'It just, again, shows how little you knew about the Royal
Family,' he points out, given that the interview had taken place
in October 2015. 'And look at how far we've come,' he adds, as if

trying to convince himself, after claims that she targeted him and had been on a mission to secure a rich and famous British husband on her trip to London.[1]

Harry said he first became aware of the actress when he was scrolling through his Instagram feed and he saw a clip a mutual friend had posted of Meghan using the dog filter on Snapchat. He was taken by her and asked the friend to introduce them. They exchanged numbers and arranged to meet for a drink in London, as she had come to the UK to watch a match at the Wimbledon tennis championships in July 2016.

Harry arrived late for the hour-long date, 'all flustered and sweaty', and Meghan found him 'refreshingly fun'. They hit it off and agreed to have dinner the following evening. After that date, both sensed a budding romance and a strong connection. A month later, they decided to meet again, this time to spend a week in Botswana, Africa. Any nerves disappeared with the first kiss. 'It just felt so right and it felt so normal,' Harry recalled.

'Thankfully, we really liked each other,' Meghan joked.

'That was when it just hit me,' said Harry, 'like, OK, this girl, this woman is amazing, is everything I've been looking for, and she's so comfortable and so relaxed in my company.'[2] They had fallen head over heels in love.

After the romance of their Africa sojourn, the couple committed to each other and agreed to meet up every fortnight. Meghan said she would visit Harry in London, but stay out of sight within the Kensington Palace compound in a bid to keep their love affair secret. Harry, who was obsessed with press intrusion, warned that once their relationship was made public, everything would change. Inevitably, the story did get out and was exclusively revealed by journalist Camilla Tominey's brilliant scoop in the *Sunday Express* on 31 October 2016.

H and M

A source told the newspaper that Harry was 'happier than he's been for many years' and 'besotted' with Miss Markle. On the same day, Meghan posted a sweet photo on her Instagram of two bananas spooning, possibly hinting at the new love in her life. The couple said they were soon being hounded by paparazzi and Meghan facing attacks in the media, because she was a biracial woman. Harry was 'terrified' for her safety, he said, and feared that history would repeat itself and she would suffer the same relentless hounding by the paparazzi that his mother endured, which he believed had led to her death. Despite that, he was sure he had found the one, and he was determined to marry her.

A few days later, on 8 November 2016, Harry confirmed his relationship with Meghan when he released a formal statement. In it he called for the press and online trolls to stop the 'wave of abuse and harassment' that had been directed at his girlfriend. He claimed he had been involved with 'nightly legal battles' to stop the media from publishing defamatory stories about Meghan and their relationship. Many thought the actress would be prepared for the attention, but she claimed she had 'never been part of tabloid culture'.

Charles, who at the time was focused on a Foreign Office-sponsored visit to the Gulf states, had just arrived in Bahrain, and did not have the opportunity to make a response to what was regarded by those close to him as an impetuous statement. He was given only twenty minutes' notice that it was going to be released. The prince had just given an important interview to the *Evening Standard* on climate change, after collecting a prestigious award for his work in this area, but his aides knew that Harry's statement, much of it drafted by the prince himself, would now dominate the news cycle.

Far from being 'crushed', as some later claimed, Charles was disappointed by his son's bad manners. 'He would never have done such a thing if the Queen was on tour. Understandably, there is a hierarchy and a grid system, but Prince Harry seemed to think when it came to Meghan Markle, she would always take precedence,' one former aide said.

William, too, privately thought his brother had overreacted. 'It was all a bit dramatic, a bit OTT,' one of his ex-aides later recalled. On 27 November 2016, William released his own statement to clear up speculation that he had been unhappy with Harry's decision. 'I absolutely understand the situation concerning privacy and support the need for Prince Harry to support those closest to him,' he stated, backing up his brother.

Dating Meghan, Harry said in their Netflix docuseries, 'became a combination of car chases, anti-surveillance driving and disguises, which isn't a particularly healthy way to start a relationship, but we always came at it with as much humour as possible.' He went on, 'To see another woman in my life, that I love, go through this feeding frenzy, that's hard. It is basically the hunter versus the prey.'

Harry felt that his father and his brother (and other men in the Royal Family) did not back him up, telling him that the treatment Meghan was getting from the press and paparazzi was par for the course.

Speaking in the docuseries, Harry said his concerns fell on deaf ears: 'But what people need to understand is, as far as a lot of the family were concerned, everything that she was being put through, they had been put through as well. So, it was almost like a rite of passage, and some of the members of the family were like, "My wife had to go through that, so why should your girlfriend be treated any differently? Why should you get special treatment? Why should she be protected?" I said, "The difference here is the race element."'[3]

William knew that Harry was smitten, and it became obvious that his brother wanted to marry Meghan almost from the moment they met. Knowing how much Harry craved the idea of being happily married and settling down, however, William urged caution. 'It might not happen, Harold, and you've got to be OK with that.' When Harry told him it *was* going to happen, William did not back down, and went on, 'She's an American actress after all, Harold, anything might happen.'[4] (Willy and Harold were the brothers' pet names for each other.)

To be fair, William had always looked out for his younger brother, so it is perhaps not surprising he was concerned that the whirlwind love affair might lead to a proposal so quickly. William's reservations were well intentioned, but they sent Harry, whose passion and protectiveness towards Meghan had reached fever pitch, into a spin. He was 'hurt' by the comment and felt nervous when he later went with Meghan to his brother's apartment at Kensington Palace to introduce her to William and Catherine.

Following their meeting, the noises came from the palace that they had 'got on fabulously'. But Meghan later revealed she thought Catherine was stand-offish. 'Even when Will and Kate came over, and I met her for the first time, they came over for dinner, I remember I was in ripped jeans and I was barefoot,' Meghan said. 'Like I was a hugger, I've always been a hugger. I didn't realise that that is really jarring for a lot of Brits. I guess I started to understand quickly that the formality on the outside carried through on the inside.'[5]

It was another swipe at Catherine and shows that relations between the two couples were less than warm from the outset.

It got worse. When Harry eventually went to tell his father that he intended to marry 'the American actress' Meghan, he already knew, as William had told him. His brother, who was present, asked again, 'Are you sure, Harold?' The record was wearing thin. 'I am, Willy,' Harry responded. He did not care about any potential difficulties. Charles then dropped a bombshell, saying he could not afford to pay for Meghan going forward as well as Camilla, and William and Catherine and their young family.[6] This understandably infuriated Harry.

Meghan spoke openly about her relationship with Harry for the first time in the October 2017 issue of *Vanity Fair*. 'We're a couple. We're in love. I'm sure there will be a time when we will have to come forward and present ourselves and have stories to tell, but I hope what people will understand is that this is our time,' she said in the cover story. 'This is for us. It's part of what makes it so special, that's just ours. But we're happy. Personally, I love a great love story.'

That month, for the first time she accompanied Harry to an official royal appearance at the opening ceremony of the Invictus Games, and they even shared a kiss at the closing ceremony, to the delight of their fans. The couple also spent time with Meghan's mother, Doria Ragland. Their engagement was finally announced on 27 November 2017 and was marked with a photoshoot and a formal interview.

Meghan, at first, was seen by the press as a breath of fresh air. She threw herself into her new role even before they married, visiting Edinburgh, Cardiff, Belfast and London, and was greeted warmly by large enthusiastic crowds wherever she went. Her biracial heritage was seen as a plus, not only by the Queen and Charles, but the people of the multicultural United Kingdom, which was a very different society to the one at Elizabeth II's accession. Charles could not have been more welcoming to his future daughter-in-law. Meghan said at the time that she was bowled over by his gentlemanly charm.

In fact, her warmth for Harry's father led to a softening of relations between father and son. Charles was captivated by Meghan's intelligence and vivacious personality. He remarked, 'She makes Harry happy. We could not like her more.' Queen Elizabeth, too, took a keen interest in Harry's bride-to-be. During the engagement interview, Harry claimed that when Meghan took tea with the Queen, the corgis took to her immediately, even going so far as to lie on her feet. It raised a few insiders' eyebrows, especially as any newcomers who tried to get into the Queen's good books by patting the dogs were sharply told, 'Don't do that, they don't like it.' The insider said, 'What she really means is, she doesn't like it.'

On the surface, everything seemed fine. But William and Charles had noticed a difference in Harry, who seemed to be permanently on edge. The stress seemed to be getting to the couple, who were being treated by an acupuncturist to the stars, Ross Barr, in the lead-up to the wedding. Barr's treatments dealt with anything from infertility to hair loss and relationship problems, but failed to have a lasting impact on Harry. Staff and family both said the normally happy and funny prince became 'petulant and short-tempered' with members of staff.

On occasion, he raised his voice and even swore. 'What Meghan wants, she gets,' he is said to have told Queen Elizabeth's dresser and loyal confidante, Angela Kelly, after she tried to advise him about a tiara for the wedding (though he has since denied saying this). When word of his tiresome behaviour reached the Queen, she addressed the issue with him personally.[7]

After the fallout over the tiara, the Queen as well as other senior aides also raised questions about why Meghan even needed a veil for the ceremony, given that this was her second marriage. *The Times* reported after the wedding that palace insiders had spoken of 'temper tantrums' when Miss Markle, now the Duchess of Sussex, was told that she would not be able to wear the tiara she had chosen.

'By tradition, royal brides wear tiaras at their weddings. In the Duchess's case, it was expected to be one lent to her by the Queen,' the story read. It went on, 'She chose one set with emeralds, but the Palace later ruled it out because of uncertainty over its origins. In the end, the Duchess wore Queen Mary's diamond bandeau tiara, made in 1932.' But it was not Meghan who threw the tantrum, it was Harry.[8]

William felt compelled to intervene in the jewellery row. He sought confirmation from the Queen about who was entitled to wear jewels that had once been worn by his late mother, Diana, Princess of Wales. His wife Catherine, due to her seniority and position as the next Princess of Wales and future Queen Consort, had, of course, been allowed to do so.

Harry felt that William did not back his marriage or approve of his choice of bride. It may have been an overreaction, but it was the beginning of a rift between the brothers that has not healed to this day. The close bond between the two siblings had been irreparably damaged. Not only was the brothers' relationship strained, but their wives were not on the best of terms either.

A story by the journalist Camilla Tominey, now assistant editor of the *Daily Telegraph*, would disclose the dynamic of the royal feud. In November 2018, she revealed in the newspaper that in the days before her wedding, Meghan had made Catherine cry over a spat involving a 'flower girl' bridesmaid's dress for Princess Charlotte to wear on Meghan and Harry's wedding day.

Meghan has confirmed that there was a disagreement between the women before her royal wedding to Prince Harry. However, during the now infamous Oprah Winfrey interview, she denied making her sister-in-law cry, saying, 'The reverse happened.' At the time, everyone kept silent, but the simmering resentment between the couples was about to blow up into a full-scale feud. To add insult to injury, Catherine would later demand an apology when Meghan offended her by talking about her hormones and saying she had 'baby brain' over tea at Kensington Palace.[9]

Like any father, Charles feared the worst when his two sons clashed, especially when the women they both loved now seemed embroiled in the ill feeling too. He knew that they were both strong-willed, stubborn even; conflict would be very difficult to manage and could have a detrimental impact on the monarchy itself. Sometimes the level of belligerence between his sons, and indeed towards him, had shocked Charles.

On occasions, both his sons have challenged him. William has even been known to speak forcefully to his father. One exchange between them was so heated that it left Charles shaken. Both of his sons' tempers are reminiscent of their mother Diana's, which Charles had struggled to cope with during their marriage. Thus the prince chose not to intervene, hoping that in time it would all blow over. But instead of a line being drawn under it, the relationship between his sons deteriorated further.

On the day of the wedding itself, the exuberant crowds were blissfully ignorant about the simmering feud between the brothers and lingering animosity between their wives. Tens of millions of people from around the world tuned in on 19 May 2018 to see Harry and Meghan wed at St George's Chapel, Windsor Castle. An A-list of celebrities such as Oprah Winfrey, David and Victoria Beckham, and George and Amal Clooney were among the 600 guests who joined the Royal Family.

The bride's father, Thomas Markle Senior, did not attend the wedding on health grounds, after suffering a heart attack. He had fallen out with the couple when it emerged that he had been paid to stage paparazzi photos. Charles agreed to step in to walk Meghan up the aisle. On the day, all eyes were on the bride, who wore a Givenchy gown for the ceremony. Among the huge, excited crowds, I saw many little Black girls dressed like princesses with tiaras. At last they had a role model in the Royal Family. One mother told me, when I complimented her five-year-old daughter Amy's outfit: 'She just wanted to dress up and see Meghan.'

One of the most touching moments came when Charles, immaculate in his grey Anderson & Sheppard morning suit and buttonhole from the garden of his Highgrove estate, smiled at Meghan and gently placed her arm under his as she approached the quire in St George's Chapel. He was delighted to be able to welcome her into his family after she had asked him to stand in for her father. Those watching could not help but be enchanted by Charles's poise at a moment that could have been awkward.

Then, in an equally heart-warming moment, Harry whispered words that seemed scarcely to register. Almost shaking with tension, he turned to his father, who had accompanied his glamorous bride down the aisle, and said, 'Thanks, Pa.' It was a sign of love between father and son.

The service combined tradition with a fresh modernity as well as the bride's African American heritage. It included uplifting gospel music from the Kingdom Choir, a group of British singers led by the award-winning conductor Karen Gibson, who had been personally invited by the Prince of Wales to perform at the ceremony.

An American bishop, Most Rev. Michael Bruce Curry, who presides over the Episcopalian Church, fervently addressed the attendees. 'There's power in love,' said the bishop. 'If you don't believe me, think about a time when you first fell in love. The whole world seemed to centre around you and your beloved.'

He concluded his passionate address by saying he had better wrap it up, as, 'We gotta get y'all married.'

The couple then exchanged vows and rings made by Cleave and Company. In her vows, Meghan noticeably deleted the promise to 'obey' her husband, while the prince broke with royal tradition by choosing to wear a wedding ring. (William chose not to wear a ring at his wedding to Catherine, and does not wear one now, as has been true of most royal men. Charles, however, wore his wedding ring from his marriage to Diana on the same finger as his signet ring.)

When Archbishop of Canterbury Justin Welby declared that the couple were 'man and wife', a huge cheer ran around the town of Windsor, where an estimated 100,000 people stood beyond the castle walls watching the ceremony unfold on big screens amid a carnival atmosphere.

The bride's mother, Doria Ragland – controversially, Meghan's only invited relative – looked an isolated, solitary figure. Dressed in a pale-green Oscar de la Renta dress, with a neat hat, an emotional-looking Doria sat silent and alone on the bride's side of the chapel for some time. Sensing her awkwardness, the Prince of Wales graciously took her hand as they left to sign the register for the royal wedding of their two children.

After the service, the couple – who had been given the title their Royal Highnesses the Duke and Duchess of Sussex, bestowed by Queen Elizabeth – kissed in front of cheering well-wishers on the steps of the chapel. A confident, beaming Meghan made the first move. 'Shall we kiss?' she asked. 'Yes,' her prince and now husband replied.

Meghan later switched to a chic Stella McCartney halter dress for the evening reception at Frogmore House with about 200 guests. At about 11 p.m., they all went outside to watch the fireworks above Windsor Castle, which surprised Charles. 'Who's paying for that?' the prince remarked half-jokingly to one of the guests, who responded, 'I believe you are, sir.'

Four days later, on 23 May 2018, the photographers' cameras went into overdrive as the royal party, led by the Prince of Wales, stepped on to the back steps of Buckingham Palace. But he knew they were not really trained on him. The four royals – Charles, Camilla, Harry and Meghan – stood underneath a specially erected awning with the words 'The Prince of Wales's 70th Birthday Patronage Celebration', topped off with his heraldic badge of three white ostrich feathers emerging from a gold coronet. A ribbon below the coronet bore the motto *Ich Dien* – 'I Serve'.

All four duly descended the steps and began working the crowd, meeting a few of the 6,000 people who were invited from 386 of Charles's patronages and 20 of his military associations. Several guests from the police, fire and ambulance services, mountain rescue and the RNLI also attended. Inevitably, though, the photographers' lenses focused on the new Duchess of Sussex, immaculate in a silk crêpe pencil dress and a Philip Treacy dome hat, as this was her first official engagement since her marriage.

Harry, now the Duke of Sussex, then marked the occasion with a speech of self-deprecation and rare warmth towards his father. 'Pa,' he said, using the term of endearment again, 'while I know that you've asked that today not be about you, you must forgive me if I don't listen to you. Much like when I was younger. Instead, I ask everyone here to say a huge thank-you to you, for your incredible work over nearly fifty years.'

Harry, whom Charles referred to as his 'darling boy', praised his father's 'selfless drive to effect change' in a heartfelt speech. 'We are here today to reflect on and to celebrate my father's dedicated support to all of you and the work that you do.' He went on,

'As I was preparing for this afternoon, I looked through the long list of those who had been invited. Pa, I was again struck by the range and diversity of the work which you are involved with. It is your selfless drive to effect change, whether that is to improve the lives of those who are on the wrong path, to save an important piece of our national heritage or to protect a particular species under threat, which William and I draw inspiration from every day.'

It was to be the high point of their father and son relationship.

CHAPTER 17

A Duchy Original

He is his own man, passionate and creative. So, this toast is to wish a happy birthday to my son, in every respect a duchy original.

HER MAJESTY QUEEN ELIZABETH II, SPEAKING AT THE
BUCKINGHAM PALACE CELEBRATION FOR THE SEVENTIETH BIRTHDAY
OF CHARLES, PRINCE OF WALES, 14 NOVEMBER 2018

'How are you feeling, Prince Charles?' asked ITN royal correspondent Chris Ship, as the prince arrived at St James's Palace with his wife, Camilla, for an engagement on his seventieth birthday on 14 November 2018. 'How am I feeling. Older, older... It's like indigestion, many happy returns aren't quite the same thing as you get older,' he joked. He was then handed a balloon with '70' on it and a gift from the royal rota press before attending a special reception of seventy people also aged seventy, who had been nominated for their work in local communities.

In Parliament, Prime Minister Theresa May paid tribute to him on his milestone birthday: 'Throughout the Prince of Wales's life his commitment to public service has been total,' she said. 'The more one looks at [his] life, the more one sees a man who has spent seventy years defying expectations and refusing to be categorised.'

That night, Queen Elizabeth hosted an elaborate dinner for her son and heir. She had instructed the Master of the Household, Vice-Admiral 'Tony' Johnstone-Burt, to ensure that the chefs, under-chefs and staff from 'F' (Food) Department pulled out all the stops. Nothing was left to chance, from the Pol Roger Brut Réserve NV champagne, a favourite of the Queen's, to the preparation of Charles's preferred Martini made relatively light on the gin, with equal parts of that and dry vermouth.

As well as family and close friends, Her Majesty had invited many of the kings and queens and senior royals from across Europe to attend the black-tie party to mark her son's seventieth birthday. Also invited were representatives from some of the 420 charities of which Charles was patron or president.

Typically for the guest of honour, Charles's day had been business as usual, for at their boss's behest the prince's team had scheduled a full day of engagements, despite it being his landmark birthday. In the morning, he met the ex-president of Kosovo, Atifete Jahjaga, who had been his host when he visited the country in 2016, and after lunch he met the Cuban president, Miguel Díaz-Canel, paving the way for a historic royal visit by the prince to the communist island country in March 2019. If it was a full day, it was also a demonstration of his statesmanship, and of how the prince, not yet the UK's head of state, was now regarded on the world stage.

To mark his big day, a photograph of Charles was taken at Clarence House, depicting him immaculately dressed in a dinner jacket, with the Duchess of Cornwall, in a navy-blue off-the-shoulder gown complete with diamond accessories, at his side. Clarence House also issued a charming family photo of Charles with his sons, their spouses, his wife and his three grandchildren, taken by Chris Jackson of Getty Images.

With her impeccable sense of timing, Queen Elizabeth saved the best until last with her tribute to her son and heir. When the moment came, Her Majesty spoke not only as sovereign and host but, most tellingly, as a mother. And in some of her warmest words about the Prince of Wales on record, she made it clear that she could not have been prouder. Her words, from a member of a family not known for expressing gushing sentiments in public, were remarkable:

> It is a privilege for any mother to be able to propose a toast to her son on his seventieth birthday. It means that you have lived long enough to see your child grow up. It is rather like – to use an analogy I am certain will find favour – planting a tree and being able to watch it grow.
>
> My mother saw me turn seventy, of course, and she was heard to observe that seventy is exactly the age when the number of candles on your cake finally exceeds the amount of breath you have to blow them out. Over his seventy years, Philip and I have seen Charles become a champion of conservation and the arts, a great charitable leader – a dedicated and respected heir to the throne to stand comparison with any in history – and a wonderful father.
>
> Most of all, sustained by his wife Camilla, he is his own man, passionate and creative. So, this toast is to wish a happy birthday to my son, in every respect a duchy original.

With that, she raised a glass and toasted her son, 'To you, Charles, to the Prince of Wales.'

Charles, not a man who enjoys being praised, particularly in public, was deeply touched, as well as a little embarrassed, by his mother's sincere and moving tribute. But at last he was getting the recognition many felt he had long deserved.

Despite his own assertion that there can only ever be one monarch at a time, since Philip's retirement at the age of ninety-six,[1] having 'done his bit', Charles had played an increasingly more important role alongside the Queen, whose great age had also forced her to slow down. So by the time he reached seventy, a more accurate description of his role ahead of becoming monarch was 'Shadow King' or 'Quasi King'. For in the twilight of her reign, it was Charles, not Her Majesty, who was undertaking the heavy lifting for the monarchy at home and abroad, while officially representing his mother, who was now the oldest reigning British sovereign.

Charles travelled hundreds of thousands of miles around the world on official business, from the tiny Lady Elliot Island, the southernmost coral cay of the Great Barrier Reef, Australia, to the former New Hebrides colony, now Vanuatu, in the South Pacific. He carried out hundreds of public duties representing the Queen in his role as heir to the throne, meeting presidents and princes as well as people going about their daily lives on visits to villages, towns and cities across the UK and the Commonwealth.

I travelled with Charles when he returned to the Caribbean in March 2019, taking in six Commonwealth countries and one overseas territory, before making a historic visit to communist Cuba, the first official visit by a member of the Royal Family, and from there on to the Cayman Islands.

Then, a month later, the world's attention turned to the birth of Charles's fourth grandchild, the Duke and Duchess of Sussex's baby, Archie Harrison Mountbatten-Windsor, who became seventh in line to the throne at birth. Once again Charles had to put duty first and make a visit to Berlin, where he met Chancellor Angela Merkel and delivered part of an important 'post-Brexit' speech in German, stressing the close relationship of the UK and Germany.

Addressing the importance of an enduring relationship between the two countries, Prince Charles switched back to say in English, 'It is a relationship in transition. But whatever the shape of our future relationship, and whatever is negotiated and agreed between governments and institutions, it is clearer to me than it has ever been that the bonds between us will, and must, endure – and that our young people, and future generations, will have as much cause to cherish those bonds as our generation has had.'

He did not forget his familial duties while away either. 'We couldn't be more delighted at the news and we're looking forward to meeting the baby when we return,' he said.

The Royal Family expressed their delight at the arrival of the Sussexes' baby boy. But, beneath the surface, tensions continued between the two brothers. While surely wanting to knock his sons' heads together, Charles stayed out of the quarrels. But Harry and Meghan were set on a course that would have far-reaching consequences, not only for Charles, but for the monarchy he serves.

From the outset, publicly all had seemed well with the so-called 'Fab Four' – a handle given to the Beatles in their heyday. The foursome of William and Catherine and Harry and Meghan had it all, with star quality in abundance. A humorous exchange at the Royal Foundation Forum on 28 February 2018, however, while giving the impression of being light-hearted banter, had begun to show the cracks. Interviewer Tina Daheley asked if they ever had family disagreements, which prompted nervous giggling from all four.

'Oh, yes,' William said in response.

'[They are] healthy disagreements,' Harry added quickly.

When Daheley asked for more detail about the disagreements, Harry sidestepped it, saying, 'I can't remember, they come so thick and fast.' When she pushed a little further and asked if any of their most recent disagreements had been resolved, William said, 'Is it resolved? We don't know,' before elaborating a little. 'We've got four different personalities and we've got the same passions to make a difference, but different opinions,' he said. 'I think those opinions work really, really well. Working as a family does have its challenges and the fact that everyone is laughing shows they know exactly what it's like. We're stuck together for the rest of our lives.'

The expression 'stuck together' seemed to say it all. Behind the stage-managed scenes and PR smiles, resentment between the brothers had been festering for some time.

When Meghan was asked how she would focus on the empowerment of women and girls through the new charity, she answered, 'Women don't need to find a voice, they have a voice and they need to feel empowered to use it, and people need to be encouraged to listen,' before adding, 'There is no better time to shine a light on women feeling empowered, and people really helping to support them,' and namechecking the #Me Too and Time's Up movements. William looked decidedly uncomfortable with Meghan taking centre stage.

The *Mail on Sunday* columnist, Rachel Johnson, the feisty sister of former prime minister Boris Johnson, saw through the slick PR. She wrote, 'This was risky on a couple of fronts. Over here, we secretly don't like women who speak out too loudly and often (I should know), let alone women who order other women to speak out and men to listen. And as a nation, we certainly prefer royal women who don't really speak, like the Queen, or the Duchess of Cambridge.

She went on to point out the problem for this cosy new arrangement for the Fab Four and their new band member. 'If you look at the Royal Foundation, it divvies things up, so Harry is armed forces, Kate is young people and mental health, and William is across conservation. Meghan – mark my words – will be banging the drum for "wimmin". We will have our first feminist-activist princess. Which is great and could be fine (though I feel women are not victims in need of charity but continued advocacy), but equally it could end up with tensions in the band – and royalty is a far harder show to keep on the road than rock 'n' roll.'

Then for the bullseye: 'Meghan would do well to remember she is becoming a member of a constitutional hierarchy, which depends on everyone knowing their exact place in the pecking order and toeing endless invisible lines.' That word 'hierarchy' was one that would return time and again.

When Charles invited the Duchess of Sussex to join him and Camilla on a private tour of his *Prince & Patron* exhibition in the state rooms of Buckingham Palace, to mark his seventieth-birthday year, Meghan accepted enthusiastically. She was keen to see a special display of more than a hundred works of art personally selected by the prince. But, when her advisers were told they would be joined by John Bridcut and the film crew for his BBC documentary, *Prince, Son and Heir: Charles at 70*, she belatedly pulled out. Cancelling on the heir to the throne after one has accepted an invitation is usually inexcusable. But Charles let it pass.

Meghan had consulted the prince about the music for the wedding, while Charles took time to explain to her the complexities of life in the Firm. It helped that Meghan was fascinated by British history, and royal history, more so than her husband, who is admittedly not a star pupil when it comes to such matters, and sources said she had been poring over notes as she studied the Commonwealth. Charles saw his work ethic and his passion for philanthropy reflected in his new daughter-in-law, who had campaigned to raise awareness of women's issues. It would not have escaped his notice that she also shared his belief in the importance of organic food.

Camilla, too, played her part as a sort of 'super-granny', dispensing humorous, down-to-earth advice to Meghan. But the duchess made it clear that she would make her own decisions. When the Queen, who had asked her then assistant private secretary Samantha Cohen to work alongside Meghan for a bedding-in period, warmly suggested that she should turn to Sophie, Countess of Wessex for support and advice, Meghan dismissed the idea, saying, 'I've got Harry.' Her response surprised the Queen.

What Harry decided to do next, however, infuriated William further and worried his father. It was the first of many betrayals that his brother would not forgive. Courting controversy, he and Meghan agreed to do a series of interviews with ITV's Tom Bradby for a behind-the-scenes documentary on their tour of South Africa, *Harry & Meghan: An African Journey*. Instead of refusing to get drawn on a deeply personal subject, Harry then spoke for the first time about his strained relationship with his brother. It came after reports of tensions between William and Harry had been stoked by a decision for them to have separate offices and to split their charitable foundation.

He said that because they were both under pressure, it was inevitable that 'stuff happens'. He added, unconvincingly, 'But we are brothers. We will always be brothers. We are certainly on different paths at the moment. But I will always be there for him, as I know he will always be there for me.'

The cat was now well and truly out of the bag, and there was no way of putting it back. The break-up of the Fab Four was now complete; over and above that, William was deeply disappointed that his brother had broken the bond of trust between them. 'To say he felt deeply let down would be an understatement, he wasn't sure if he could ever fully trust his brother again. That was a loss to him,' said one member of his circle.

Meghan spoke out too about the difficulties of living under the intense media scrutiny she had experienced ever since she married into the Royal Family. 'I never thought that this would be easy, but I thought it would be fair and that's the part that's really hard to reconcile,' she said. She explained, 'I've said for a long time to "H" – that's what I call him – it's not enough to just survive something, right? That's not the point of life. You've got to thrive; you've got to feel happy. I really tried to adopt this British sensibility of a stiff upper lip. I tried, I really tried. But I think that what that does internally is probably really damaging.'

In the same interview, Meghan disclosed that her British friends had warned her against marrying Prince Harry. 'When I first met Harry, my friends were so excited. My US friends were happy because I was happy,' she said. 'But my British friends, they were sure he was lovely, but they said I shouldn't do it because "The British tabloids will destroy your life".'

Asked by Tom Bradby how she was coping, Meghan said, 'Thank you for asking, because not many people have asked if I'm OK. But it's a very real thing to be going through behind the scenes.' Bradby then added, 'And the answer is, would it be fair to say, not really OK? That it's really been a struggle?' Looking close to tears, she replied, 'Yes.' It was a theme Harry and Meghan would return to again and again.

The Sussexes' tour of southern Africa, which ran from the end of September to early October 2019, had been going smoothly. The first section of the tour appeared to have gone well. They had posed beautifully for a photo opportunity with Archie and the revered anti-apartheid campaigner the late Archbishop Desmond Tutu, in Cape Town. Ironically, they would later use one of those photos in a trailer for their Netflix docuseries to try to highlight paparazzi intrusion, despite the fact that it was taken from that accredited pool position, arranged by them and policed by their press secretary Sara Latham, who stood next to the three British media outlets picked to report on the moment outside Archbishop Tutu's private residence.

Later they danced and spoke eloquently in Nyanga township on the outskirts of the city, and Harry then went on to visit Angola, Malawi and Botswana for his charity work, accompanied mainly by television crews, as it was too expensive for most print media to follow.

On 8 April 2021, it was reported in *The Times* that William had broken off his decades-long friendship with ITN news anchor Bradby because of his relationship with the Duke and Duchess of Sussex. William, the newspaper reported, was left frustrated that the former royal correspondent and host of *News at Ten* on ITV appeared to have sided with his brother and sister-in-law in their break from the Royal Household.[2]

Rather like the original Fab Four, the Beatles, who split after bitter infighting, the same fate would befall the royal quartet, only it took months, not years. On 14 March 2019, it was officially announced that William and Harry's households were to split up to create separate courts. Palace spin doctors tried to dress it up as being part of a natural plan, but could not explain why there had been such a media fanfare for the Royal Foundation the previous year. The imminent arrival of the Sussexes' first child was seen as the perfect moment to act.

Harry and Meghan had rejected a proposed move next door to William and Catherine's palatial Apartment 1A at Kensington Palace. The move was turned down, it emerged later, due to timing and not to the fact that the two brothers did not want to be neighbours. When they had gone round to have drinks at William's apartment while living at the compact Nottingham

Cottage opposite, Harry and Meghan had been piqued by the disparity between the two households. The royal hierarchy, to them, seemed imbalanced.

Tired of being cooped up in their own modest accommodation inside the Kensington Palace 'compound', they accepted an offer to move to Frogmore Cottage, Windsor. This, aides said, would give them autonomy. Stories soon began to emerge in the press that the Sussex household was not a happy place to work. Claims of bullying were alleged, along with complaints about what some staff deemed to be unacceptable behaviour by the duchess.

The shake-up left William with all the key players from their communications team, and civil service high-flyer Simon Case, briefly director of strategy at GCHQ, was appointed as his new private secretary.[3] This left Harry floundering.

The Sussexes enlisted Amy Pickerill, who had worked for the joint Kensington Palace team in communications, as Meghan's first private secretary, and American Sara Latham as the couple's communications secretary. Pickerill did not last long. She quit in May 2019, becoming the fourth member of Meghan's team to leave in quick succession, following the planned departure of the Queen's former assistant private secretary, Samantha Cohen, and the resignation of Meghan's personal secretary Melissa Touabti. Her female personal protection officer also left after the visit to Australia, Fiji and Tonga.

The palace tried to dismiss rumours that Meghan was difficult to work with. Privately, however, the duchess said that the palace aides and the Royal Family were briefing against her and trying to discredit her, as bullying accusations then emerged. One courtier said that the duchess 'governed by fear'. The swirl of negativity around Meghan helped her and Harry to make up their minds that leaving the Firm was the right thing for them to do.

In a BBC documentary *The Princes and the Press*, presented by BBC media editor Amol Rajan in November 2021, Schillings lawyer Jenny Afia denied that the Duchess of Sussex ever bullied staff, or inflicted 'emotional cruelty' on them that 'drove them out'. Ms Afia insisted that Meghan did not 'repeatedly and deliberately hurt anyone'. But she added that she 'wouldn't want to negate anyone's personal experiences. She also claimed there were 'massive inaccuracies' in the story in *The Times* by Valentine Low, who had been the first journalist to publish the allegations by Harry and Meghan's staff. The veteran reporter responded via Twitter, saying, 'How odd. Perhaps she would care to let me know what they were.'

It emerged later that the Sussexes' former communications secretary, Jason Knauf, had submitted the bullying allegations to the palace Human Resources department in October 2018. He also emailed Prince William's private secretary Simon Case, after raising bullying concerns with the head of HR, Samantha Carruthers. Knauf had become communications secretary to the Duke and Duchess of Cambridge in 2015, before taking on the same role for the Duke and Duchess of Sussex after they married in 2018. One month after reporting the allegation, Mr Knauf handed in his notice, before leaving and then returning to head up the Cambridges' new Royal Foundation.

Knauf, who would stand down from his role as CEO of the Royal Foundation in December 2021, had verbally advised Meghan on the letter she wrote to her father that was at the centre of her privacy action against Associated Newspapers, publisher of the *Mail on Sunday*. William was concerned that the situation was out of control, but his relationship with his brother had deteriorated so badly that he could not go to him and ask him to try to calm the situation down by speaking to his wife. There was no turning back.

The Sussexes decided they wanted a new life, away from the palace and the press, and even the Royal Family.

Harry claimed later in their Netflix docuseries that it had become a 'dirty game'. There is a 'hierarchy in the family', Harry said, and there was 'leaking but there's planting of stories'. Meghan was even more harsh in her assessment, claiming she had not just been 'thrown to the wolves', but was being 'fed to them'. It was now only a matter of time before they would quit Britain for good.

CHAPTER 18

Grandpa Wales

*The great thing is to encourage them. Show them things
to take their interest. My grandmother did that, she was
wonderful. It is very important to create a bond when
they are very young.*

**THE KING COMMENTING ON HOW HE SEES HIS ROLE
AS A GRANDFATHER**

William and Catherine's children call King Charles 'Grandpa Wales' – from the time he was Prince of Wales – and they 'absolutely adore' him. When he reads to them, doing the voices of all the characters, he has them spellbound; they particularly like J.K. Rowling's Harry Potter books. William praised his father on how good he is with his and Catherine's children, Prince George, Princess Charlotte and Prince Louis, but added that his devotion to duty means he is not around enough. William said, 'When he's there, he's brilliant,' but 'we need him there as much as possible.'[1]

Sadly, due to the sorry current state of his relationship with Harry and Meghan, and their decision to live in the USA, Charles has very little to do with his other two grandchildren, Archie and Lilibet, whom he has seen only fleetingly.

Charles had become a grandfather for the second time on 2 May 2015, with the arrival of the Cambridges' baby girl, Charlotte. William and Catherine had both privately hoped for a little girl.

Charles, too, was thrilled at the news, and he and Camilla issued a statement saying they were 'absolutely delighted' by the arrival of the little princess. The palace simultaneously announced that the baby girl, at this stage unnamed, had been born at 8.34 a.m., weighing 8lb 3oz, as her proud parents introduced her to the waiting press. She was covered in a shawl and with a bonnet over her head to protect her from the early-evening chill.

'She's fast asleep,' said Catherine to her husband, on the steps of the Lindo wing of St Mary's Hospital. William told the press they were 'very, very pleased'. After resting up for two days at Kensington Palace, the Cambridges then headed with their young family to Anmer Hall in Norfolk, which they announced would become their main residence.

The royal baby was just the fillip the country needed after the humdrum general election that had been dominating the UK news. Charles was very pleased too when William and Catherine named their baby Charlotte Elizabeth Diana of Cambridge, a homage to her grandfather Charles, with Charlotte being a feminisation of his name, along with the Queen and his late mother Diana. Charles had a real connection with her and could not stop talking about the new royal baby. While taking tea with Second World War veterans at Clarence House, the doting grandfather revealed that Charlotte was 'already sleeping through the night and was much easier on Mum than Prince George.'

So serious were the Cambridges about switching their life to Norfolk, it caught many off guard when, instead of George being enrolled in a London nursery, it was announced that he would be attending a Norfolk school a few days a week, starting in January 2016, the £33-a-day Westacre Montessori school, in East Walton near King's Lynn, a short distance from their home, Anmer Hall. It was another example of the couple putting family first.

Charlotte was christened at the Church of St Mary Magdalene, Sandringham, on Sunday 5 July 2015. She was baptised at the Lily Font by the Archbishop of Canterbury. The princess, wearing the royal christening robe, was taken to church in a Millson pram, previously used for Prince Andrew and Prince Edward, and members of the local community were invited to join in the occasion outside the church. She might be Her Royal Highness Princess Charlotte of Cambridge, but to her mother she would be 'Lottie' and to her devoted father 'Mignonette', which is French for cute little thing.

With the birth of their third child, Prince Louis, at 11.01 a.m. on 23 April 2018, the Cambridge family was complete. He was born weighing 8lb 7oz at St Mary's Hospital, in London. It was later announced that they would name their child Louis Arthur Charles, a nod to Lord Louis Mountbatten, Charles's mentor and great-uncle, who had been murdered by the IRA in 1979, and Charles was touched by the gesture.

A republican self-publicist, shouting at the top of his voice on a megaphone, was loudly booed and drowned out by the cheers of royal fans as Prince William and Catherine emerged on the steps of the maternity wing with their baby, wrapped in a G.H. Hurt & Son shawl. The following day Charles said the birth of his third grandchild was a 'great joy'. He added affectionately, 'The only trouble, is I don't know how I am going to keep up with them.'

Like his brother, Louis would later be baptised in the Chapel Royal at St James's Palace. The little prince was the first royal child to be affected by the change to the ancient, feudal law of male-preference primogeniture, which received royal assent in April 2013 and commenced on 26 March 2015. Absolute primogeniture, for those in the line of succession born after 28 October 2011, means that the eldest child, regardless of sex, precedes any siblings, so male heirs will no longer automatically leapfrog girls. Louis had replaced his uncle Harry as fifth in line to the throne, but, due to the new rules, he was still ranked lower than his sister, Charlotte.

Charles dotes on Louis, who has formed a close bond with his grandfather. In April 2020, Charles's team released a photograph to celebrate Louis's second birthday. The black and white picture, which was posted on the official Clarence House Instagram page, showed the intimate bond between them, with Charles hugging Louis, who cuddled up to his grandfather. The caption read: 'A very Happy Birthday to Prince Louis, who turns two today. The young prince enjoys a hug from his grandfather, The Prince of Wales.' During the late Queen's Platinum Jubilee Pageant, Louis stole the show by pulling faces at his mother Catherine during the long parade. He only behaved himself when he ran to his grandfather and sat on his lap, much to the delight of the photographers and TV cameras.

As the King, Charles plans to honour his granddaughter and the change in hereditary law by granting her the title Duchess of Edinburgh, one of the most senior royal dukedoms in the Royal Family, on her wedding day.[2]

For years it was expected that Charles's brother Prince Edward, Earl of Wessex, the third son of the Queen and Prince Philip, would be granted the rank. It was promised to him. But Charles, determined to reduce the size of the Royal Family, wants such senior titles to be given only to its working members and stop it expanding further. The move by the King to focus on the line of succession is significant, as Charles III plans a modernised, slimmed-down monarchy.

'Edinburgh as capital of Scotland is seen as an important UK city,' said a senior palace source, 'and as the Dukedom of Edinburgh is one of the most important it was felt it should pass to one of the senior members of the Royal Family going forward. Technically by law and practice if Edward was given it, it would mean his son

Viscount Severn would have expected to inherit the title. So when it came up for discussion it was first felt best if it went to Charlotte given that she is third in line to the throne, rather than those on the edges, who in the coming years really won't have any role.'

It is understood, however, that after the exclusive story appeared in the *Mail on Sunday* the King had a change of heart and, not wanting to break a promise made by his late father to Edward, privately agreed that he would grant his youngest brother the title 'Duke of Edinburgh' eventually, with his sixtieth birthday earmarked. The proviso being that the title will revert to the Crown on Edward's death and not pass to his son, Viscount Severn, leaving it free for Charlotte at a future date. The days of rows of royals waving from the palace balcony are over for good.

Following newspaper speculation that he felt edged out by Catherine's parents, Michael and Carole Middleton, Charles began to spend more time with the Cambridges' children, and matters improved. He revealed too that he shares precious moments with his grandson, George, messing around in his garden at Highgrove. 'The most important thing is I got him planting a tree or two,' he said. For a time, there was some friction between father and son, particularly when William felt his father was 'using' George's popularity in what could be perceived as PR opportunities, which baffled Charles as it had not even occurred to him.

During a media day, the prince's PR team revealed how a 'doting' Charles had turned his garden at Highgrove into what was described as a 'toddler's paradise'. It was reported in 2015 that the heir to the throne, whose gardens at his private Gloucestershire home are his life's work, had recently refurbished the tree house once played in by William and Harry for the little prince to inherit. To cap that he had also installed in his wildflower meadow a £20,000 handmade artisan shepherd's hut, complete with a little bed, wood-burner and French oak wooden floors, for George, then two, to enjoy.

Despite his father's good intentions, the fact that this was made public irritated William. He was also reportedly unhappy when photographs of his children even appeared in the background of official photographs of his father without being cleared by him first. 'He can be a bit of a control freak when it comes to things like that,' said one former member of the Royal Household. So it was a little surprising that, for his seventieth-birthday exhibition at the palace – *Prince & Patron*, for which Charles loaned out his favourite artwork, trinkets and family photos to help present a glimpse of his home life – among them was a never-before-seen photograph of him cradling his firstborn grandson, George, with his elder son William by his side.

'Ha, perhaps William is mellowing,' an inside source told me. 'The Prince of Wales would have to have got sign-off on that before allowing it in the exhibition.'

The three future kings look relaxed, with baby George fast asleep in his grandfather's arms. Charles and William are both wearing open-necked shirts, in a casual family photograph likely taken at Clarence House or Kensington Palace in 2013. It was the first time such a candid family photograph of the three direct heirs together had been shown to the public, and obviously would have had to be cleared by the censor – William – to be allowed to be shown.

Another senior household figure said of William, 'He can be difficult. He is a driven person and that can make him impatient. He also does not possess the intellectual capability or the patience of his father.' That can make William short-tempered when dealing with Charles. 'He lacks his father's charm too,' said another. One well-placed source remarked, 'The Boss has a temper, too, but it does not go on and on. He can get frustrated and flare up and then, in an instant, it is forgotten about. With William it is rarely forgotten. He will never say resolving a situation, such as posing for a family portrait for his father's seventieth birthday, is easy. His default position is always, "It's difficult…"'

Charles has always disliked direct confrontation, but fathers and sons rarely see eye to eye when the children are finding their feet as young men. Charles, as a single father, throughout his sons' development tried his best to avoid tension with them. While he expected his sons to be well mannered, he was not a disciplinarian. If a senior aide tried to discuss issues with him about things they did not want to do, he rarely intervened.

It happened to one senior courtier when Charles and his sons were staying at the five-star Walserhof Hotel during a ski trip to Klosters, when they were teenagers. The boys refused to turn the music down as she attempted to talk to them about a media op. When she tried to get Charles to take charge, he just shrugged his shoulders, as if to say, 'they are a law unto themselves'.

The prince did, however, intervene when he felt passionately about something. For example, he clashed with William over his comment about destroying the priceless ivory collection at Buckingham Palace. Charles told William he was being 'naive' during a 'frank exchange of views' five years ago, according to an informed source. He rebuked William for telling the eminent zoologist and chimpanzee expert, Dr Jane Goodall, he would 'like to see all the ivory owned by Buckingham Palace destroyed'. William was left in no doubt after the conversation with his father that he should have chosen his words more carefully.

Charles, while appreciating his son's passion and agreeing with its sentiment, believes there is a vast difference between calling for action against illegal traders now and ordering Buckingham Palace to destroy an enormously important and historical collection of artefacts that form part of the Royal Collection Trust. Items include an Indian throne and footstool (1840–50), carved from ivory and the centrepiece of the Indian section in the Great Exhibition of 1851, and a pair of late-eighteenth-century, seven-storey ivory pagodas acquired by George IV.

The idea of such historic pieces being broken up, along with other items such as Henry VIII's quill pen, filled Charles with dread. That said, there are many who know William and his stubborn streak and believe he will take some form of action when he is king, despite his father's heartfelt protestations.

Unfortunately, due to the poor relationship with his second son Prince Harry and his wife Meghan, Charles has spent hardly any quality time with his other grandchildren, Archie and his sister, Lilibet Diana Mountbatten-Windsor. But those close to him say they are always in his heart. It is one of the reasons he finds the estrangement from his second son so difficult to cope with.

A week after Archie was born in May 2019, Charles had gone to see Harry and Meghan at Frogmore Cottage, and was thrilled as he cradled the baby boy in his arms. But even then, the Sussexes were planning their escape from the Firm. With his wife reportedly suicidal and himself deeply depressed, Harry knew he had to do something. As Christmas 2019 approached, he told his father that he and his wife no longer wished to serve as full-time working royals.

They wanted to come up with a workable plan for them to be part in and part out – splitting their time between the UK and North America. He also said that he and his wife would be heading back to Canada to spend Christmas there, and not with the Queen and the rest of the royals at Sandringham, a place he referred to as 'Hotel Granny'. Harry explained that he wanted to find a satisfactory balance between his private life and his public duties.

Charles, who was used to his son letting off steam periodically, listened but eventually said that his idea was unworkable. He told him to go away and come up with a better plan. They continued to exchange emails, but no plan was forthcoming.

On 8 January, Dan Wootton, then assistant editor of the *Sun*, revealed that Harry and Meghan planned to 'quit the Royals'. The headline writers coined the term 'Megxit' for the banner headline – a slang term for the decision of Meghan and Harry to step back from their senior roles in the British Royal Family – which would later become one of the ten 'Words of 2020' in the *Collins English Dictionary*. Within hours, the Duke and Duchess of Sussex issued a statement that they were looking to 'carve out a progressive new role' for themselves within the monarchy and would divide their time between North America and the UK, confirming Wootton's scoop.

Charles was understandably upset and concerned. Nothing acceptable had been proposed by the couple and certainly nothing had been agreed. The Sussexes staked everything on their belief that, if Charles refused to back them, then the Queen would. It was a punt too far and, as we saw played out, it would backfire spectacularly.

A 'summit' meeting involving the Queen, Charles and William was hastily arranged on 14 January at Sandringham, where Her Majesty was in residence. The Queen was so concerned about privacy that, on taking advice, she had the library where the meeting was to take place swept for bugs. There was a suggestion that Meghan should join them via video link from Canada, but the Queen ruled that her attendance in any form was 'not necessary' as Harry would represent her. The royals also felt it was not secure, as they would not be able to tell who was listening in to the conversation other than Meghan, or whether the meeting was being recorded.

Funding and security for the couple were among the many issues discussed at the summit. It was also agreed that the Sussexes' departure would be subject to a twelve-month review. Ultimately, Harry left the meeting with very little from his and Meghan's wish-list. Queen Elizabeth released a statement that read:

> Today my family had very constructive discussions on the future of my grandson and his family. My family and I are entirely supportive of Harry and Meghan's desire to create a new life as a young family. Although we would have preferred them to remain full-time working members of the Royal Family, we respect and understand their wish to live a more independent life as a family while remaining a valued part of my family. Harry and Meghan have made clear that they do not want to be reliant on public funds in their new lives. It has therefore been agreed that there will be a period of transition in which the Sussexes will spend time in Canada and the UK. These are complex matters for my family to resolve, and there is some more work to be done, but I have asked for final decisions to be reached in the coming days.

For Harry and Meghan, it was a bitter pill. They had made their play and lost. On 31 March, the Sussexes completed their final official engagements before leaving for a new life across the Atlantic. They flew to Canada before making the inevitable move to California, Meghan's home state.

Talk of a private, quiet existence started to unravel almost immediately. In April details emerged of the couple's new foundation, called Archewell, after their son, which was to replace their now-defunct 'Sussex Royal' brand. In May, it emerged that a book about the Sussexes called *Finding Freedom* was to be published, written by journalists Omid Scobie and Carolyn Durand, who were sympathetic to their cause. It was said to have been written with the Sussexes' blessing (although the couple denied it), giving what the authors claimed was an 'accurate version' of the couple's relationship and departure from Britain.

Then, in September, the couple signed a mega multi-million-dollar contract with Netflix to provide 'content that informs but also gives hope'. Ultimately, this deal would produce the controversial docuseries aired in December 2022 and called a 'global television event' by the streaming service. Once it was signed, it was made public that the couple had paid back the £2.4m of taxpayers' money used to renovate Frogmore Cottage, where the couple had lived in the UK before they emigrated

Big commercial deals kept coming and, with each one, increasing cynicism in the UK from the public and media alike. Fleet Street's editors slammed Harry and Meghan as hypocrites and charged them with selling out for a fistful of dollars. Even the previously pro-US media joined in the chorus of disapproval.

Under the headline, 'Hypocrites Meghan and Harry beg for privacy – but are hungry for attention', *New York Post* columnist Maureen Callahan criticised them in an op-ed on 3 October 2020. She wrote:

> It's only been ten months since Prince Harry and Meghan Markle announced they were leaving the British Royal Family in search of 'privacy' – yet they have never been so much in our faces, sanctimoniously and hypocritically telling us how to live and who to vote for, all while signing a reported $100m deal with Netflix. Also, Markle is reportedly eyeing a run for president of the United States in 2024. Yes,

this formerly unknown C-list actress who couldn't hack the cosseted existence of a senior royal, whose entire adult life has been spent in search of a spotlight she now claims to disdain, thinks she has the grit, intellect and real-world experience necessary for the top job.

Harry and Meghan knew they had to change the narrative back in their favour. On 11 February 2021, it was announced that Meghan had won her High Court privacy case after a two-year legal battle with the *Mail on Sunday*, with the judge granting a summary judgment in Meghan's favour over the newspaper's publication of a 'personal and private' handwritten letter from the duchess to her estranged father, Thomas Markle.

In her statement, Meghan spoke of 'illegal and dehumanising practices'. She went on, 'These tactics – and those of their sister publications Mail Online and the *Daily Mail* – are not new... For these outlets, it's a game. For me and so many others, it's real life, real relationships, and very real sadness. The damage they have done and continue to do runs deep.'

Three days later, on Valentine's Day, they had announced that they were expecting another baby. The Queen, Charles and William publicly congratulated them. Then they dropped a bombshell, by confirming they had agreed to be interviewed by Oprah Winfrey on her television show. The announcement came just as the Duke of Edinburgh was being admitted to hospital in central London for what was to be the beginning of his last great fight. He would be dead within weeks, aged ninety-nine.

On 19 February, when Harry and Meghan's departure deal was confirmed, it left the prince in no doubt that he had been cut adrift. He and his wife were stripped of their patronages and Harry, a proud military man, had several honorary titles removed as well, including Captain General of the Royal Marines. In what was widely seen as a cheap shot, the Sussexes released another statement, in which the couple said they 'offered their continued support to the organisations they have represented regardless of official role', ending with a swipe at the royal triumvirate of the Queen, Charles and William, who had moved decisively, by saying 'service is universal'.

Harry seemed unconcerned that Queen Elizabeth and his father would be caught in the crossfire. First, he appeared on *The Late Late Show with James Corden*, claiming he had 'stepped back, not stepped away', because his mental health was being 'destroyed', and insisted that his 'life is public service'. Compared to the Oprah interview, it was tame.

The trailer for Harry and Meghan's interview with Oprah was packed with jaw-dropping soundbites. In one, Harry said his biggest fear was that 'history would repeat itself', a reference to the death of Diana. Then, in another, Oprah asked Meghan how she felt knowing that the Royal Family would be hearing her speak out about them. 'I don't know how they could expect that after all of this time we would still just be silent when there is an active role that the Firm is playing in perpetuating falsehoods about us,' she said. 'And if that comes with [the] risk of losing things… there's a lot that's been lost already.'

When the full interview aired on 7 March 2021, nearly fifty million viewers tuned in. Meghan, at first interviewed without her husband, came out firing in all directions, not seeming to care who she took down, or what the wider implications might be for the Queen, Charles and her husband's estranged family. She claimed that becoming a member of the British Royal Family had left her feeling suicidal.

Then she said that that Archie, their mixed-race son, was not given a princely title due to the colour of his skin. 'In those months when I was pregnant,' she said, 'we have in tandem the conversation of "you won't be given security", "not going to be given a title", and concerns and conversations about how dark his skin might be when he's born.' Oprah did not ask Meghan to back up the veracity of her claims.

When Harry eventually appeared in the hot seat, he contradicted his wife about the timing of the so-called racist comment and her version of what had happened. He went on, 'That conversation, I'm never going to share. But at the time, it was awkward. I was a bit shocked. That was right at the beginning when she wasn't going to get security, when members of my family were suggesting that she carries on acting because there's not enough money to pay for her, and all this sort of stuff.'

When accusations against specific members of the family followed the interview, Harry ruled out his grandmother, the Queen, and his seriously ill grandfather, Prince Philip. But the furore over racism and the royals would have a devastating impact on the monarchy.

Charles was accused by online trolls of making the crass remark about the possible colour of his future grandchild's skin. Camilla, known for her risqué sense of humour and for previously using an inappropriate novelty key ring, also came under scrutiny. For years, however, Charles had moved to improve diversity within his household and, now as King, he has asked William to do the same.

One senior member of the Royal Household dismissed talk of Charles having made a racist comment. 'It goes against everything The Boss [Charles] believes in. He believes diversity is the strength of our society. It is a bit rich coming from Harry, given the prince had to defend him when he was forced to apologise for dressing up in a Nazi uniform and filming himself making a racist remark to a fellow Sandhurst officer cadet from Pakistan back in 2009.'

It was not the first time Harry had been admonished for what he now calls his 'unconscious bias'. When he was a little boy, around eight years old, his mother took him and William for a ride on a London bus as a treat, arranged by her police protection officer, Inspector Ken Wharfe. On the bus, Diana had to tell Harry to stop mimicking the Sikh bus conductor's pronounced Punjabi accent every time a passenger pressed the bell to get off. The conductor, a jovial chap wearing a bright-yellow turban, was relaxed about Harry's casual racism, but Diana was mortified.

The princess was so embarrassed that she eventually told Ken Wharfe to abandon the trip. Diana, Ken, William and Harry all got off at Green Park and Diana immediately smacked Harry and told him, 'Don't you ever do that again.' She was so incensed that she even made Harry write to Inspector Wharfe to apologise for his behaviour and for spoiling the day he had arranged for the boys.

I have spoken to Wharfe, who confirms the incident, and I have also seen the letter, still in his possession, in which Harry jokes about the phrase he used. As he was still a child, I suppose Harry can be forgiven, but it demonstrates clearly that Diana would not tolerate any form of racism from her two sons.

At another moment in the Oprah interview, with echoes of his late mother's BBC *Panorama* interview, in which Diana suggested her husband was not suited to the top job as King, Harry claimed that both William and Charles were 'trapped' by their roles, explaining: 'I was trapped but I didn't know I was trapped. Like the rest of my family are, my father and my brother, they are trapped. They don't get to leave, and I have huge compassion for that. For the family, they very much have this mentality of, this is just how it is. This is how it's meant to be. You can't change it. We've all been through it. What was different for me was the race element, because now it wasn't just about her. It was about what she represented.'[3]

Harry's comments cut Charles and William to the quick. They were deeply upset by Harry's arrogance, furious that he had the audacity to speak about *their* feelings. 'They were both deeply disappointed in him. He had no right or authority to speak on their behalf,' said a senior Royal Household source.

When a reporter shouted out a question asking if he had seen the Oprah interview, Charles, who was wearing a face mask due to the COVID-19 restrictions in operation at the time, chose to say nothing as he departed a visit to a pop-up vaccine clinic in a London church. Two days later, William hit back, albeit spontaneously. During a visit to School 21, a pioneering high school in Stratford, east London, Sky News reporter Inzamam Rashid drew a response from the Duke of Cambridge with his loaded question. William, who was also wearing a face mask, said: 'We're very much not a racist family.' Asked if he had spoken to his brother, he added, 'No, I haven't spoken to him yet, but I will do.'

In the aftermath of the Oprah interview, William went to his father and told him that the Royal Family needed a clear strategy in dealing with the Sussexes, the renegade royals. He became a key figure in the ongoing conversations between the Queen and Charles on how to counter the 'groundless' verbal attacks. Of course, Her Majesty would have the final say, but she needed Charles and William to guide her. What concerned both Charles and his eldest son was Harry's total lack of discretion; neither felt they could fully trust him again and they decided not to meet him alone in future.

The first test of that trust came in 2021, when the two brothers were reunited for the Duke of Edinburgh's funeral on 17 April. Tensions were running high between them at the funeral ceremony in Windsor Castle, which Harry attended without his wife, and their first cousin Peter Phillips walked between them as they followed their grandfather's coffin. After the service in St George's Chapel, Catherine appeared to try acting as peacemaker, but there was no great reconciliation.

Almost three months later, Harry returned for the unveiling of a statue of their mother at Kensington Palace, on what would have been Diana's sixtieth birthday on 1 July 2021. The brothers posted a joint statement: 'Today, on what would have been our mother's sixtieth birthday, we remember her love, strength, and character – qualities that made her a force for good around the world, changing countless lives for the better. Every day, we wish she were still with us, and our hope is that this statue will be seen forever as a symbol of her life and her legacy.'

Again, neither were inclined to engage in any meaningful conversation. Harry made no attempt at a rapprochement with his father either. He returned to Meghan in Montecito, California, under no illusions: he was now an outsider. If anything, the cold shoulder he received from his father and brother only strengthened his resolve.

CHAPTER 19

Last Farewells

You have met us and talked with us. You laugh and cry with us and, most importantly, you have been there for us, for these seventy years.

CHARLES'S SPEECH AT THE END OF THE PLATINUM JUBILEE
CONCERT OUTSIDE BUCKINGHAM PALACE, WHEN HE ADDRESSED
THE QUEEN ON 5 JUNE 2022

As ever, he had walked into King Edward VII's Hospital in London, but, when the Duke of Edinburgh left on 16 March 2021 after twenty-eight days of professional care, his longest ever hospital stay, he was in a wheelchair. He was ninety-nine and still very frail, but he had made it clear to his medical team and Charles, who had visited him in hospital, that he wanted to return to live out his final days at Windsor Castle. As he approached his hundredth birthday, Prince Philip admitted to those around him that life had finally caught up with him and gone was the old gusto that drove him on.

In his last conversation with Charles, hours before he died, the duke retained his blunt sense of humour. When Charles told his father, 'We're talking about your birthday,' he had to repeat himself and speak louder as Philip was now going deaf. 'We are talking about your birthday, and whether there's going to be a reception!'

Philip replied, 'Well, I've got to be alive for it, haven't I?'

Charles said, 'I knew you'd say that!'[1] Sadly, his father died a few hours later at Windsor Castle, on 9 April 2021.

Like so many fathers and sons who both possess sharp minds and for both of whom their forthright beliefs are at their core, the two men had clashed frequently over the years – not on trivial matters, but often on big issues such as organic and genetically engineered food production and how to save the planet. It is understood, however, that Philip and Charles had found much common ground in the old man's twilight years, particularly in the last few months of his life.

'They had both mellowed,' said a well-placed source. 'In recent years they were much more accepting of the other's point of view. They had always loved one another very much – that had never been in question. But there was a deeper respect, and it was growing as time went by. They shared common ground on the future direction of the monarchy, on religious issues – even on the environment. They both believed in interfaith dialogue and that talking openly and honestly can only help strengthen communities and understanding.'

Following months of mounting pressure over Prince Andrew's disastrous television interview in 2019, in which he discussed his friendship with convicted sex offender Jeffrey Epstein and allegations of sexual abuse with an underage girl, Virginia Roberts Giuffre, it was Philip, behind the scenes, who orchestrated the crunch meeting between his two sons at Sandringham. It was also Philip who met with Andrew first – to soften the blow of the news that the Duke of York would have no choice but to step away from royal duties. They knew the situation had to be dealt with decisively, for the sake of the Queen and the monarchy going forward.

One of Charles's circle of friends added, 'The idea that these are two men who spent a lifetime at loggerheads, and that the Princess Royal was the son he wished he'd had, is out of date and wrong.

A much more accurate picture over the last ten years is of two very strong-willed people who came to understand each other's point of view. A father and son who loved each other and enjoyed a relationship of mutual respect and affection. Over the last year of Philip's life, they were the closest that they've ever been.'

Although resting at Windsor, Prince Philip deteriorated further after his period in hospital and his heart operation. But he had vowed never to go back. When the moment came, the duke told his family he would die in his own bed. Being forced as they had to shield together during the COVID-19 lockdowns at the castle and for a time at Balmoral in August, the Queen had spent much more time with her husband, giving her what aides described as a 'new lease of life' in lockdown. The duke had been at her side as she dealt with the fallout of the Sussexes fleeing to Canada and then the USA.

Queen Elizabeth enjoyed the rare opportunity to spend an extended period of quality time with Philip again, cared for by a small team of loyal staff dubbed 'HMS *Bubble*'. They had time to relax and, at last, to live at an appropriate pace for their ages. They were rarely seen in public, although they were pictured together during the surprise wedding of their granddaughter Princess Beatrice on 17 July 2020 to property entrepreneur Edoardo Mapelli Mozzi, at a private ceremony in the Royal Chapel of All Saints at Royal Lodge, Windsor.

Prince Philip made his final public appearance at a ceremony on 22 July 2020, when he handed over the keys of Colonel-in-Chief of The Rifles, a merger of four infantry regiments that was now the largest infantry regiment in the British army, to his daughter-in-law Camilla. Immaculately dressed in a blazer, regimental tie and highly polished brogues, he stood tall in front of the cameras within the walls of Windsor Castle.

Last Farewells

In the final weeks of Philip's life, the Queen became so concerned about her husband's loss of energy and lack of interest in life that she contacted his long-term companion Penny, Countess Mountbatten, wife of Philip's second cousin, the 3rd Earl Mountbatten of Burma, and asked her to join him at the castle.

Penny, thirty-one years Philip's junior, enjoyed a 'highly personal' relationship with the duke spanning many years. She had been so much a part of royal life that household staff nicknamed her 'And Also', because whenever Philip listed guests who were to be invited to a royal event, he would end with 'and also Penny'. Queen Elizabeth was known to have been irritated by the talk of her husband's flirtations, but what mattered to her was Philip's love and his loyalty that, as far as she was concerned, was always unquestioning. She hoped that Penny's presence would help him to regain his 'zest for life'. He did rally, those close to the Queen said, but it was short-lived.

It was no surprise then, when his passing came, that Penny was one of the mourners present, despite the limited numbers due to COVID restrictions. She remains popular at the new King's court and is still invited to royal gatherings, such as the pre-Christmas luncheon for the extended Royal Family that he hosted at Windsor Castle in December 2022.

The relationship between Charles and Philip began to look very much like a partnership towards the end of the old duke's life, as they worked together behind the scenes to support the Queen. A warmth came to the fore and Charles felt that his father finally trusted him to take on his mantle once he was gone. That bond was evident in Charles's televised tribute to his 'dear papa', in which he described his father as a 'much loved and appreciated figure', and a 'very special person'.

His feeling of loss was etched on Charles's face as he led his family at the head of the short funeral procession following Philip's coffin, which was transported to St George's Chapel in the specially modified Land Rover that the duke had designed. His widow Queen Elizabeth broke with royal protocol and followed her family by car, accompanied by her lady-in-waiting Lady Susan Hussey. Charles stood behind his father's coffin next to his sister, the Princess Royal, leading the country in a poignant and powerful tribute to the late Duke of Edinburgh. As the Queen left her car, she briefly looked back at her husband's coffin before heading inside the church with the Dean of Windsor.

Inside the chapel, Her Majesty cut a lonely, isolated figure, sitting several seats apart from other guests due to government COVID-19 restrictions. Visibly moved, Charles was sitting next to Camilla, who squeezed his hand in a loving gesture of support. Throughout his long life, Prince Philip had been a stickler for precision and military detail. Before his death he had laid out specific instructions for his own funeral, codenamed 'Operation Forth Bridge', and it all went to plan, with the minimum of fuss.

At least Charles could be comforted by all the letters the two men had written to each other. It was their way of exchanging views without falling out, often when Charles was away on overseas tours. 'It was a way they shared ideas,' confided a friend.

The prince had his own issues as a father to contend with. In his book *Spare*, Harry reveals that after the funeral Charles stood between his two warring sons and pleaded with them, 'Please, boys, don't make my final years a misery.' The meeting between them in the garden of Frogmore Cottage at Windsor was short and 'painfully tepid', recalls Harry, who admits he was 'nervous' and 'fighting to keep his emotions in check' as he tried to explain his side of things.

Harry was itching to speak to his father, but he felt that

Charles and his brother William had come 'ready for a fight'. He says he was left flabbergasted when his brother told him that he 'honestly' had no idea why Harry had left the country. His father said nothing but his expression, according to Harry, indicated, 'Neither do I.'[2] Charles was not in the mood to listen on the day of his father's funeral. After half an hour they had reached an impasse. Charles wanted time to grieve alone and he headed to his sanctuary, Llwynywermod, his Welsh home adapted from a former model farm in Carmarthenshire, to read and answer letters of condolence.

Yet again Harry returned to the USA having effectively been given the cold shoulder by his close family. Charles wrote that his father's death marked 'the end of an era' and that Prince Philip would be greatly missed by so many people in the UK and around the world. He was touched by the outpouring of love for Philip after his 'memorable lifetime' was over.

The death of his father did not technically change Charles's status; he was still the Prince of Wales and heir to the throne (although he did inherit his father's title, Duke of Edinburgh, albeit briefly until he became King, when the title reverted to the Crown), but it did change the family dynamic. In effect, Charles became the paterfamilias in place of his father, who had been the patriarchal head of the Firm. This is the mantle Charles will now assume. It was a difficult role to take on at a hard time. Charles's siblings took a while to adjust to his new role, particularly Prince Andrew, because it was not easy for them to envisage their elder brother in the same way as they had done their father.

In fact, Charles had been effectively the head of the Royal Family for some time with the decline in the Duke of Edinburgh's health and his retirement from public life. The Queen turned to him more and more, not only to take her place when she was unable to carry out engagements at home and abroad due to her age, but also for advice.

Whenever he was due to host an investiture at Windsor Castle, Charles arranged to stay the night there and have dinner with his mother, instead of returning to Highgrove in Gloucestershire. He appreciated that his mother was also nearing the end of her life, and he wanted to be there for her.

Charles, now fully prepared for the top job, understood that when it came it would mean any overt 'lobbying' would have to be sacrificed. As the time of his reign as monarch approached, he increasingly used his position as a statesman to influence the influencers.

President Donald Trump's state visit in 2019 was a landmark event for Charles and, when Trump breezed into Britain on 3 June, the prince played a central role in all the proceedings as his mother's right-hand man.

It was Charles who strode out confidently, his wife Camilla at his side, to greet the US president and his first lady Melania Trump as they stepped from Marine One in the bright sunshine at Stansted airport. 'Hello, Donald,' he said, stretching out his hand to the president. Trump looked very comfortable with the prince greeting him like an old friend, pulling him in for a close-up handshake that would last a full ten seconds.

Later, Queen Elizabeth officially welcomed the president at Buckingham Palace, before it again fell to Charles to accompany Trump out in the palace garden as he inspected the assembled guard of honour formed by Nijmegen Company, Grenadier Guards, in their splendid scarlet tunics and black bearskins, before the party went back inside for lunch.

That afternoon, the two men had afternoon tea at Clarence House, accompanied by their wives. Charles did not waste his face time with the president and climate change was top of his list of topics to discuss. But the talks were calm and friendly. In an interview with television presenter Piers Morgan, broadcast on the final day of the visit, the president said he had been deeply impressed by Charles's passion for saving the planet for future generations.

Trump said, 'He [Charles] is a very good person who wants to have a world that's good for future generations. That's what impressed me the most, his love for this world. We were going to have a fifteen-minute chat and it turned out to be an hour and a half and he did most of the talking. He is really into climate change, and I think that's great… He wants to make sure future generations have climate that is good climate as opposed to a disaster. And I agree.'

Asked whether he was able to give Charles 'comfort' that he was taking climate change seriously, he replied, 'I think I was, yes.'[3]

President Trump's state visit proved a triumph for Charles. No one would be impolite enough to use the word 'handover', but his central role was a defining moment for him. With so many of his views, on everything from climate change and food production to dialogue with the Muslim world, diametrically opposed to those held by President Trump, Charles took a significant step by demonstrating that when he became King he would put duty and country first.

The days of personal protest, such as his famous boycotting of a state banquet in honour of Jiang Zemin in 1999 – a decision motivated by his admiration for the Dalai Lama, Tibet's exiled leader, whom the Chinese regard as a dangerous separatist – have been over for some time. He may still be a 'dissident at heart', but he is a king to the core.

As more royal records toppled, with Elizabeth II becoming the first British monarch in history to mark her Platinum Jubilee, it fell on Charles as her liegeman to lead the celebrations. Frail and, it is understood, stricken with a form of myeloma (bone marrow cancer),[4] Queen Elizabeth did her very best to avoid letting anyone down, but she increasingly had to rely on her son and heir to take the lead. Palace officials tried to play down her immobility issues, but that was becoming harder to justify. The fact remained that she was having to use a wheelchair, and, like her late husband before he died, she did not want to be seen using it.

On 23 May, Her Majesty made her annual visit to the Chelsea Flower Show in London. This time, however, she arrived at the event in a special buggy to tour the gardens and exhibits. Before her attendance, she had a disagreement with her grandson, William, who defied her wishes by taking a helicopter flight to Norfolk with all his immediate family. She had warned him against flying with his eldest son and heir George, in case of an accident, because he always had to be aware of the succession.

The Queen had been locked in discussions with William and Charles about her errant grandson Harry after he quit royal life. Queen Elizabeth was at first mystified by Harry and Meghan's behaviour. She described it as 'quite mad' and said she believed Harry was 'so consumed' by his love for his wife that it was 'clouding his judgement'. In fact, the Queen also admitted to someone in her close circle that when Meghan was introduced she did not fully appreciate her heritage as a biracial woman, because she had not been briefed.

Not that it would have caused her any concern. The impeccable household source added, 'Her late Majesty was the oldest, longest-reigning, most travelled British monarch ever. She met and forged friendships with men and women of all faiths and different ethnicities and colours in her role as Head of the Commonwealth.'

The Queen felt let down by the Sussexes. She was not only disappointed in Harry's decision to abandon his royal duty, but she also saw their departure as a missed opportunity. She was wearied by the volatile exchanges during which Harry claimed it had been 'terrifying' to have William 'scream and shout' at him and his father lie in front of the Queen.[5] He also spoke of the 'wedge' between him and William and being disappointed that his brother was 'now on the institution's side'. When stories appeared in the press about William allegedly treating Meghan badly and 'bullying' his brother, the palace released a joint statement from both princes denying the claims.

'No one asked me for permission to put out a statement like that,' Harry said. 'Within four hours they were happy to lie to protect my brother and yet for three years they were never willing to tell the truth to protect us.'[6]

Queen Elizabeth, like Charles, warmly welcomed Meghan into the Royal Family. She was pleased that Harry had at last found love. She also felt, when she discovered that Meghan was a woman of colour, that she would be a great asset to a modern Royal Family and to her vision of the Commonwealth. She envisaged that Meghan's Black heritage and her confident presentation skills, which she had honed as an actress, would see her hailed as a great champion for young women as she worked alongside Harry in his role as a Youth Ambassador with the Commonwealth Youth Programme.

Indeed, Harry had invited his then wife-to-be to share the job with him and she was said to be 'hugely excited about it'. Within months of the Queen's death, however, the couple released their documentary that branded the Commonwealth, Her late Majesty's legacy, as 'Empire 2.0'.[7]

The Queen hoped that her grandson, having decided to live in Canada and then California, would find peace and happiness living the life he had chosen. But Harry was regularly trying to contact his grandmother and, in the end, she asked him to speak directly to his father. A source said, 'Her Majesty found Prince Harry's calls quite difficult and wearisome. She didn't want to interfere in the father/son relationship and would urge him to speak to his father.' Charles stopped taking the calls, however, after his son had sworn at him and repeatedly asked for funds in their tense calls. When the Queen asked him why, Charles told her that he was not a bank.

The Queen also had to contend with her favourite son, Andrew, who had sunk into a depression after being stripped of his royal patronage and military associations over his friendship with the paedophile Jeffrey Epstein, who had killed himself in jail; ultimately he settled out of court with Virginia Roberts Giuffre[8] over claims that he sexually assaulted her on three occasions when she was seventeen, allegations he has repeatedly denied. Andrew had been constantly asking his mother for a way back into public life. But it wore the monarch down.

The Queen did meet Harry and Meghan at Windsor Castle when they had a stopover in April 2022, en route to Holland for his Invictus Games. She agreed to see him on the proviso that he met and talked to his father too. The couple were welcomed warmly by the Queen, in what turned out to be the last time Harry saw his grandmother. Charles was also at the castle – along with Camilla – where he was standing in for his mother at the annual Maundy Thursday service. To add insult to injury, Harry and Meghan turned up late, meaning the meeting lasted less than fifteen minutes.

In the spirit of reconciliation, it was agreed that the Sussexes should join the rest of the Royal Family for the Queen's Platinum Jubilee. As non-working royals, there were restrictions. They were left in no doubt that the Netflix film crew accompanying them for their docuseries would not be allowed access to royal palaces or members of the family. Nevertheless, when the couple arrived at St Paul's Cathedral on 3 June for the National Service of Thanksgiving for the Queen (which she could not attend), some in the large crowd outside booed them.

The celebrations to honour the monarch for her Platinum Jubilee culminated in a four-day bank holiday weekend on 2–5 June. It included everything from street parties across the country to Trooping the Colour and a star-studded concert led by Diana Ross, as well as a final balcony appearance by the Queen herself. But she was not strong enough to make them all.

Charles paid tribute to his mother at the BBC's *Platinum Party at the Palace*, where he began his address, 'Your Majesty, Mummy.' Thanking her for a 'lifetime of selfless service', he told her during the televised concert, 'You continue to make history.' Referring to the Queen's absence from the celebrations, after she was said to have experienced 'some discomfort' during Trooping the Colour two days earlier, he said, 'We might have been celebrating that Derby winner this evening… next year, perhaps?' Then, addressing the crowd, he added, 'But I know what really gets my mother up in the morning is all of you – watching at home. Represented here tonight in this great audience.'

Behind the scenes, the Queen had been feeling very frail. Her doctors said the earlier appearances on Thursday, when she took the salute and watched the fly-past during the Trooping the Colour ceremony, and her second appearance later that day as she triggered the lighting of the principal Jubilee beacon at Windsor Castle, had taken their toll. Her Majesty had previously filmed the highly acclaimed TV sketch of a computer-generated Paddington Bear taking afternoon tea with her and thanking her 'for everything'.

Charles felt it was imperative, for history, that the Queen acknowledge the crowds with a wave from the Buckingham Palace balcony at the end of the jubilee celebrations. He implored her to make the appearance and a military-style exercise was put in place to ensure – on her insistence – that she made it without being seen in public or by the press in the wheelchair she had to use.

Ever the stalwart, and in considerable discomfort, Her Majesty was taken by wheelchair to the helicopter pad at Windsor and, after it landed at the palace, taken again by wheelchair right to the balcony door, before being helped to her feet so that she could stand alongside the other royals. It took real strength and courage for her to do so. She wore a vibrant Stewart Parvin outfit, an emerald double crêpe wool dress and coat, adorned with the Bow Brooch, finished off with a Rachel Trevor-Morgan hat with a black pompom, pearl jewellery and white gloves, so that she could be seen by the cheering crowd.

Bravely holding on to her walking stick, the Queen stood on the balcony alongside Charles and Prince George, flanked by William and Catherine, Charlotte, Louis and Camilla. After the family and the flag-waving crowd packed along The Mall sang 'God Save the Queen' enthusiastically, and a display of red, white and blue fireworks was launched from the stage on the Victoria Memorial, Queen Elizabeth II smiled with delight.

It was to be her final salute to her people.

CHAPTER 20

Destiny

You only have to look at Shakespeare's plays, Henry V *or*
Henry IV Parts I *and* II, *to see the change that can take place*
because if you become the sovereign, then you play the role in
the way that it is expected.

CHARLES INVOKING THE TALES OF SHAKESPEARE,
IN WHICH THE WAYWARD PRINCE HAL TRANSFORMS INTO
THE HEROIC KING HENRY V, WHEN ASKED ABOUT THE
TRANSITION OF THE CROWN[1]

The official statement on the Royal Family website, alongside a
black and white portrait of the Queen, was posted at 6.30 p.m.
It read simply, 'The Queen died peacefully at Balmoral this
afternoon. The King and The Queen Consort will remain at
Balmoral this evening and will return to London tomorrow.'
Her late Majesty's death certificate, made public later, recorded
that the Queen died at 3.10 p.m. on 8 September in Balmoral
Castle, at the age of ninety-six. There were subsequent reports that
the prime minister Liz Truss, whom the monarch had met for the
kissing hands ceremony only two days earlier, had been privately
notified at 4.30 p.m. by Simon Case, her most senior civil servant.

The Princess Royal, who had been at her mother's side when
she passed away, gave the information to the authorities about
the Queen's death. The only other people in the room were King

Charles, the Queen Consort Camilla, and Her late Majesty's apothecary Dr James Glass, who had treated the Queen for more than thirty years. For 'occupation' of the deceased, the official form said, 'Her Majesty the Queen'. Her cause of death was recorded as 'old age', thus maintaining the curtain of privacy around the Queen's health that she had been afforded in her final years.

Her loyal aide, Angela Kelly, had the job of collecting the Queen's possessions, including her priceless jewellery. She brought them with her to Windsor, where Kelly lives, and handed them to a senior member of the King's staff.

The following day the new King and his wife returned to Buckingham Palace, where he was touched by the reaction of people in the crowd, who applauded and cheered him during a twelve-minute walkabout outside the gates, with several shouting 'God bless you, Charles' and 'God save the King'. Flanked by his vigilant Scotland Yard protection officers, he stopped to speak to some of the people who had waited to greet him. One woman, Jenny Assiminios, from Cyprus, even hugged Charles and kissed him on the cheek as he stopped in front of her, but the new monarch appeared unconcerned and took it in his stride. Before walking through the palace gates, the royal couple went to look at the bouquets of flowers laid to honour the late Queen.

In a nod to modern times, for the first time in history the proclamation was broadcast on live television; at 10 a.m. on 10 September, Charles was proclaimed King before the Accession Council in the red-carpeted Throne Room at St James's Palace. Years earlier, he had seriously considered the idea of using another of his names and becoming King George VII, and even had the documents drawn up, but he changed his mind.[2] At the ceremony, the King gave a short speech to accept the role of sovereign, saying, 'It is my most sorrowful duty to announce to you the death of my beloved mother, the Queen. I know how deeply you, the entire nation – and I think I may say the whole world – sympathise with me in the irreparable loss we have all suffered.'

By now the King was clearly fatigued and his short temper beginning to show, as he was seen on camera signalling irritably towards his private secretary, Sir Clive Alderton, to move a box for his pen and an ink pot, a gift from his sons, from the small desk where he signed the proclamation documents. These were then witnessed by William and Camilla, his two gatekeepers and most loyal lieutenants.[3]

At 11 a.m. the Garter King of Arms, David Vines White, stepped out to a trumpet fanfare from the Friary Court balcony at St James's, with gun salutes fired in Hyde Park and at the Tower of London, and began the proclamation ritual. As is convention, a second proclamation would be read at the Royal Exchange in the City of London at 12 p.m. and further proclamations took place over the coming days when the King travelled to Scotland, Wales and Northern Ireland.

In Belfast, the King would show his frustration once again when signing the visitors' book at Hillsborough Castle. After being told that he had signed the wrong date, his fountain pen started to leak, causing him to complain, 'Oh, God, I hate this [pen].' He then walked out of the room, rubbing ink from his fingers and mumbling, 'I can't bear this bloody thing... every stinking time.'

On 12 September, Charles addressed both MPs from the Commons and peers from the House of Lords in Westminster Hall for the first time as monarch. In a poignant speech from the gilded lectern, he said his beloved mother had 'set an example of selfless duty which, with God's help and your counsels, I am resolved faithfully to follow.' He went on, 'As Shakespeare said of the earlier Queen Elizabeth, she was a pattern to all princes living. As I stand before you today, I cannot help but feel the weight of history which surrounds us and which reminds us of the vital parliamentary traditions to which members of both Houses dedicate yourselves with such personal commitment, for the betterment of us all.'

The King looked deeply emotional as the Commons Speaker, Sir Lindsay Hoyle, expressed his condolences, and said, 'Deep as our grief is, we know yours is deeper.' He also seemed close to tears as the hundreds of dignitaries then stood for the national anthem for the first rendition of 'God Save the King' for seventy years.

Amid all the family grieving, on 10 September William and Harry had called a truce in their bitter dispute and put on a show of unity at Windsor to view the floral tributes at the castle, after William invited his brother and Meghan to join him and Catherine there. Harry and Meghan held hands together before all four of them walked forward to greet the crowds. For the cameras, at least, it was as if they had slipped straight back into being the so-called Fab Four again. Nothing could be further from the truth, as close sources have confirmed: Catherine later admitted to a senior royal that it was one of the hardest things she ever had to do, such was the ill feeling between the two couples.

Next day, the Princess Royal and her husband Vice-Admiral Sir Tim Laurence accompanied the Queen's coffin by hearse in the funeral cortège of seven vehicles on the 170-mile, six-hour long procession to Edinburgh from Balmoral Castle, where the coffin had been resting in the ballroom. Thousands of people packed the streets to watch it pass before it went on public view.

The convoy of cars made its way through the small villages of Ballater and Aboyne in the heart of Deeside. On the way, Scottish farmers paid their respects by lining the procession route with dozens of tractors; some had their front loaders raised in salute as the Queen's coffin passed by them. After a stunning route that also took in the Forth River and Edinburgh's Royal Mile, the coffin was carried by a guard of honour into the Palace of Holyroodhouse, the official residence of the monarchy in Scotland. Princess Anne dropped a curtsey to Elizabeth II's coffin as the oak casket was carried into the palace.

The following afternoon, a bagpipe lament was the only sound as kilted soldiers from the Royal Regiment of Scotland bore the casket from the palace, and then a gun salute boomed out from a battery on Edinburgh Castle as the hearse moved off on its way up the Royal Mile. A single round was fired each minute of the procession as the royal party walked to St Giles's Cathedral, where Her Majesty's coffin would remain for twenty-four hours.

King Charles and his siblings, Anne, Andrew and Edward, held a silent vigil at the side of their mother Queen Elizabeth's coffin as it lay at rest in Edinburgh's historic cathedral, with thousands queuing for hours to pay their respects to Britain's longest-serving monarch. With his head bowed, Charles, wearing a kilt, stood solemnly for ten minutes next to the oak coffin, draped with the Royal Standard of Scotland with a wreath of white flowers and the Crown of Scotland. Then the late Queen's four children left the cathedral to applause from onlookers.

Her late Majesty was then taken from Scotland to England by RAF C-17 plane, accompanied by the Princess Royal and Tim Laurence. When the plane carrying her coffin landed at London's RAF Northolt, her daughter Anne issued a moving tribute to her mother, saying she was 'fortunate' to be able to share 'the last twenty-four hours of my dearest mother's life', adding, 'It has been an honour and a privilege to accompany her on her final journeys. Witnessing the love and respect shown by so many on these journeys has been both humbling and uplifting.'

Her late Majesty's family witnessed the arrival of her coffin at

Buckingham Palace, which she had affectionately called the office. There it lay for one night in the Bow Room, a circular room with full-length windows and marble columns in between each bay, before the family finally handed the monarch back to her people for them to pay their last respects at Westminster Hall, where she would lie in state for four days as more than 250,000 people queued for many hours to view the late Queen's coffin, draped in the Royal Standard.

What followed was a spectacle like no other, a demonstration of British military precision and pageantry, heralding the end of an era and the passing of the most beloved Queen. The heart of a family and a nation may have been broken, but her devoted people were determined to give their late sovereign the most rousing of send-offs.

The state funeral was held at 11 a.m. on Monday, 19 September at Westminster Abbey, filled with 2,000 VVIPs, with royals and their foreign cousins, presidents and prime ministers, in the biggest gathering of world leaders in a generation, as well as Britons selected by the Queen for their contribution to society.

After the poignant service, sombre crowds filled The Mall, Whitehall and Parliament Square and watched as her coffin was carried from the Abbey by a gun carriage that dated back to Queen Victoria's reign. An estimated two million well-wishers then lined the streets as the cortège drove from west London to Windsor, where thousands more waited to pay their respects as the coffin was conveyed along the Long Walk to the Castle.

The final service, in St George's Chapel at Windsor Castle, was private, for members of the Royal Family only. Afterwards, the Queen's coffin was borne to its final resting place in the King George VI Memorial Chapel, an annexe to the chapel. It was commissioned by the Queen in 1962, in line with her late father's wishes. There,

Destiny

Her Majesty joined her father, mother and sister Margaret. Prince Philip, whose casket had been in the Royal Vault since his funeral in 2021, was later moved to lie beside his wife in the chapel.[4]

The new stone now contains, in list form, 'George VI 1895–1952' and 'Elizabeth 1900–2002' followed by a metal Garter Star, and then 'Elizabeth II 1926–2022' and 'Philip 1921–2021'. All four royals were members of the Order of the Garter, which has St George's Chapel as its spiritual home. The stone is made of hand-carved Belgian black marble with brass letter inlays, to match the previous ledger stone.

The funeral of Elizabeth II was watched by an estimated 4.1 billion people globally. It was the biggest television audience in history.

King Charles's moment of destiny had arrived. His devoted wife never doubted his courage and conviction. Asked whether she thought her husband's future as king weighed heavily on his shoulders, she once replied, 'No, I don't. I think his destiny will come, he's always known it's going to come, and I don't think it does weigh on his shoulders at all. It's just something that's going to happen.'[5]

She was right, for when his moment came Charles rose to it and the people agreed. A YouGov/*Times* survey taken after the Queen's funeral in September 2022 showed that attitudes towards the new King had already shifted substantially. Of those asked, 63 per cent said they thought Charles would do a good job as monarch, markedly up on polls taken when he was heir to the throne, and 73 per cent said he provided good leadership.

Only Harry's constant televised complaints threatened to upset the harmony of the new reign. With each interview, he made the chances of healing any rift with his father, which he claimed he wanted, look even less likely. Ahead of publication of his book

Spare in January 2023, Harry gave another interview in which he once again complained about the press and palace officials, without taking any responsibility himself for the breakdown in relations with his family.

He told Tom Bradby, the ITN news anchor and his go-to friendly UK journalist: 'It never needed to be this way. The leaking and the planting [of stories]. I want a family, not an institution. They feel as though it is better somehow to keep us as the villains. They've shown absolutely no willingness to reconcile. I would like to get my father back. I would like to have my brother back.'

Harry's dwelling on his version of the past has left many senior members of the Royal Family cold. He told US broadcast journalist Anderson Cooper, son of heiress Gloria Vanderbilt, on CBS' *60 Minutes*, that every time he tried to meet his family privately there had been 'briefings and leakings and planting of stories about me and my wife. You know the family motto is never complain, never explain, but it's just a motto. There's been a lot of complaining and a lot of explaining... being done through leaks.'

He claimed the palace press office would protect other royals but would not do it for him and his wife. 'There comes a point when silence is betrayal,' he said.

In fact, Charles instructed a wall of silence about the Netflix docuseries and his son's book *Spare*, not wanting to dignify some of the elaborate claims. One senior figure said, 'Some blame Meghan Markle for the fallout, ignoring the fact that Harry seems to be the driving force in everything that happened. There was a point when officials joked Harry was the victim of Stockholm syndrome, and he was Meghan's hostage, but now most just feel Harry has turned his back on everything he has known.' Either way it has left Charles torn between love and duty and deeply saddened.

The idea of stripping Harry, and therefore Meghan too, of his title the Duke of Sussex has been discussed at the highest level. The King is said not to be in favour of it, but other senior royals are less indulgent. Only time will tell.

Throughout his working life, Charles has striven to make a real difference and to enlighten others. He has championed organic farming and spoken up for sustainable urbanism, emphasising the need for local character to be preserved. He has encouraged a more balanced approach to business and healthcare and a more benign holistic approach to science and technology.

In doing so, he has placed himself in the firing line and faced widespread criticism for daring to challenge the current orthodoxy and the conventional way of thinking. However, what he has been revealing is that these areas are totally interrelated, and we must see what he often calls 'the big picture' to appreciate the problems that we all, as humanity, face.

Despite his considerable wealth and resources, Charles devoted his entire life as the Prince of Wales to service and duty, supporting the late Queen in her role as head of state as well as being an incredibly successful global philanthropist. His Prince's Trust, the charity that he founded in 1976 to help young people forge careers, and get access to education and training, has also guided more than 90,000 entrepreneurs to start their own businesses.

Now he is King, as he wrote in a private letter in 1993, Charles is 'entirely motivated by a desperate desire to put the "Great" back into Great Britain.' Those close to him are confident he will not be suffocated by the limitations and restrictions of the role of the top job, and will continue to support causes that he believes in. He will not be so outspoken, and will be guided by the relevant ministers, but he will use his convening powers to bring influential people together to address the big issues of the day.

King Charles, on his accession, inherited his mother's considerable wealth alongside assets belonging to the Crown. The monarch's largest land and property holdings are managed by the Crown Estate and include properties in areas of central London such as Regent Street and St James's, as well as farmland, offices and retail parks around the country. Since 1760, the estate's net income has been handed to the government in return for a fixed annual payment, now called the Sovereign Grant.

The grant for 2021–22 was set at £86.3m and is used to fund official travel, property maintenance and the operating costs of the King's household. In addition, he gets private income from the Duchy of Lancaster and property he personally owns. The duchy had nearly £653m of net assets under its control at the end of March 2022, which provided a net surplus of £24m to the monarch, at the time Queen Elizabeth.

These funds pay for the smooth running of the monarchy and the extended Royal Family. In the first one hundred days of his reign, Charles deliberately did not make major changes to the way the Royal Household operates, but those close to him say it is only a matter of time. After the coronation he is expected to start making efficiency savings. As it stands, his old Clarence House staff have been merged with the veritable army of the late Queen's household. He and the Queen Consort, insiders say, have already noted it is 'top heavy'.

'Some of Her late Majesty's team are already finding the King's way of doing things challenging. When he says he wants something done, he expects it to be acted on immediately,' said one insider. 'Those who worked for the late Queen and in the last reign are finding that when they say, "But that's how we have always done it," it won't wash.'

As the King has so many more responsibilities, he has turned to the Queen Consort to start the ball rolling over the staff merger and she has already begun making subtle changes where she sees fit. Informed sources say there were raised eyebrows when it emerged that the Master of the King's Household, Vice-Admiral Sir 'Tony' Johnstone-Burt, who held the same position under the late Queen and runs below-stairs operations, had produced a 'mission statement' for household staff. Every worker was handed a document that read: 'One Team, One Standard'. 'It makes working for the Royal Household very corporate, like a hotel,' one aide said. The motto may be one of the many things to change in the coming months.[6]

Charles showed his tolerance and forgiveness at his first family Christmas at Sandringham. Among those invited to the festive lunch and traditional Boxing Day pheasant shoot was Andrew's ex-wife and champion, Sarah Ferguson. It was her first invitation for decades and came after she and the Queen Consort had forged an unlikely friendship. Sources say the two women have grown very close. Whether that hand of forgiveness will be extended to Harry and Meghan remains to be seen, as it may be an even harder road back.

In time, I believe, history will be kind to King Charles III. His reign will probably be short, in contrast to the longest wait to attain it, and, as a result, in historical terms his time on the throne may not be a remarkable one.[7]

His contribution to the world during his working lifetime, however, certainly has been remarkable. His legacy, whether as prince or as king, will be as a royal philosopher, property developer and artist, a courageous man prepared to take risks for what he sees as the greater good, and an unselfish and unflinching advocate for peace and global sustainability. During his stewardship as Prince of Wales, the scope and diversity of the prince's work was wide-ranging, from state occasions through to work supporting the military, not to mention communities of every faith and of every ethnic origin, helping to bind all people together as a single United Kingdom.

According to an independent study in 2017, the prince had contributed £1.4bn of value to society in the previous decade alone. His charities raised £170m in a year, a figure they have achieved repeatedly. On the environment, he practises what he preaches, with his household recording that 85 per cent of its energy now comes from renewable sources, including all its electricity.

Despite all this devotion to duty, some still dismiss Charles as a pampered, over-opinionated hypocrite, who has his elevated wealth and status only through the good fortune of his birth. If one chooses to ignore the facts about the man, it is easy enough to argue that point. After all, as heir to the throne Charles had a personal staff of over 120, a figure perhaps more suited to a Tudor monarch than a modern-day, pared-down prince. Prince William has already started streamlining his own team and has gone on record saying that as heir to the throne he will ultimately employ far fewer people on his staff, once he has had a chance to assess the needs of a modern monarchy.

When the time comes to evaluate Charles's legacy, one must examine his public role in its entirety, not just as King. For it is his role as a pioneer for which he should be best remembered. As King, he has already encountered some frustrations. The work can be 'rubber-stamping' his government's decisions, rather than making a real difference.

His first, albeit short-lived, prime minister Liz Truss effectively stopped him attending the COP 27 conference in Sharm El-Sheikh, Egypt, despite officials claiming he was never planning to go. Charles only discovered via the media he was not going, when it was reported that Downing Street felt it was not the 'right occasion' for him to attend and it was 'unanimously agreed'. Buckingham Palace officials played down any suggestion of a conflict, saying the move was made on the government's advice and was 'entirely in the spirit of being ever-mindful as King that he acts on government advice'. In truth, the way it was handled irked him considerably.

The monarch, a veteran campaigner on environmental issues, had been invited to the 27th UN climate change conference and it was even listed that he would make the second speech. Ahead of the conference, on 4 November, he hosted a reception for business figures at Buckingham Palace, and Charles had the last laugh when he welcomed more than 200 guests, including his new prime minister Rishi Sunak, the first British Asian to hold the position, who reversed his own decision to skip the UN climate change meeting.

Even as King he has already shown his convening power, hosting many Buckingham Palace receptions, sometimes twice a day, to honour those who have contributed to our society, from Olympians to small business owners. Those close to him say he will do his best to find ways to advance society and will continue to give a platform to those who share his beliefs.

Now that he is King, he is still behind a global sustainability revolution to make world leaders – indeed all of us – think more deeply about how we are treating nature and our planet, and to understand that our lifestyles must change for the sake of future generations. More than anyone, Charles has led the charge in altering how people think and increasing recognition that, as he would say, 'Right action cannot happen without right thinking.'

In a clear sign that the King wants to use his position to benefit society wherever possible, particularly with regard to sustainability, in January 2023 he gave up the opportunity to benefit from a £1bn-a-year windfall from a major expansion of green energy. Mindful of the cost-of-living crisis facing the UK, he asked Rishi Sunak's government to change the way the monarchy is funded in order to ensure that the extra revenue from six new offshore wind farm projects, which was estimated to bring the Crown Estate an extra £250m annually and almost quadruple his current income from the taxpayer, is used for the 'wider public good' instead.

The wind farm projects – three in the North Sea off the Yorkshire and Lincolnshire coast and three off North Wales, Cumbria and Lancashire – are expected to bolster Britain's efforts to reach net zero greenhouse gas emissions by 2050. It shows Charles's determination as the King to still have a positive influence on the areas which he has been passionate about all his life.

He will also continue to travel overseas on behalf of his government, with planned state visits to our pre-eminent European neighbours France and Germany planned for the spring ahead of his coronation. He is expected to visit the realm of Canada, where he remains King, in the autumn of 2023.

In King Charles III, we are blessed to have a monarch of high intelligence, vision and drive. He is a deep-thinking, spiritual man, not cynical but intuitive and instinctive. He cares very strongly about the world and environment we live in, today and for the future. He may have been born into huge wealth and privilege, but he has always tried his best to justify that good fortune by working to improve the lot of others.

Speaking from the Quire of St George's Chapel, Windsor, in his first Christmas Day message – the first by a king to be televised – Charles spoke of his late mother's belief in the power of the 'everlasting light' that was an essential part of her faith in God, but also in people, which he said he shared 'with all his heart'. He also spoke of his strong support for people of all faiths, as well as for those without religious beliefs.

In a nod to the cost-of-living crisis in the UK, he went on, 'And at this time of great anxiety and hardship – be it from those around the world facing conflict, famine or natural disaster, or for those at home finding ways to pay their bills and keep their families fed and warm – we see it in the humanity of people throughout our nations and the Commonwealth who so readily respond to the plight of others.'

In what was seen as a political intervention at a time when nurses were taking industrial action over their pay and conditions, he also praised the selfless NHS workers. He said, 'I particularly want to pay tribute to all those wonderfully kind people who so generously give food or donations, or that most precious commodity of all – their time – to support those around them in the greatest need, together with the many charitable organisations which do such extraordinary work in the most difficult circumstances.'

He concluded, 'While Christmas is, of course, a Christian celebration, the power of light overcoming darkness is celebrated across the boundaries of faith and belief. So whatever faith you have, or whether you have none, it is in this life-giving light, and with true humility that lies in our service to others, that I believe we can find hope for the future. Let's celebrate together and cherish it always.'

His first Christmas Day message attracted the highest viewing figures this century for the monarch's traditional festive address, with a combined audience of 10.7 million. Just ahead of the message being broadcast, the King announced that he was also giving money donated in memory of Queen Elizabeth to the Fuel Bank Foundation charity, helping people who were unable to pay their fuel bills. The Fleet Street headlines that followed dubbed him the 'Caring King'.

Charles plans to turn Buckingham Palace, the residence of British sovereigns since 1837, into more of a 'people's palace', as well as his office. While in London, the King will continue to live at Clarence House and travel to the palace daily to work, but he also wants it to be used for more national celebrations. Neither Charles nor Camilla is in any rush to move in permanently until the £369m renovations there are nearing completion.

In the early days of his reign, Charles has been spending two or three days a week at Windsor Castle, where he uses his father's old rooms. Meanwhile William, whose family has moved to Adelaide Cottage[8] in Windsor Home Park, has also investigated the idea of taking a wing of the castle for his staff and possibly as residential quarters later.

Two separate meaningful conversations I have had with Charles have helped greatly to shape my understanding of the man. On 10 April 2018, at a reception at Government House in Darwin, the final engagement of the visit, the two of us had another, much shorter exchange.

Vicki O'Halloran, administrator of Australia's Northern Territory, escorted Charles, and I was formally introduced to the prince, as is the custom, even though we both knew perfectly well who the other was.

I informed him how well he personally, and the monarchy as an institution, had fared in a poll that day in *The Australian* newspaper. It reported my comment that support for the monarchy Down Under was at an eighteen-year high. Perhaps I should have known better. The prince merely smiled, then shrugged his shoulders. 'Polls mean nothing to me,' he said, before looking me straight in the eye and adding, 'You see, I'm in it for the long term.'

In September 2018, shortly before my first biography of Charles was published, I was invited to a dinner at Dumfries House, the eighteenth-century Palladian country house west of Cumnock in Ayrshire, Scotland, designed by the architects John and Robert Adam and Robert Weir Schultz, which he helped to save from ruin in 2007. At a reception afterwards, I asked Charles, who is an excellent watercolourist, if he was still painting. As we waited for the piper to play, he pondered for a second or two, before looking at me and replying, with a touch of regret, 'I haven't got time.'

It was, perhaps, a metaphor for his life; for our King, who was after all the longest-serving heir to the British throne and is the oldest man ever to become sovereign, at seventy-three years and 298 days.[9]

Charles has always been a man in a hurry. He knows, as he said to me that evening in Scotland, that for him the clock is ticking.

Appendix

The coronation of King Charles III will take place on Saturday, 6 May 2023 at Westminster Abbey in London, and will be conducted by the Archbishop of Canterbury, whose task this has been almost always since the Norman Conquest in 1066. The current Archbishop is the Most Reverend and Right Honourable Justin Welby. Buckingham Palace has also confirmed that the Queen Consort will be crowned alongside the King. The service will be followed by a series of events over the Coronation Weekend, which includes an extra bank holiday on Monday, 8 May, so that members of the public around the United Kingdom can join together to celebrate this historic occasion.

During the solemn ceremony, Charles III will be crowned with St Edward's Crown, as was his late mother Queen Elizabeth II on 2 June 1953. It was removed from the Tower of London in December 2022 to be resized for the King's coronation. The centrepiece of the Crown Jewels has also been taken for some modification work ahead of the historic ceremony. He will wear the Imperial State Crown during the service, but it is understood that the event will be very different to his mother's service and will reflect the King's vision for a slimmed-down, more modern monarchy.

At its heart a coronation, is an Anglican service, but the ceremony also combines aspects of Britain's unwritten constitution as well as pomp and pageantry. King George V wore the cap of state, his robes, and a tunic and breeches for his arrival at Westminster Abbey in June 1911. Charles's grandfather George VI arrived in a similar outfit for his crowning in 1937. Charles is expected to ditch the breeches in his smaller, less formal ceremony and to arrive in military unform.

There will be a state carriage procession, known as 'The King's Procession', from Buckingham Palace to Westminster Abbey, followed by another procession inside, then the Recognition, the Anointing, the Coronation Oath, the Homage and finally 'The Coronation Procession' back to Buckingham Palace. Their Majesties will then appear on the palace balcony accompanied by members of the Royal Family.

The only part of the Coronation ceremony that is required legally is the Coronation Oath, when the King swears to govern the people of the United Kingdom and the Commonwealth Realms 'according to their respective laws and customs'.

The UK government pays for the coronation as it is classed a state event, but its organisation involves input from government ministers, the Royal Household, the Church of England and the Commonwealth Realms. A Privy Council 'Coronation Committee' oversaw the planning for this special occasion, and its Executive Committee was chaired by the Earl Marshal, a hereditary royal office holder and chivalric title. The current duke, a Roman Catholic, is Edward Fitzalan-Howard, 18th Duke of Norfolk. To encourage celebration, the government has announced that public houses will be able to stay open until

1 a.m. for the coronation to allow patriotic revellers to 'raise a glass' to the King.

The day after the ceremony, on Sunday, 7 May, neighbours and communities across the UK have been invited to come together at Coronation Big Lunches in streets, gardens and parks in a nationwide act of celebration and friendship. The Big Lunch is an idea from the Eden Project, sponsored by the National Lottery, and brings millions of people together annually to boost community spirit, reduce loneliness and support charities and good causes. The Queen Consort has been patron of the Big Lunch since 2013.

On Sunday evening, there will be a Coronation Concert at Windsor Castle, which will feature performances by many global music icons, as well as stars of stage and screen, dancers and a world-class orchestra. The audience will include volunteers from the King and Queen Consort's many charity affiliations, and several thousand members of the public selected through a national ballot to be held by the BBC.

The show will also see an exclusive appearance by the Coronation Choir, created from community choirs and amateur singers around the UK, such as Refugee choirs, NHS choirs, LGBTQ+ singing groups and deaf signing choirs, alongside a performance by the Virtual Choir, made up of singers from across the Commonwealth. The centrepiece of the Coronation Concert will be 'Lighting Up the Nation', when iconic locations in the United Kingdom will be lit up using projections, lasers, drone displays and illuminations.

On the bank holiday Monday, 8 May, a special event called the Big Help Out will take place, in tribute to the public service of the King and organised by the Together Coalition, along with partners such as the Scouts, the Royal Voluntary Service and faith groups nationwide. The aim of the Big Help Out is to encourage people to try volunteering for themselves in their local areas and to create a lasting legacy of volunteering from the Coronation Weekend.

The Coronation of King Charles III will be an historic occasion and a time for celebration – for the man, the monarch and the country.

Acknowledgements

I have spent the last thirty-three years of my professional life chronicling the highs and lows of the House of Windsor. In that time, as a journalist, broadcaster and author, I have travelled around the UK and the world alongside our new King – as the Prince of Wales, and now, since his accession, as monarch – observing, up close, the man and how he carries out his public role.

I have been fortunate to have seen first-hand the impact he has had on others and his ability to convene people to try to make the world we all share a better place. I have interviewed him too on matters that he finds compelling, for which I am very grateful. In the journey of writing this biography of our King, I have been assisted by close and inside sources, both on and off the record. Many of those sources I cannot identify, for obvious reasons, but I am and remain deeply indebted to them for their confidence and for their honesty.

During my research I read many speeches by the King, as well as books and newspaper and magazine reports written about him, spanning his life. With that in mind, I would like to acknowledge those authors for their insight, in particular Jonathan Dimbleby,

Acknowledgements

Penny Junor, Anthony Holden, Ross Benson and Alan Hamilton. I would also like to thank the writers Sally Bedell Smith, Catherine Mayer, Tom Bower, and of course Prince Harry, Duke of Sussex, whose memoir *Spare*, written by his ghostwriter J.R Moehringer – in which he dubbed me 'Pa's Hack Biographer' – I found to be compelling. I may not share some of their views about the King, but I respect their insight and integrity.

I would also like to express my appreciation to Inspector Ken Wharfe MVO, Ian Walker, Arthur Edwards MBE, Patrick Jephson LVO, Richard Kay, Geoffrey Levy, Charles Anson CVO, DL, Colleen Harris MVO, Ailsa Anderson LVO, Emily Nash, Rodney Cook, Bernice King, Matt Wilkinson, Doug Wills and my editor at the *Evening Standard*, Jack Lefley. I am also most grateful to two wonderful former palace courtiers, now sadly no longer with us, the late Geoff Crawford CVO and the late Felicity Murdo-Smith CVO.

Further thanks are due to my colleagues with whom I have travelled the world on countless overseas royal tours and who have made them such fun: Robin Nunn, Alan Jones, Kent Gavin, Michael Dunlea, Chris Jackson, Matt Wilkinson, Kate Mansey, Russell Myers and Tim Rooke.

I would like to acknowledge my publisher in the United Kingdom, John Blake Publishing, now an imprint of Bonnier Books UK, for supporting this project. I would particularly like to thank editorial director Ciara Lloyd for her vision in backing me, and for uniting me with my editor Barry Johnston, whose hard work and talent helped make this a much better book. I would also like to thank CEO of Bonnier Books UK, Perminder Mann, for her foresight and believing in me and this project.

Finally, I again thank my late father, Vic, who instilled in me the drive to do what I wanted and to strive to do it to the very best of my ability; and my beloved mother, Jean, who encouraged my love of history and writing and who has always been there for me. I would also like to thank my son Charlie for his love and for always making me proud.

Selected Bibliography

Bedell Smith, Sally, *Prince Charles: The Passions and Paradoxes of an Improbable Life* (Random House, 2017).

Benson, Ross, *Charles: The Untold Story* (Gollancz, 1993).

Bower, Tom, *Rebel Prince: The Power, Passion and Defiance of Prince Charles* (William Collins, 2018).

Bower, Tom, *Revenge: Meghan, Harry and the War Between the Windsors* (Blink, 2021).

Brandreth, Gyles, *Elizabeth: An Intimate Portrait* (Michael Joseph, 2022).

Dimbleby, Jonathan, *The Prince of Wales: A Biography* (Little, Brown, 1994).

Hamilton, Alan, *The Real Charles* (Fontana, 1988).

Hewitt, Gavin, *A Soul on Ice: A Life in News* (Macmillan, 2005).
Hoey, Brian, *Prince William* (The History Press, 2003).

Holden, Anthony, *Prince Charles: A Biography* (Bantam Press, 1998).

Jephson, P.D., *Shadows of a Princess* (Harper Collins, 2000).

Jobson, Robert, *The New Royal Family* (John Blake, 2014).

Jobson, Robert, *Diana's Legacy: William and Harry* (MPressmedia, 2019).

Jobson, Robert, *Charles at 70: Our Future King* (John Blake, 2019).

Junor, Penny, *The Firm* (Harper Nonfiction, 2011).

Junor, Penny, *Prince William: Born to be King: An Intimate Portrait* (Hodder & Stoughton, 2012).

Junor, Penny, *The Duchess: The Untold Story* (William Collins, 2017).

Lacey, Robert, *Battle of Brothers* (William Collins, 2020).

Levin, Angela, *Camilla: Duchess of Cornwall – From Outcast to Future Queen Consort* (Simon & Schuster, 2022).

Low, Valentine, *Courtiers: The Hidden Power Behind the Crown* (Headline, 2022).

Lownie, Andrew, *The Mountbattens, Their Lives and Loves* (Blink, 2019).

Lownie, Andrew, *Traitor King: The Scandalous Exile of the Duke and Duchess of Windsor* (Blink, 2021).

Mayer, Catherine, *Charles: The Heart of a King* (WH Allen, 2016).

Morton, Andrew, *Diana: Her True Story – In Her Own Words* (Michael O'Mara, 2017).

Morton, Andrew, *The Queen: 1926–2022* (Michael O'Mara, 2022).

Selected Bibliography

Nicholl, Katie, *Kate: The Future Queen* (Hachette, 2015).

Scobie, Omid & Durand, Carolyn, *Finding Freedom* (HQ, 2020).

Seward, Ingrid, *The Queen & Di: The Untold Story* (Arcade, 2001).

Seward, Ingrid, *William & Harry: A Portrait of Two Princes* (Arcade, 2003).

Seward, Ingrid, *William and Harry: The People's Princes* (Welbeck, 2008).

Seward, Ingrid, *My Husband and I: The Inside Story of 70 Years of the Royal Marriage* (Simon & Schuster, 2017).

Shawcross, William, *Counting One's Blessings: The Collected Letters of Queen Elizabeth the Queen Mother* (Pan, 2013).

Sussex, Duke of, Prince Harry, *Spare* (Bantam, 2023).

Wharfe, Ken & Jobson, Robert, *Diana: Closely Guarded Secret* (John Blake, 2016).

Wharfe, Ken & Jobson, Robert, *Guarding Diana* (John Blake, 2017).

Source Notes

Chapter 1: My Beloved Mother

1 Former foreign secretary Liz Truss gained notoriety as the shortest-serving UK prime minister, resigning after just forty-four days on 25 October 2022.

2 From an interview with the *Guardian*, 9 September 2022.

Chapter 2: Born to Be King

1 Lt Commander Michael Parker CVO was a close friend of Prince Philip's from his Royal Navy days and was his private secretary from 1947 to 1957. They would remain friends after he left royal service.

2 When Princess Elizabeth was born at 17 Bruton Street, Mayfair, at 2.40 a.m. on 21 April 1926, her parents the Duke and Duchess of York invited the home secretary, Sir William Joynson-Hicks, to be present at the birth, despite the government being embroiled in a row with coal miners and the threat of a General Strike.

3 'Roosie', as Philip called her, was a kind and loving nanny to him and instilled in Philip a sense of Englishness. She also stressed to the young Philip the importance of speaking the King's English, which was his first language. He once declared, 'Nobody's allowed to spank me but my own nanny,' when his friend's nanny was about to discipline him for breaking a vase.

4   Ingrid Seward, *My Husband and I*, Simon & Schuster, 2017. Lieutenant Commander Parker was divorced by his wife Eileen on the grounds of adultery in 1958.

5   Nanny Lightbody was fired in 1956 after she refused a 'request' by Elizabeth that Charles, then eight years old, be given a special pudding that she thought he might like. The nanny crossed the dessert off the menu. It was the last straw after several similar disagreements over her being too stern with Charles. The prince continued to visit Miss Lightbody after she had left the palace. She was invited in 1969 to his investiture as Prince of Wales and to his twenty-first birthday party. She died aged seventy-nine in a nursing home in Hawick, Scotland in 1987.

6   Elizabeth II became the first British monarch since George I in 1714 to become British sovereign while outside the UK.

7   Sagana Lodge was a wedding present to the Duke and Duchess of Edinburgh in 1947 from the colony of Kenya. The lease to the lodge was returned to Kenya in 1963.

8   The Cullinan Diamond is the largest gem-quality rough diamond ever found, weighing 3106.75 carats, discovered at the Premier No. 2 mine in Cullinan, South Africa, on 26 January 1905. It was named after Thomas Cullinan, the owner of the mine.

Chapter 3: Colditz in Kilts

1   Queen Victoria's great-granddaughter, Princess Alice was born at Windsor Castle in 1885 and her mother was Princess Victoria of Hesse and by Rhine, a granddaughter of Queen Victoria. Alice's father was Prince Louis of Battenberg.

2   Later, of course, Charles would become an accomplished rider, especially on the polo field.

3   William Shawcross, *Counting One's Blessings,* Pan, 2013.

4   At first Buckingham Palace denied the underage drinking allegations, but later had to admit the story was true. Soon afterwards, Charles's personal protection officer, Don Green, was moved to other duties.

5   Penny Junor, *The Firm*, Harper Nonfiction, 2011.

6   In February 2022, Prince Andrew settled a New York federal lawsuit for an undisclosed sum that alleged he had sexually assaulted Virginia Roberts Giuffre when she was under the legal age of consent. Giuffre claimed that Andrew abused her after she was directed to have sex with him by his friends Jeffrey Epstein and Ghislaine Maxwell. Jeffrey Epstein killed himself in jail after he was charged with child sex trafficking. Ghislaine Maxwell was later convicted of procuring underage girls for Epstein.

7   There had been a number of terror threats. The mastermind of a Welsh bombing campaign in the 1960s later claimed that the terrorist group he led could have killed Prince Charles during his investiture. John Barnard Jenkins plotted a long and audacious bombing campaign with the Welsh nationalist group Mudiad Amddiffyn Cymru ('Movement to Defend Wales' – generally known as MAC), which caused damage to water pipes and government buildings throughout Wales from 1963 to 1969.

In a new biography of Jenkins, he claimed: 'We could have killed him… For one thing, I was a sergeant in the British Army's Dental Corps and was on duty in Caernarfon that day.' During the period leading up to the investiture many targets were bombed, with one device killing two of the bombers themselves in Abergele. The intelligence services had also picked up chatter of terrorist threats.

8   Jonathan Dimbleby, *The Prince of Wales: A Biography*, Little, Brown, 1994.

Chapter 4: The Feeling of Emptiness

1   Actress Amanda Barrie, who later came out as a lesbian, claimed she was approached by the actor James Robertson Justice, a friend of Prince Philip, who was one of eight people selected to help 'launch the royal males into their future life' and to choose anyone they thought would be suitable to teach Prince Charles about sex.

2   Alice Keppel met the Prince of Wales, Prince Albert Edward, in 1898 when he was fifty-six and she was twenty-nine. They stayed together for twelve years, through his coronation as King Edward VII until his death in 1910.

Source Notes

3 Catherine Mayer, *Charles: The Heart of a King*, WH Allen, 2016.

4 She later married merchant banker Lord Anthony Tryon, one of Charles's oldest friends, in 1973, with whom she had four children. While undergoing treatment at Farm Place, Surrey, Kanga fell from a high window, shattering her spine. As she lay in hospital recovering, she claimed to have been pushed. Towards the end of her life, she was wheelchair bound and suffered from depression. She died from septicaemia on 15 November 1997, aged forty-nine.

5 The term 'global warming' was brought into common use in the 1970s by geoscientist Wallace Broecker, who initiated key research into the history of the Earth's climate and humans' influence upon it.

6 *Harmony: A New Way of Looking at Our World* is a 2010 book written by Charles, Prince of Wales, with Tony Juniper and Ian Skelly. The book was published by HarperCollins and focuses on the world's environment, which includes climate change, architecture and agriculture. It is Charles's blueprint for a more balanced and sustainable world. He described the book as his 'call to arms to save the planet from ecological devastation'. The *Independent* in its review called it, 'An important book... By promoting the idea of a revolution in consciousness as the remedy for contemporary ills, the prince shows he is a modern man.' The *Daily Telegraph* said it was, 'A bold and courageous book.'

7 Since then, Charles's focus on climate change and the environment has been a big part of his work over several decades, and he recently set up the Sustainable Markets Initiative and Council, which is supported by the World Economic Forum, to help financial markets become more sustainable.

Chapter 5: End of an Era

1 At the time the republican debate was high on the political agenda. Charles delivered the speech after the commotion ended. In it he said, 'Some people will doubtless prefer the stability of a system that has been reasonably well tried and tested over the years, while others will see real advantages in doing things differently. The point I want to make here, and for everyone

to be perfectly clear about, is that this is something which only you – the Australian people – can decide. Personally, I happen to think that it is the sign of a mature and self-confident nation to debate those issues and to use the democratic process to re-examine the way in which you want to face the future. Whatever course you ultimately decide upon, I can only say that I will always have an enormous affection for this country.' In a 1999 referendum, 55 per cent of Australians voted against ending ties with the Crown and establishing a republic.

2   Kang was charged with threatening unlawful violence and he did 500 hours of community service. He later qualified as a barrister.

3   Close sources told the author.

Chapter 6: Lady Di

1   Diana was honoured on 29 September 2021 with an English Heritage London blue plaque that was unveiled by her former flatmate Virginia Clarke, marking Coleherne Court on the Old Brompton Road as being where Diana lived at Flat 60 from 1979 to 1981, when she became engaged to the Prince of Wales.

2   Lady Pamela Hicks told Sally Bedell Smith, author of *Prince Charles: The Passions and Paradoxes of an Improbable Life*, that she had read the letter. Some writers, including Bedell Smith, say Charles felt he was 'bullied into marriage'.

3   Robert Jobson, *Charles at 70: Thoughts, Hopes and Dreams*, John Blake, 2018. From information obtained by the author from an inside source.

4   Even the BBC compounded a myth involving the duchess that riles Charles even now. In 2001, the BBC website published a story saying: 'But, for the woman who has in the past suffered such indignities as being labelled the "Rottweiler" and having bread rolls thrown at her by Diana fans, to have come this far down the Highgrove path without facing further hostility must in itself count as a significant achievement.'

Source Notes

Chapter 7: Son and Heir

1 Dr McGlashan's letter was revealed in a *Mail on Sunday* exclusive story on 23 September 2017 by reporters Ian Gallagher and Barbara Jones.

2 Charles II was succeeded by his Roman Catholic brother James II. He was overthrown in the 'Glorious Revolution' by William III, after a group of Protestant nobles appealed to Dutch prince William of Orange, husband of James's older, and Protestant, daughter Mary. In November 1689, William landed with an army in Devon. Deserted by an army and navy whom he had completely alienated, James lost his nerve and fled abroad. In February 1689, parliament declared that James's flight constituted an abdication, and William and Mary were crowned joint monarchs. The Hanoverians, from whom William's father is directly descended, came to power in difficult circumstances that could have undermined the stability of British society. George I was only 52nd in line to the throne, but given that the Act of Settlement required a Protestant ruler, he was the nearest in line.

3 Andrew Morton, *Diana: Her True Story – In Her Own Words*, Michael O'Mara, 2017.

4 Ibid.

5 The name given to reporters and photographers assigned to cover the House of Windsor story.

6 Now known by the indigenous name Uluru.

7 A uniquely Australian name for a man working on a sheep or cattle station to gain experience.

Chapter 8: Spare

1 Morton, *Diana: Her True Story – In Her Own Words*.

2 Ibid.

3 Ibid.

4   Charles detests foie gras, as ducks and geese are force-fed until their livers swell up to ten times their natural size before the animals are slaughtered. He banned it from royal residences within weeks of becoming King.

5   Frances and Johnny Spencer separated in 1967. She went on to date Peter Shand Kydd, the heir to a wallpaper fortune in Australia, whom she met the year before her separation. Peter was then married to his wife, Janet Shand Kydd, who named Frances as 'the other woman' in her divorce from her husband. Frances and Peter were married on 2 May 1969.

6   *Diana: Her True Story – In Her Own Words.*

7   Prince Harry, Duke of Sussex, *Spare*, Bantam, 2023.

8   Penny Junor, *Prince William: Born to be King*, Hodder & Stoughton, 2012.

9   Ingrid Seward, *The Queen & Di: The Untold Story*, Arcade, 2001.

10   Prince Harry, *Spare*.

11   Ibid.

12   From an interview by Hannah Booth with Wayne Sleep in the *Guardian*, 14 July 2014.

Chapter 9: Taking Sides

1   Ken Wharfe & Robert Jobson, *Diana: Closely Guarded Secret*, John Blake, 2016.

2   Ibid.

3   Wharfe & Jobson, *Diana: Closely Guarded Secret*.

4   Written on Buckingham Palace headed paper and dated 28 March 1988, Charles's letter was written to the former tapissier of Sandringham House in Norfolk, Robert Marrington.

5   Many Iranians were still angered by the British support given to Iraq during the eight-year Iran–Iraq War. On 2 August 1990 the first Gulf

War, spearheaded by US forces alongside a 34-country coalition including the UK, was triggered by Iraq's invasion of Kuwait, and ended with the liberation of Kuwait on 11 April 1991.

Chapter 10: An Unfortunate Year

1   Princess Anne married former equerry Commander (later Admiral) Timothy Laurence at Crathie Kirk, near Balmoral, on 12 December the same year.

2   In an interview with the author for this book.

3   The 8th Earl Spencer LVO, who had served as a captain in the Royal Scots Greys and landed on the Normandy beaches on D-Day as was mentioned in Dispatches. He served as equerry to King VI and Queen Elizabeth II between 1950 and 1954.

4   From an interview by the author with Inspector Ken Wharfe.

5   James Gilbey was a friend of Diana's from childhood. He denied he and Diana ever had an affair, but the nature of their conversation showed that they were intimate.

6   Later British Ambassador to the USA.

7   Dimbleby, *The Prince of Wales: A Biography*.

8   Charles once said it was his former private secretary's idea for him to admit publicly to being unfaithful to his wife Diana in the Dimbleby TV interview, according to royal writer Valentine Low in his 2022 book, *Courtiers: The Hidden Power Behind the Crown*. *The Times* correspondent wrote that the confession caused Charles 'untold reputational damage'.

9   Although Andrew Parker Bowles felt publicly humiliated by Charles's admission of adultery with his wife Camilla, he was not totally innocent and was reportedly having an affair of his own with Rosemary Pitman, a friend of Camilla's. They wed in 1996, but sadly she passed away from cancer in 2001.

10   This phrase was first used in *The Duchess: The Untold Story* by Penny Junor, which focused on describing the aftermath of Princess Diana's untimely

death in 1997. She wrote: 'Prince Charles made it perfectly clear to anyone who listened that Camilla would always be a part of his life. She had rescued him from the depths of depression, had shown him love, comfort, approval and tenderness that had been so woefully lacking from any other quarter.'

11   Tiggy Legge-Bourke brought a defamation suit against the BBC over their 'false and malicious' allegations that she had an affair with Prince Charles in 1995 whilst she was working as his personal assistant. The High Court in London was told how Tiggy was falsely accused of falling pregnant with Charles's baby and having an abortion.

12   Miss Legge-Bourke married former Coldstream Guards officer Charles Pettifer in October 1999. In 2022, she was offered 'significant' damages by the BBC for the distressing and groundless smears spread by Martin Bashir, who also apologised in a statement for mocking up the fake documents.

13   Prince William went further than anyone expected him to in his recorded statement, saying the *Panorama* interview 'holds no legitimacy and should never be aired again'. He went on: 'It effectively established a false narrative which, for over a quarter of a century, has been commercialised by the BBC and others. It is my view that the deceitful way the interview was obtained substantially influenced what my mother said. The interview was a major contribution to making my parents' relationship worse and has since hurt countless others. It brings indescribable sadness to know that the BBC's failures contributed significantly to her fear, paranoia, and isolation that I remember from those final years with her. But what saddens me most is that if the BBC had properly investigated the complaints and concerns first raised in 1995, my mother would have known that she had been deceived. She was failed not just by a rogue reporter, but by leaders at the BBC who looked the other way rather than asking the tough questions.'

Chapter 11: Death in Paris

1   From the Oxford Films 2017 documentary, *Diana, Our Mother: Her Life and Legacy*.

2   *Spare*.

3   Ibid.

4 Ibid.

5 Ibid.

6 Nine months after the crash in Paris in August 1997 that claimed Diana's life, Camilla did finally meet Prince William at St James's Palace. It was said to be a chance meeting, but this was untrue. In fact, William requested the meeting so he could ask her personally to help him organise a surprise early fiftieth birthday party for his father.

7 *Harry: The Interview,* with Tom Bradby, ITV, 8 January 2023.

8 *Spare.*

9 Ibid.

Chapter 12: Dissident at Heart

1 Blair was made Knight Companion of the Most Noble Order of the Garter, the most senior knighthood, in the Queen's New Year Honours list, 2021.

2 The UK and US governments argued the invasion of Iraq was not illegal as UN Security Council Resolution 1441, passed by unanimous vote in November 2002, made clear that it was the status quo in Iraq that was illegal. Dictator Saddam Hussein had already violated seventeen previous resolutions demanding his verifiable disarmament. He was therefore put on notice by Resolution 1441 that continuing this was emphatically unacceptable.

3 Quote from John Bridcut's documentary, *Prince, Son and Heir: Charles at 70*, aired on BBC 1, November 2018.

4 In interviews by the author with unnamed senior sources.

5 Charles is quoted in the *Daily Telegraph* in 2013 as saying: 'I tried to learn it (Arabic) once, but I gave up. It goes in one ear and out the other.'

6 With the ceremony being held on the Sabbath, Chief Rabbi Mirvis is according to Jewish law unable to drive or travel by car to the location. Instead, he and his wife will spend the night at Clarence House. By attending the ceremony, even on a Saturday, the chief rabbi is continuing a 120-year-old tradition set by former Chief Rabbi Hermann Adler, who

attended the coronation of King Edward VII in 1902, an event that also took place on Shabbat.

7   The expression is normally used to mean that bad things someone has done in the past will come back to bite or haunt the individual.

Chapter 13: Home and Dry

1   *Spare.*

2   Gavin Hewitt, *A Soul on Ice: A Life in News*, Macmillan, 2005.

3   According to Charles's biographer Jonathan Dimbleby, who told the BBC's *Panorama* programme.

4   The Queen first acknowledged the work of the Duchess of Cornwall in 2012, when she awarded her daughter-in-law her highest personal honour, Dame Grand Cross of the Royal Victorian Order, to mark the seventh anniversary of her wedding to Prince Charles.

Chapter 14: Defender of the Faith

1   Princess Victoria Alice Elizabeth Julia Marie of Battenberg (1969–1885) was the mother of Prince Philip, Duke of Edinburgh. In 1949 she founded a nursing order of Greek Orthodox nuns, the Christian Sisterhood of Martha and Mary, and moved to the island of Tinos.

2   The title Defender of the Faith was bestowed on the tyrannical Henry by Pope Leo X on 11 October 1521 because he was a good Roman Catholic. Ironically, the title was originally conferred on Henry in recognition of his treatise *Assertio Septem Sacramentorum* (Defence of the Seven Sacraments), which defended the sacramental nature of marriage and the supremacy of the Pope. When Henry broke with Rome nine years later in 1530 and was established as head of his new Church of England, the title was revoked by Pope Leo's successor, Pope Paul III, and the king was later excommunicated. In 1544, the English Parliament conferred the same title, 'Defender of the Faith', on the king and all his successors, now not for defending Catholicism but for his role and position in the new Anglican faith, of which they

remained Supreme Governors, except for Henry's Roman Catholic daughter Mary I.

3   Dimbleby, *The Prince of Wales, A Biography.*

4   Since Queen Elizabeth II's deeply religious coronation, the status of the Church of England, which is called the established church, has been undermined over the years by dwindling congregations. Today, only 15 per cent of people in Britain consider themselves Anglican, half the proportion who said this in 2000. The number of people describing themselves as Catholic has remained relatively stable at around 10 per cent over the past thirty years, while around 6 per cent of people now belong to non-Christian religions. In 2014 Nick Clegg, the deputy prime minister, suggested that the church and state should be separated over time and 'stand on their own two separate feet'. But the prime minister, David Cameron, spoke out against disestablishmentarianism and insisted on maintaining the status quo that he said worked well.

Chapter 15: New Beginnings

1   Charles bought Diana's engagement ring for £47,000 (equivalent to around £300,000 in 2022) from the jewellers Garrard. It features a 12-carat oval Ceylon sapphire set in 18-carat white gold and is surrounded by fourteen solitaire diamonds. Royal jeweller Harry Collins of G. Collins and Sons added small platinum beads inside the band to reduce its diameter, which is why the alteration has not been visible from the exterior.

Chapter 16: H and M

[insert endnote 1: From the Netflix documentary series *Harry and Meghan*, December 2022.]

1   Ibid.

2   Ibid.

3   Ibid.

4   *Spare.*

5   *Harry & Meghan.*

6   *Spare.*

7   After the publication of my first book on the King, *Charles at 70: Thoughts, Hopes and Dreams*, this story caused a furore in the British press. The *Sun*'s executive editor, Dan Wootton (now a presenter with GB News and columnist on the MailOnline), investigated further and wrote an exclusive piece in November 2018, in which he corroborated my revelation that Her Majesty had warned Harry over his behaviour before their wedding. The article in the *Sun* reported that Meghan had her heart set on this tiara, which is set with emeralds, and that Harry had hit the roof when told no. There were concerns that it might have once belonged to the Imperial Russian royal family before it had been smuggled out of Russia ahead of the revolution of 1917 and the assassination the following year of Tsar Nicholas II.

8   In his book *Spare*, Harry contends that they had picked out a tiara with the Queen's blessing and she had advised Meghan to practise putting it on. When they contacted Angela Kelly about it, she did not respond to their messages. When she did reply, Kelly told them that to get the tiara to them at Kensington Palace would need an orderly and a police escort, which she later said 'can't be done'. Harry claims that she was being 'obstructive' and in his mind was a 'troublemaker', but he did not want to be her enemy.

9   *Spare.*

Chapter 17: A Duchy Original

1   With perfect timing, the Duke of Edinburgh had walked off the royal stage in a summer downpour on 2 August 2017 at Buckingham Palace, doffing his bowler hat as he departed. He marched off the forecourt as the Plymouth Band of the Royal Marines played 'For He's a Jolly Good Fellow'.

2   In May 2021, Bradby surprisingly spoke out and said the brothers had been arguing for the previous eighteen months. He told *The Times* that the princes' relationship had 'slowly descended into something that was difficult – personally and publicly'.

Source Notes

3   Simon Case was soon poached back by prime minister Boris Johnson in September 2020, after two years as William's right-hand man, to run Whitehall as head of the Civil Service. At forty-two, he became the youngest ever cabinet secretary, replacing Sir Mark Sedwell. Case was then replaced in 2021 by Jean-Christophe Gray, forty-seven, a former official spokesman at No. 10 to prime minister David Cameron.

Chapter 18: Grandpa Wales

1   Quote from John Bridcut's documentary *Prince, Son and Heir: Charles at 70*.

2   First reported by the newspaper's award-winning journalist and assistant editor, Kate Mansey, in the *Mail on Sunday* on 27 November 2022. The title Duke of Edinburgh has been granted three times in the history of the British monarchy. It was created in 1726 by George I for his grandson Prince Frederick, who was in the direct line of succession and later became Prince of Wales. The second was Queen Victoria's second son Prince Alfred, who was also the sovereign duke of Saxe-Coburg and Gotha from 1893 until his death in 1900. Philip, the third duke, was given the title by the King before his marriage to Princess Elizabeth in 1947. Charles inherited the title on his father's death. The title merged in the Crown on Charles's accession.

3   *Oprah with Meghan and Harry*, Harpo Productions, CBS/ITV, 7 March 2021

Chapter 19: Last Farewells

1   From the documentary entitled *Prince Philip: The Royal Family Remembers*, broadcast on BBC 1.

2   *Spare.*

3   The president claimed that statistics showed the United States to be among the cleanest climates and 'it's getting better'. Regarded as a climate-change denier himself, he highlighted that the pollution problems of the world stem from China, India and Russia. He also stopped short of admitting that he believed in climate change, saying instead that he believes

in 'extreme weather'. In 2018, the president accused climate experts of having a 'political agenda', while his decision to withdraw from the Paris Agreement in 2017 led to widespread criticism.

4 Officially, the cause of the Queen's death would be 'old age'. But former MP and respected royal author, Gyles Brandreth, spoke further on the topic in his excellent new biography, *Elizabeth: An Intimate Portrait*. He reported in his book: 'I had heard that the Queen had a form of myeloma – bone marrow cancer – which would explain her tiredness and weight loss and those "mobility issues" we were often told about during the last year or so of her life.' This author was told the same by an impeccable source.

5 Harry said in the *Harry & Megan* docuseries: 'It was terrifying to have my brother scream and shout at me and have my father say things that just simply weren't true, and my grandmother quietly sit there and sort of take it all in.'

6 *Harry & Meghan*.

7 In the third episode of Harry and Meghan's docuseries, the writer and broadcaster Afua Hirsch – author of the 2018 memoir *Brit(ish)* – described the Commonwealth as 'Empire 2.0' and Harry as 'anti-racist'.

8 In February 2022, the Duke of York, then sixty-one, had settled the sexual assault case filed against him in the USA by Virginia Roberts Giuffre, thirty-eight, for an undisclosed sum and with no admission of guilt. Doing so spared him the humiliation of giving evidence in a trial and protected the Royal Family from further reputational damage.

Chapter 20: Destiny

1 *Prince, Son and Heir: Charles at 70.*

2 The negative connotations from the two predecessors bearing his name, the Stuart kings Charles I and Charles II, had been the driving force behind the idea. Eventually he settled on King Charles III, as it is the name that everyone associates with him.

3 A clip of him pointing at the items, showing the King's frustration as

he requested the items be removed, went viral on social media immediately afterwards.

4   Designed by George Pace and completed in 1969, it is a simple, intimate place, just 5.5 metres (18ft) high and 3 metres (10ft) wide, with a depth of 4.25 metres (14ft). No official reason is given why Princess Margaret's name is not on the gravestone, other than it is reserved for monarchs and their partners.

5   *Prince, Son and Heir: Charles at 70.*

6   On 22 December 2022, Buckingham Palace announced that the Queen Consort had taken over Prince Andrew's role as Colonel of the Grenadier Guards. The changes also saw the Princess of Wales promoted to her first Army role, taking over as Colonel of the Irish Guards, while her husband, the Prince of Wales, switched to become Colonel of the Welsh Guards. King Charles holds the appointment of Colonel-in-Chief of the Regiments.

7   If you exclude the disputed reign of Lady Jane Grey, the eldest daughter of Henry Grey, Duke of Suffolk and the great-granddaughter of Henry VII, whose nine-day reign was seen by many historians as a failed coup by her father; the shortest reigns in English royal history are Queen Mary I (5 years, 121 days), King James II (3 years, 309 days), King Richard III (2 years, 57 days) and Edward V (4 months and 23 days in 1483). The shortest reign by a British monarch was King Edward VIII, who reigned for 10 months, 21 days before his abdication in 1936, and King William IV (6 years, 11 months, 24 days from 1830).

8   The house was built in 1831 for Adelaide of Saxe-Meiningen, wife of William IV.

9   The oldest British king to accede the throne before Charles III was King William IV, the uncle of our monarch's great, great, great-grandmother Queen Victoria. He was sixty-one when he became King of the United Kingdom of Great Britain and Ireland and King of Hanover; he reigned from 26 June 1830 until his death in 1837 and died with no legitimate heirs. The third son of George III, William had succeeded his elder brother George IV, becoming the last king and penultimate monarch of Britain's House of Hanover.